WITHDRAWN

D0316735

Individuals in Groups and Organizations

03

LIVERPOOL JMU LIBRARY

3 1111 00750 1545

Individuals in Groups and Organizations

Bobbie Turniansky
and A. Paul Hare

SAGE Publications
London • Thousand Oaks • New Delhi

© Bobbie Turniansky and A. Paul Hare 1998

First published 1998

All rights reserved. No part of this publication may be
reproduced, stored in a retrieval system, transmitted or
utilized in any form or by any means, electronic,
mechanical, photocopying, recording or otherwise, without
permission in writing from the Publishers.

 SAGE Publications Ltd
6 Bonhill Street
London EC2A 4PU

SAGE Publications Inc.
2455 Teller Road
Thousand Oaks, California 91320

SAGE Publications India Pvt Ltd
32, M-Block Market
Greater Kailash – I
New Delhi 110 048

British Library Cataloguing in Publication data

A catalogue record for this book is available from
the British Library.

ISBN 0 7619 5720 0
ISBN 0 7619 5721 9 (pbk)

Library of Congress catalog card number 98–061166

Typeset by Photoprint, Torquay, Devon
Printed in Great Britain by The Cromwell Press,
Trowbridge, Wiltshire

CONTENTS

PREFACE

This book grew out of a collaboration between a psychologist and a sociologist, each of whom has taught organizational subjects for a number of years. When we reached the decision to write the book, we decided to approach the topic of individuals and groups in organizations from a slightly different direction from that which we usually see, because of the difficulties we have had with the majority of books already available. Most of the books on organizational behaviour are directed at business-school students. The examples they use are almost exclusively from 'business' organizations located in the USA. Strange as it may seem, organizational behaviour is also taught in psychology departments and schools of education and social work, as well as in countries other than the USA. Most books are also either 'academic' books for the university or 'how-to' books for the practitioner.

This book has a different emphasis. The primary audience is practitioners – a wide category under which we include managers, co-ordinators, consultants and (dare we say it) even workers. But since our emphasis is on the practitioner who is also interested in theory, in what has been said and done during the last few years in the organizational field, the book can also be used by students looking for current material about organizations. Although it has a practitioner focus, it is more academically than 'recipe' focused. Since we were also interested in breaking the 'American business' mould, we have tried to include examples and research from additional domains as varied as the Israeli kibbutz, Dutch schools and Hallmark Cards. We have attempted to provide a book in which school principals, human resources managers, work team members and college students from different places in the Western world can all find their place and feel comfortable.

If this *was* a 'how-to' recipe book, we could say that in it you will find entrées of reports of academic research both from the laboratory and the field, stirred in with information from daily newspapers and news magazines and peppered with a small bit of 'how to' advice. We feel that all of these pieces are important. The academic basis is of limited practical use if we do not know what is going on in the 'normal' world.

The book is set out in, what seems to us, a logical progression. The view we take is that employees are first and foremost people. They have wants, needs and complex life situations which they bring to work with them and which are influenced by that work. These people come in different 'types' which we usually call men and women. As much as we might like to think that there is no need to refer to this situation when discussing organizations, reality tells us otherwise, and so from looking at 'people' we move on to looking at 'gender'. From this point, our next large topic is flexibility and this chapter acts as a transition from the individual level to the group and organizational level. Here we look at personal flexibility in terms of careers and functions, technological flexibility, and spatial and temporal flexibility. We then move on to groups in organizations and examine some of the possibilities for team-based work organizations. Learning and creativity finish off the list of large topics that we present.

This is not a book which needs to be read in any particular order, although the order in which the topics are presented 'makes sense' to us. Within each chapter, it is also possible to select a certain topic which is of interest at a particular time. We hope that each of you will find what you are looking for.

This is the place where we also want to thank the other people involved in bringing the book to publication, and to remind everyone that any deficiencies are still our responsibility. There are the people who read and commented on it: June Hare, Julia Chaitin, Barabra Rosenstein and Herb Blumberg. And, of course, the people at Sage who have been so helpful: Rosemary Nixon, Hans Lock, Pascale Carrington, the copy-editor Neil Dowden and all the other people who have helped create this book.

On a more personal note, I (Bobbie) would like to thank you (Paul) for guiding me through the book-writing process. It was certainly an adventure! And Reuven, even though you never believed we would actually finish it, thank you for being so understanding about it.

INTRODUCTION

The typical text on organizations has chapters about motivating the individual worker, about the influence of small groups in enhancing or retarding productivity, on leadership and on change. The text usually serves as an introduction to the main features of social psychology for students in business schools or for organizational managers or consultants. Here, without ignoring the more traditional topics, we propose to provide an overview of research on individuals and groups in organizations by considering six topics of interest to persons who wish to maintain organizations, make them more effective, or implement change. The topics, ordered from a focus on the individual to that of the group and organization, are:

1 People
2 Gender
3 Flexibility
4 Groups
5 Learning
6 Creativity

Each of these topics has been written about in numerous books and articles. We're not going to claim that we're going to tell you everything about each one of them. What we *will* try to do is present some of the current work being done and put it into an understandable framework.

Interspersed with some theoretical notions and summaries of current research, we will include several cases to illustrate some of the units of analysis and relationships that are important for understanding the role of the individual in the group, the group in the organization and the organization in the environment.

Although more bits of theory will be introduced as we go along, we find it useful to have in mind five sets of ideas that are based on functional analysis. The first idea is that every social system, be it a work group or an organization, has four functions that must be maintained for the system to survive: economic (supply of resources); political (exercise of control in reaching the goal); legal (norms, roles); and values in its culture (that give meaning to the exercise). We will refer to these functions respectively as resources (R), goal-attainment (G), integration (I) and meaning (M). (These concepts are fully developed in Effrat, 1968; Hare, 1992a; and Parsons, 1961.)

The second idea is that these functions exist in a cybernetic hierarchy with Meaning (having the most 'information') at the top and resources (with the most 'energy') at the bottom. The goal-attainment function is just above resources and the integrative function is above that.

The third idea is that the overall development and change in an organization or group usually goes through four phases: beginning with a definition of the values that will guide the activity and the goal to be achieved (meaning); then securing or making the resources necessary for the task (resources); next developing the roles and level of morale required by the participants (integration); and finally coordinating the activity, through leadership, to use the resources and the behaviour in roles to produce specific outcomes that are in line with the overall goal (goal-attainment). There is a fifth phase at the end of the life of the group or organization when the meaning of the activity needs to be reassessed for the individuals, when they must give up their roles and their control, and distribute the remaining resources.

The fourth idea is that, in addition to paying attention to the four internal problems, an organization as a unit in a society must relate to other organizations in the same sector and in other sectors, and also to the physical environment, which according to some calculations is rapidly being depleted.

The fifth idea is to recognize that the four system levels of biological, personality, social and cultural also form a cybernetic hierarchy. Additionally, environment is at the bottom of the hierarchy since it acts on the biological system. In recent years dealing with environmental problems has provided a significant challenge. We also divide the social system level into subsystems for a finer grain analysis, including the work group, organization and network of organizations within a nation. In addition we recognize the problems faced by multinational organizations as they operate in different national cultures and structures.

Within the same functional area, providing resources for example, we expect the amount of influence on individual behaviour by groups and organizations will be positively correlated with the system level. When different functions are involved, say, meaning versus resources, we expect that the amount of influence will be correlated with the position of the functional area in the cybernetic hierarchy (meaning = high, resources = low). For example, the classic Western Electric studies (Roethlisberger and Dickson, 1939) revealed that the informal work group of women in the 'relay assembly test room' could raise productivity above the standard set by management, while the informal group of men in the 'bank wiring room' could lower productivity. In this case the organization provided pay as a motivation for work (resources level), but the informal groups influenced the meaning of the work and also provided social support (integration level).

Some texts emphasize 'systems theory' in which they categorize various elements or activities as 'inputs', 'processes' and 'outputs' where the process supplies some 'value added' aspect to the input. The example usually given is when some raw material, say cotton balls, are run through a process (cotton gin), to produce an output (cotton ready for spinning and weaving). However, in groups and organizations, not all the inputs are physical raw materials. Further, with the typical raw material example, it is assumed that all four aspects of the system do not change while the process is going on. With a functional perspective we can sort out the inputs according to their functional category. An input at the top of the cybernetic hierarchy, in the values and goal of the system, can be expected to produce the greatest change (for example, the shift from a system based on cooperation to one that favours individual enterprise); next an input that requires changes in the individual roles or in the support that members give to each other (for example, the introduction of cross-training for members of a work group so that each individual needs to be able to play at least two roles); next a change in the control of the process (for example, introducing self-managed work groups); and finally, at the bottom, changes in technology (for example, computers) or raw materials (plastics).

Throughout the text we will be using these ideas drawn from functional analysis to classify issues such as aspects of gender segregation at work, perspectives on organizational reality, types of organizational flexibility, career contracts, support for technological change, patterns of career experiences, anchors and competencies, group attributes, functions within functions, types of groups, organizational cultures and organizational vision statements. We will also suggest how some aspects of organizations can be seen to form a cybernetic hierarchy or how they might fit in some way into the general scheme of things. If you are interested in some of the key words and ideas we look for when coding the various types of individual, group or organizational activity, then you may wish to look at Table I.1. If you have had enough theory for a while, you may prefer to skip the next few paragraphs.

Looking at the table, we can see that for each functional area there is a generalized medium of exchange (assets, power, influence and commitments). Exchanges may be made within a functional area, for example exchanging money for information, or from one area to another, for example exchanging commitment for power.

There is a value principle which guides action in each area. In the short term, resources are judged by their utility, goal-attainment by its effectiveness, integration by the extent to which it produces solidarity or role clarity, and meaning to the extent to which it upholds the integrity (or *gestalt*) of the organization and leads to a coherent vision.

Table I.1   *Media of exchange, value principles and evaluative standards for four functional problems*

Functional problem	Resources	Goal-attainment	Integration	Meaning
Medium of exchange	Assets (money, information, skills, materials)	Power	Influence (based on social capital)	Commitments
Value principle	Utility	Effectiveness	Solidarity, role, clarity	Coherent vision
Coordinative standard	Solvency	Success	Cohesiveness	Consensus

There is also a long-term standard of evaluation for how well activity in each area has been coordinated. Activity in the resources area is effective if the books show a positive balance or the shelves in the stockroom are neither bare nor overstocked. That is, the organization is solvent. The criterion for the goal-attainment area is success, for integration it is cohesiveness showing solidarity and role clarity, and for meaning, consensus about the culture and its values.

We use these key concepts to classify an activity of an organization (or individual or group) as belonging to one of the four functional areas. For example, an activity that has to do with facilities, such as raising money or securing raw materials, to be used for the general purposes of the organization, where the focus is on utility with a concern for solvency, would be classified as in the R or resources area. In contrast, an activity that is related to the values of the organization as set out in the vision statement as part of the organizational culture, that has to do with basic commitment to the organization, is concerned with coherence and is related to consensus, would be classified in the M or meaning area. In a similar way, other activities would be classified as being related to integration or goal-attainment functions.

Throughout the text we will provide more examples of the way the four functional categories can be used, for example to classify steps in reaching consensus. But we will not be using this classification at every opportunity both because there is not always sufficient information upon which to base a decision and because there are other factors that are important to organizational behaviour which are not captured by the model. One of the things which we must continually remember is that organizations, and what goes on in them, are very complex phenomena. Because of this complexity, from time to time we will introduce more concepts to elaborate the functional perspective. However there is still a gap between existing theories of organizations and the day-to-day activities they seek to explain. At some point we will stop theorizing and simply tell you what we see or what others have seen. If you wish to use the functional categories for analysis in some of your own work, more examples are given in Hare (1993).

One other idea which will show up now and then is that we create our reality and that what is important is our perception of it and the meaning we attach to it. Of course, we do not do this alone. We influence and are influenced by others in our social settings. We test our perceptions on others and try, sometimes actively, other times less so, to arrive at shared meanings.

1

PEOPLE

More and more employers are opening their eyes to the fact that employees are people too. They are complete human beings with needs, motivations, concerns, emotions and lives that cannot be shut off when they enter the workplace. The work organization is embedded within the total life sphere of the person and what happens within it both affects, and is affected by, that life sphere. The question of where the person stops and the employee begins is a complicated one. How much can the employee express his or her 'real self'?

An organizing theme for this chapter is identity. According to social identity theory (Abrams and Hogg, 1990; Tajfel and Turner, 1985) people classify themselves as members of social groups, a process known as self-categorization (Turner et al., 1987). Group membership results from perceptions or cognitions, not from interpersonal affections. Social categories provide members with a social identity that is both descriptive and prescriptive – a definition of who one is and a definition of appropriate behaviour for your kind of group member. The self-concept is the sum of an individual's beliefs or knowledge about his or her personal qualities, and social identity is the part of the self-concept that comes from group membership.

We have different 'selves'. Some of our behaviours, thoughts and feelings depend on what we are doing and who we are with (Markus and Wurf, 1987). We probably feel and act differently when we are at home and when we are at work. To deal with all of the varying information about ourselves, we organize it according to our various roles, activities and relationships (Carver and Scheier, 1981; Rogers, 1981). The extent of identification with each role varies and is influenced by factors such as shared goals (Turner, 1984). Situations act to 'switch on' different social identities (Turner, 1982) and the individual reacts to changes in situational cues by assuming different identities. Accessibility is the readiness with which a given stimulus will be identified with a given social identity and fit is the degree to which the stimulus matches the specifications of a given category. Both factors influence the likelihood that a given social identity will be switched on in a given situation (Turner et al., 1987).

A self-aspect summarizes what we believe we are like in a particular role or activity and people differ in self-complexity – the number and diversity of the self-aspects they develop for different roles, situations or relationships. People with few, relatively similar self-aspects are said to have low self-complexity while those with many independent self-aspects are described as high in self-complexity (Linville, 1985). High self-complexity seems to protect people from swings in self-esteem since a bad event (or a good one) is likely to have a direct effect on only a limited number of self-aspects. If people have many independent self-aspects, only a small part of their self-concept will be affected by such an event. Linville (1987) suggests that self-complexity can be increased by being involved in many roles and activities but also by seeing the various roles and activities as involving somewhat different selves.

A working person plays multiple roles and has multiple identities – both within and outside the workplace. As mentioned above, and as will be expanded below, this is probably a healthy phenomenon. However, at some stage people try to fit all of the different pieces of self-knowledge, the identities, into a coherent whole and are usually successful in doing so. But there are factors that can aid or hinder the balancing and integrating of those roles and these are some of the topics we look at in the following pages.

Stress, Burnout and Coping

As we will see in this chapter, the actions that organizations take do not remain in a vacuum. They have effects not only on the 'bottom-line' but also on the lives of their employees. The most common problem of everyday life may be stress and there is little disagreement that costs to individuals and organizations resulting from stress and its related illnesses are great (Matteson and Ivancevich, 1987). In the USA, the annual cost of stress-related absence and sickness, reduced productivity and associated health and compensation costs is estimated at more than $150 billion a year (Karasek and Theorell, 1990). The estimate of all job accidents that are stress related ranges from 60 per cent to 80 per cent (Cartwright and Cooper, 1996)

Studies of organizational stress and burnout are often done on selected worker populations such as social workers (Bennett et al., 1993; Poulin and Walter, 1993), teachers (Capel, 1987), police officers (Beehr et al., 1995; Golembiewski and Kim, 1990; Hart et al., 1995), active union members (Nandram and Klandermans, 1993), nurses (Parasuraman and Hansen, 1987) and airline pilots (Little et al., 1990). Stress is not only a problem for workers but affects supervisors as well (Erera, 1991).

There are three main perspectives on stress (Ross and Altmaier, 1994): stress as the internal response of the individual (typified by the work of Selye, 1956); stress as the accumulation of difficulties in an individual's environment (for example, the work on stressful life events done by Holmes and Rahe, 1967); and stress as the interaction of characteristics of the person and factors in the environment. It is the interaction approach that will concern us here since if we accept that stress is almost inevitable (or avoidable only at great societal cost), as assumed by the first two perspectives, then there is little that can be done in an organizational context to reduce it. As opposed to the first two perspectives that emphasize either internal process or external events, the view of stress as an interaction between the person and the environment is more useful to understanding what occurs in organizations.

Lazarus is the father of the transactional (interactional) model of stress or, as he called it, a cognitive-phenomenological theory (Lazarus, 1981; Lazarus and Folkman, 1984). In brief, the model defines stress as occurring when there is an imbalance between demands and resources. As opposed to some other stress models, stress is not seen only as the result of major events – there is also an emphasis on 'daily hassles', chronic external conditions, as stressors. This model views the influence process as bi-directional – people can influence environments and environments can influence people. The model is flexible and dynamic; things can change over time, the appraisal of demands and resources is not static.

In accordance with the transactional model, occupational stress can be defined as the 'interaction of work conditions with characteristics of the worker such that the demands of work exceed the ability of the worker to cope with them' (Ross and Altmaier, 1994: 12). Not all people will show stress reactions to the same situation. The person–environment relationship is mediated by three types of cognitive appraisal which will be described below. The appraisal process is not only perception; it is '. . . the process of categorizing an encounter, and its various facets, with respect to its significance for well-being' (Lazarus and Folkman, 1984: 31).

The appraisal process follows a temporal sequence and begins with primary (initial) appraisal – the event is evaluated with respect to its significance to personal well-being. In this respect, the stimulus is deter-mined to be benign, stressful or irrelevant (positive, negative or neutral). Secondary appraisal is a judgment about how damage can be minimized or gain maximized. It is about coping – what can be done about the stressful encounter, what resources are available. The process may be iterative and therefore the third appraisal is reappraisal, another appraisal cycle activated by new information. For example, is the coping attempt having the desired effect?

Theoretically, the model is very attractive. In reality, the process may be problematic. The first problem comes up with the secondary appraisal process. Both the range of alternatives that can be considered and the time available to consider them is questionable. In all probability, both are limited and a satisficing, rather than an optimizing path is taken

(Edwards, 1988). The reappraisal process also raises questions. In 'real life' the feedback process that allows the individual, or the organization, to assess the effectiveness of any response may be delayed and, as with many behaviours taken within a system, a 'bad' or maladaptive response may be continued if it is not realized that the effect may only occur after some time has passed (Senge, 1990).

For organizational psychologists and others interested in organizational issues, it is not enough to identify the stressors. We must also concentrate on the organizational (and extra-organizational) factors or variables that precede the stressors – that is, their organizational causes. Stressors in organizational settings should be looked at not just as independent variables but also as dependent variables. Questions should be asked about properties of organizations that have the consequence of creating stressors (Kahn and Byosiere, 1992).

As Kahn and Byosiere (1992) point out, there are many disagreements among stress researchers as to definitions but there is agreement on three aspects of stress that are important to study:

1 identification of objective sources of stress-indicative responses;
2 immediate cognitive or affective responses to them; and
3 long-term effect on psychological, physiological and behavioural functions.

In a study of Swedish workers, Alfredsson and Theorell (1983) found that men whose jobs were characterized by high psychological demand and low control (autonomy) were at twice the risk for myocardial infarction than men employed in other occupations. Continuing along these lines, a study done jointly in the USA and Sweden on the social and psychological aspects of work situations that are risk factors for coronary heart disease found that the primary work-related risk factor appears to be a lack of control over how skills are used and job demands are met (Karasek and Theorell, 1990). Using two concepts, skill discretion (or task variety – the breadth of skills workers can use on the job) and decision authority (or autonomy – workers' authority over decision making), Karasek and Theorell (1990) present a combined measure which they call decision latitude or control. It is important to emphasize that the control dimension is control over one's own activities and skill usage, not control over other people. By looking at the interactions between decision latitude and high or low psychological demands (defined as 'how hard you work', including deadlines, widgets/hour, mental load, role overload, stressors arising from personal conflicts, and so on), they arrive at a four-level classification of jobs. As shown in Figure 1.1 (Karasek and Theorell, 1990: 32), a combination of low psychological demand and high decision latitude results in low strain, while the opposite combination of high psychological demand and low latitude results in high strain. The other two possibilities result in

Psychological demands

		Low	High
Decision latitude (control)	High	Low strain (repair-man, architect)	Active (lawyer, teacher, physician)
	Low	Passive (watchman, custodian)	High strain (machine-paced jobs, waiter)

Figure 1.1   *Psychological demand/decision latitude model*

active jobs (high on both dimensions) and passive ones (low on both dimensions).

Schaubroeck and Merritt (1997) point out that although the decision latitude model has formed the underlying theoretical basis for most large-scale studies of job stress in the last 10 years, the research support for it has been mixed. They propose that the mixed results stem from at least one unmeasured variable – self-efficacy. The researchers maintain that the model assumes that most employees have a high level of self-efficacy, and suggest that for those with low self-efficacy control may even have adverse health consequences. As defined by Wood and Bandura (1989: 408), self-efficacy refers to 'beliefs in one's capabilities to mobilize the motivation, cognitive resources, and courses of action needed to meet given situational demands'. It is self-efficacy that affects an individual's ability and willingness to exercise control (Litt, 1988). Reviewing stress studies, Fisher (1984) suggested that for individuals with lower self-efficacy, lower control may reduce stressfulness since it would allow for situational attributions of failure rather than self-attributions. Research results predicting blood pressure bore out these predictions (Schaubroeck and Merritt, 1997).

The Case of New Technology

An area of special concern with relation to stress is technology. In modern organizations computer systems are fairly standard. In most cases they are no longer feared and are accepted as part of working life (see Chapter 3). But technology implementation does not stop with the first installation. The pace of change in computer hardware and software is rapid. This means that workers in many situations have to adjust to a state of permanent innovation. Looking at new technology from an interactional perspective, it is clear that some people will react positively to the challenge of constant innovation, while others will find it very stressful. In 1987, a heart attack suffered by a clerk when his workplace introduced computers was recognized by the Israel National Insurance Institute as a work accident. The worker claimed that his heart attack was the consequence of severe stress and anxiety, a result of not knowing how he would cope with the new technology (*Jerusalem Post*, 1987). There are three situational variables that can act as stressors in the case of new technology: lack of predictability, lack of control and lack of understanding. In addition to the issue of constant upgrading with its attendant need for learning and opportunities for failure, there are other possible sources of stress connected with information technologies. These include ergonomic factors leading to physical strain, computer 'crashes' and the resulting loss of work, the opportunity to make mistakes with far-reaching consequences due to the complexity and interconnectedness of the system, a feeling of loss of control when program directives that contradict the worker's pattern of thinking and reasoning must be followed and feelings of dependency on experts because of lack of technical knowledge. This is by no means an exhaustive list, just a sample. The effects of the technology on job and skill content are also potential sources of stress but, as will be shown in Chapter 3, there is very little determinism in the implementation of new technology. Effects are not pre-ordained. It is not the technology *per se* but the organizational culture and the way it is implemented that will have an effect on many outcomes including stress. Again, it must be remembered that the perception of stress is very individual and these factors may or may not influence a particular employee.

Stress Responses and Consequences

Stress responses are usually categorized as physiological, psychological or behavioural (although there are overlaps). In organizational research, the inclusion of physiological responses is much rarer than the other two categories. Kahn and Byosiere (1992) conclude that the psychological effects of work-related stressors are fairly well established as opposed to their implications for illness. But the psychological effects in and of themselves are very real, very painful and very costly and are not limited to work roles and work performance. The most common expression of stress is job dissatisfaction but it can also be manifested in aroused affective states (frustration, hostility) or passivity (boredom, helplessness, depression). On the behavioural side, there can be direct disruption of the work role as a result of accidents or use of drugs or alcohol, aggressive behaviour such as sabotage, stealing, flight or withdrawal (absenteeism, turnover), disruption of other life roles and self-damaging behaviour (smoking, drugs, alcohol). There is also evidence that the pressures of the job are not left behind and that there is 'spillover' into the home environment (Bacharach et al., 1991; Burke, 1986). The behavioural responses affect the person, the organization and the person's extra-organizational life and relationships and, again, the costs can be very high.

The potential consequences of stress include not only the immediate experience of the stress and responses to it, but also longer-term consequences for organizational performance as a whole and the health of the individual. Tetrick (1992) found evidence that the perception of role stress influences perceptions of other aspects of the work environment. For example, perceived role stress was found to have a stronger impact on perceived work group supportiveness than the other way round. This is viewed as an attempt to maintain cognitive consistency among higher order perceptions, beliefs and needs. So in addition to physiological, psychological and behavioural responses to stress, perhaps we need to add perceptual responses as well.

There is some suggestion that reactions to job-related stress may differ for blue-collar and white-collar workers. Some differences between white-collar and blue-collar workers in the relationship between job insecurity and employee psychological adjustment were found by Kuhnert and Vance (1992). Blue-collar workers who were low in organizational commitment and low in job security experienced the greatest psychological adjustment problems, but no significant results were found for white-collar workers in the same organization.

As with many other areas of research on work experiences, most of the research on stress and health has been done on men (Chusmir et al., 1990). But, as will be seen in Chapter 2, managerial and professional women as a group can no longer be ignored – it is a group growing in importance and size. Along with the usual job stressors such as role overload, conflict and ambiguity common to both female and male managers, women in the workplace also face unique stressors, some of them resulting from overt and more subtle gender bias. As we will see, their situation gives ample opportunity for stress stemming from factors such as the glass ceiling, differential rewards, sexual harassment, and so on. The next part of this chapter on the integration of work and home also points out many chances for additional 'women's stressors'. Issues relating specifically to women and workplace stress will be looked at in the next chapter.

However, we do not want to give the impression that employees are passive vessels, filling themselves up with whatever stressors the environment throws their way. To some extent, individuals select occupations with stress levels suited to their temperament and coping abilities. Different occupations and different hierarchical levels in organizations will have characteristically different stressors. It is not chance that there are few people who fight oil-well fires. Anticipation of the stressors at a higher organizational level may lead to employees turning down promotions or actively seeking them. This is not to say that employees deserve what they get because they chose it. Often the stressors are not well understood or coping capabilities are over-evaluated. And often choice is *not* present. A blue-collar worker did not necessarily choose that occupation because the work is machine-paced. In more than a few cases, the job was 'chosen' because it was the only job available or the best of a few bad options. Any work setting in which organizational problems create dysfunctional stress reactions needs to be examined from the organizational point of view.

There are also workplace stressors over which the employee can exercise little or no control and circumstances in which the employee may have no past experience to draw on. One example of this can be found in the results of waves of cutbacks, reorganizations, rationalization, or whatever the organization chooses to call the process. Besides having questionable economic results for the organization, they have some obvious results for their employees and ex-employees such as problems of poor morale, rumours and mistrust (Curtis, 1989). A classic study of a plant closing in Michigan (Cobb and Kasl, 1977) showed that not only were there physical, psychological and economic costs to unemployment, but also that the *threat* of unemployment triggered some physiological changes long before there was actual job loss. After re-employment, most of the physical indicators returned to normal.

Greenhalgh and Rosenblatt developed a model of the causes, effects, and organizational consequences of perceived job insecurity. They define job insecurity as 'perceived powerlessness to maintain desired continuity in a threatened job situation' (1984: 438). Loss of continuity may range from permanent loss of the job itself to loss of a subjectively important feature of the job but insecurity occurs only in cases of involuntary loss. Employees receive information from intended and unintended organizational messages and from rumours. The individual derives a subjective threat from objective threat, a process influenced by individual differences and social support. Reactions to job insecurity may include decreased effort, increased propensity to leave and resistance to change. On an organizational level, these reactions have a negative impact on organizational effectiveness because of increased turnover and reduced productivity and adaptability. Other examples include mergers, acquisitions and corporate restructurings of various kinds.

Burnout

One of the outcomes of untreated job stress may be burnout (Pines and Aronson, 1981). Although there is consensus about the burnout concept, there has not been a clear distinction made between burnout and stress. It has even been argued that burnout is a type of stress – a chronic affective response pattern to stressful work conditions that feature high levels of interpersonal contact (Ganster and Schaubroeck, 1991). The three parts of burnout are physical exhaustion, emotional exhaustion and mental exhaustion. Burnout may cause people to leave their profession or, worse, stay in it and turn into 'dead wood'.

The three-component conceptualization used by Maslach and colleagues is probably the most accepted definition of burnout (Maslach, 1982; Maslach and Jackson, 1981; Pines and Maslach, 1980):

- *emotional exhaustion* – a lack of energy and a feeling that one's emotional resources are used up;
- *depersonalization* (dehumanization) – treatment of clients as objects rather than people;
- *diminished personal accomplishment* – tendency to evaluate oneself negatively and a decline in feelings of job competence and achievement.

Briefly, the burnout process can be understood as follows (Cordes and Dougherty, 1993). Burnout is a set of responses to a chronic high level of work demands entailing important interpersonal obligations and responsibilities. As a result of the high level of arousal, employees begin to feel emotionally exhausted after repeated exposure to these demands and depersonalization of clients is used as a coping strategy. In the end, they begin to feel a diminished sense of personal accomplishment, especially in situations where the work environment provides little feedback and few rewards for accomplishments.

The issue of interpersonal contact needs some refinement as not all contacts are equal. Cordes and Dougherty (1993) suggest a contact classification based on the two dimensions of frequency and intensity. For example, a librarian might have a high frequency of contact but the contacts are of low intensity and the level of predicted emotional exhaustion is moderate as opposed to forest rangers (low) or social workers (high).

Coping

Coping is a complex combination of things that people can do to deal with stress. Dewe et al. (1993) say there has to be a clear distinction between coping style and coping behaviour. Coping style is context-free while coping behaviour is context-dependent.

Certain traits seem to be linked with successful coping, such as a sense of coherence (Antonovsky, 1987). A sense of coherence includes comprehensibility, manageability and meaningfulness. Comprehensibility refers to the belief that life and life experiences are ordered, structured and predictable rather than random and confusing. Manageability is the belief that the person has resources that are adequate to meet demands placed on them. Meaningfulness is the belief that life and their experiences make sense and that many of the problems and challenges they must face are worth an investment of time and energy.

Dunahoo et al. (1996) come out against the traditional individualistic perspective that characterizes coping research and prescribed coping methods. This is a perspective in which control and action are valued and social and communal aspects of coping are ignored. Therefore, the emphasis is on active, problem-focused coping and the social context in which the coping occurs is dismissed. They put this down to the fact that, as with the rest of the research on stress, most of the coping research has focused on males and there is a bias towards viewing men as better copers even though research results do not always support this claim. And it is not only in the research realm that activity is valued. Dunkel-Schetter and Skokan (1990) found that people who cope more actively are given greater support in response to their efforts. Schwartz and Stone (1993) found that work-related problems tended to be addressed with more active problem-focused coping responses than non-work related problems.

Coping responses can be adaptive (effective) or maladaptive. Effective responses reduce the harmful impacts of stress and improve well-being. Maladaptive strategies are actions taken to temporarily alleviate stress that are usually effective in the short term but may have a negative impact on health and well-being if continued (Cartwright and Cooper, 1996). Examples are drinking or eating, which may provide temporary comfort, but lead to long-term problems, possibly more severe than the original stressor.

Coping responses can be classified according to the focus of coping (Lazarus and Folkman, 1984) or the purpose of coping (Pearlin and Schooler, 1978). Coping can be focused on the problem (responses that eliminate or modify the problem) or on emotion (responses that manage the emotional consequences of the stressor). The purpose of the coping can be to change the situation, change the meaning of the situation so that stressful consequences are less likely, or control the stressful consequences after they occur.

One of the most frequently identified stress buffers is social support (Cobb, 1976), which helps by buffering the individual against possible negative effects of stressors (Cohen and Wills, 1985). The buffering can occur through the provision of tangible assistance (providing a loan or information), through help in reframing the situation and looking at it from another perspective (moving to a new job as an opportunity not a threat), and/or through bolstering self-esteem as a result of feeling accepted and loved.

Other potential buffers against stress have been proposed by Sutton and Kahn (1987): the extent to which the onset of the stressor is predictable; the extent to which it is understandable; and the extent to which aspects of the stressor are controllable by the person experiencing it. The support for these predictions comes mainly from laboratory studies and not the field of organizational research. However, they present promising leads and, as we have seen above, may present some of the keys to dealing with stress produced by technological change.

Some workplaces see themselves as partially responsible for helping workers (or soon to be ex-workers) cope with the stressful positions they have been placed in by the organization. For example, job termination, especially for high-status workers, may be accompanied by outplacement services. These are viewed less in terms of their practical advantages – helping the terminated employee find new employment – and more in terms of their use as a device for enabling the individual to protect himself, to find a way to cope with the emotional problems that termination brings with it (Miller and Robinson, 1994). Schweiger and DeNisi (1991) found that a communications programme relating to a merger had a positive impact on job satisfaction and employee perceptions of organizational honesty, caring and trustworthiness.

It has been pointed out several times that activities and suggestions aimed at prevention and intervention have several shortcomings when viewed from the side of the organizational psychologist (Kahn and Byosiere, 1992; Karasek and Theorell, 1990). For example, most work looks at reducing the effects of stress rather than reducing the presence of stressors at work and most 'stress cures' focus on the individual – what he or she has to do to relieve the stress, rather than the organization. Most of the burden for adapting or increasing resistance to stress is placed on the individual. If job characteristics can help cause heart disease because of stress, then it is the job characteristics that should be changed – not necessarily the cognitive 'interpretation' of those characteristics by the worker or the worker doing the job.

In a study of police officers, Greller et al. (1992) found that social support from the supervisor was a unique form of buffer, altering the impact of strain-producing events so that their association with strain was weaker. They propose that this result is because the supervisor is in a position to provide all three factors that contribute to buffering: information, support and esteem (Cohen and Wills, 1985). The implications for organizations as proposed are quite clear: 'Effective management may permit employees to work comfortably in environments that would otherwise produce high levels of strain. Conversely, managed badly enough, employees can experience high levels of strain in situations that would otherwise be quite bearable' (Greller et al., 1992: 45). Again, here there is a plea for changing the nature of supervision – an organizational intervention, not changing the way employees think about the stress.

There are three possible foci of intervention (Ivancevich and Matteson, 1988; Murphy, 1988):

- *primary*: stressor reduction – modifying environmental stressors to reduce their intensity and number to decrease or eliminate their negative impact on the individual;
- *secondary*: stress management – improving employee coping methods and strategies by various methods including helping them modify their perception or appraisal of a potentially stressful situation;

- *tertiary*: outcome management – dealing with the outcomes of the stress process (e.g. Employee Assistance Programmes).

Although there is a lot of potential for reducing or eliminating stressors, most interventions again focus on individuals – on enhancing their resources, physical and psychological, and helping them cope with stress. This is usually done by improving their adaptability to the existing work environment, by changing their behaviour and improving their lifestyle or stress-management skills. That is, even from an organizational standpoint, the efficiency of these measures must be questioned. As long as organizational conditions remain unchanged and what is changed is the employee, then these are interventions that must be applied again and again. Every time there is turnover, promotion or any change in employees, there will be the potential for the new employee to experience the same stress as the former one, and the intervention will have to take place once more (assuming it was effective the first time). And if the intervention was successful and stress symptoms are reduced but the individual returns to a workplace that has not changed, job satisfaction will probably not improve. Coping responses may result in positive individual outcomes, but there may be negative organizational outcomes. Research has shown that overall job satisfaction and specific job stressors are important predictors of the extent to which individuals will seek to cope in a way that is consistent with organizational goals (George et al., 1991).

To the observer, this situation seems puzzling but Cartwright and Cooper (1996) offer some reasons why secondary and tertiary interventions are more popular:

- *savings* – cost–benefit analyses of these programmes produce impressive results;
- *comfort* – the 'interventionists' responsible for health care are more comfortable with changing individuals than changing organizations;
- *ease* – it is thought to be easier and less disruptive to change the individual than to embark on an extensive and, possibly, expensive organizational programme that may have uncertain results;
- *public relations* – organizations are seen to be 'doing something' about stress – an important message to both employees and the external environment.

Caring for the Caregivers (Kahn, 1993)

Caregiving organizations are defined as organizations such as hospitals, schools and social service agencies that serve their clients primarily through personal relationships between caregivers and care-seekers. In a caregiving situation, the caregivers give of themselves emotionally, physically and intellectually. They run a more than usual risk of becoming burnt-out. As discussed earlier, there are many interventions which may help prevent or halt the process. Kahn proposes that peer support interventions '. . . allow caregivers to be, for a time, care-seekers and have others personally attend to them in the service of their growth and healing' (1993: 540). Kahn proposes an organization-level view of job burnout. He views caregiving organizations in terms of networks of caregiving relationships among the members and proposes that existing patterns of caregiving, within the organization, help create the conditions in which burnout is more or less likely to occur in systematic ways as a result of the caregivers being emotionally supported or drained in co-worker relations.

In this study, the organization is a social service agency providing homeless children with adult volunteers as role models. Qualitative data were collected from the 11 staff members of the agency: social workers and their supervisor, the executive director, fund-raiser and office manager.

Kahn found five patterns that characterized recurring acts of caregiving and withholding care:

- *flow* – caregiving flowing from agency superiors to subordinates during role-related interactions. The members with the responsibility for directing, coaching, managing and supervising others exhibit caregiving behaviours towards their subordinates.
- *reverse flow* – subordinates giving unreciprocated care to superiors. Roles are exchanged.
- *fragmented* – a cycling of caregiving between a superior and a subordinate who care for each other while withholding care from others for whom they are responsible. There is a split between those who receive care and those who do not.
- *self-contained* – a temporary retreat of members into mutual caregiving outside the hierarchical structure. Support groups form because the members are abandoned by those who can, but do not, provide care.
- *barren* – mutual lack of caregiving between hierarchical superior and subordinates. Characterized by relating at a distance, bitterness and frustration.

In the agency in question, caregiving did not flow from the administrative branch (executive director and office manager) to the social work branch. Reverse flow was the only caregiving that crossed the boundary. As Kahn remarks: 'The indication here, then, is that the social worker branch (including the supervisor) not only remained unfilled with caregiving by the administrative branch, but was drained by a reverse flow (from supervisor to executive director)' (1993: 557). The social workers were the only members who did not receive caregiving from others while, at the same time, regularly providing caregiving to their supervisor and clients. They are 'in debt' – giving more care than they received. The social workers became a closed unit and replenished themselves; often, however, using up their collective resources.

The method was useful for the short term but eventually their energy was drained. The social workers became emotionally overdrawn, and withdrew both from clients and co-workers. The emotional withdrawal became translated into temporary, and often permanent, physical withdrawal – turnover.

Emotional Labour

Emotions have to be understood in their social context since they are not only mental and physical states but are also social constructs (Hearn, 1993). Emotions are not absolute – they are open to construction, interpretation and choice. Rosenberg defines emotion as 'internal states of arousal that are subjected to interpreted processes' (1990: 4). Today's prevailing view is that emotions are caused by cognitive appraisals of an object or event that is relevant to the self (Frijda, 1986; Roseman et al., 1990; Scherer, 1988). Different appraisals of the same situation can produce different emotions, and if emotion is at least partly a social construction, its experience and expression can be, and often is, subject to external direction, suppression or enhancement (Ashforth and Humphrey, 1995). Emotions affect our bodily responses as well as our thought processes and their focus. Because of the associations between these components, any one of them can start the chain that engages the rest. Our inward and outward expressions of emotion are intertwined and bodily expressions of emotion often lead to stronger emotional feelings (Adelmann and Zajonc, 1989; Ekman, 1992). For example, unclenching the jaw and taking a few deep breaths in a tense situation will alleviate the feeling a bit. This is a case of emotion following behaviour and facial expression.

Emotions play many roles. They signal that something important is happening, force us to pay attention to significant events, tell us about the nature of those events and direct behaviour towards a goal.

Morris and Feldman (1996: 987) define emotional labour as 'the effort, planning, and control needed to express organizationally desired emotion during interpersonal transactions'. This definition is in line with the social constructionist view mentioned above. To this we can also add a look at the ways in which organizations direct and use emotional labour – how the privately determined expression of emotion is turned into a marketplace commodity. According to Putnam and Mumby (1993: 37), emotional labour '. . . is the term used to typify the way roles and tasks exert overt and covert control over emotional displays. Through recruitment, selection, socialization, and performance evaluations, organizations develop a social reality in which feelings become a commodity for achieving instrumental goals.' With emotional labour, organizations direct and control how their employees present themselves to others. Display rules are standards or norms that indicate both the appropriate emotions to show and the method of their expression (Ekman, 1973), and emotional displays can be characterized as positive, neutral or negative – each with its own function. Positive emotional displays are aimed at increasing liking between customers and employees; neutral displays communicate status and authority; negative displays are often used for intimidation or to subdue the other party (Wharton and Erickson, 1993).

However, as with many other subjects, it must not be forgotten that what is desired, appropriate or demanded is a culture-bound issue. The strategy of the organization, the demands of the customers from a particular organization and national culture all combine to determine whether the required emotional displays will have positive or negative organizational outcomes. For example, Disney is probably one of the best-known users of emotional labour and its employees are heavily trained and indoctrinated as to the emotions they are supposed to display. However, when Disney tried to export the identical emotional displays used in its US theme parks to Paris Disneyland (Euro Disney), those same displays were proposed as one of the reasons for the poor performance of the European site (Rudolf, 1993). The positive emotions and endless smiling were not appreciated by the Europeans who were the target audience.

The operative word in this discussion is 'display'. Although Hochschild (1983) talked about the *feelings* that employees were expected to experience, here we will take the perspective that concentrates on the *display* of appropriate emotion as emotional labour (Ashforth and Humphrey, 1993; Rafaeli and Sutton, 1989). Hochschild (1983) viewed the outward display as the expression of an inner emotion and referred to the 'management of feeling', but emotional labour can be considered impression management (Ashforth and Humphrey, 1993) – an act. The act can be either the outcome of surface acting, in which emotions are simulated but not felt, or deep acting, in which an attempt is made to experience the emotions that will be displayed (similar to Konstantin Stanislavski's 'method acting'). To this distinction, Ashforth and Humphrey add the type of emotional display that is the result of spontaneous and genuine felt emotion – cases in which the employee feels the emotion that he or she is expected to express. Morris and Feldman (1996) argue that even when the felt emotion and the organizationally desired emotion are congruent, there is still labour involved in translating the felt emotion into the appropriate outward emotional display.

The other side of the emotional part of work has to do with those emotions that *cannot* be expressed. Many organizational roles also carry the requirement to suppress overt displays of certain emotions. Doctors, psychologists and dentists cannot express sexual attraction to their patients but salespeople can flirt with their clients and are often expected to do so. The organizational suppression of emotions can lead to disagreements being suppressed, blocks in the information flow, a shutdown of employee voice, a rise in overall stress and lowered job satisfaction (Rutter and Fielding, 1988; Waldron and Krone, 1991). There are also other results which, in addition to the harmful effects on the individual employee, have organization-wide effects, such as a lessening of the organization's ability to learn and a blocking of creativity – subjects that will be addressed in later chapters.

Sometimes, both sides in the transaction realize they are participating in a play (Wouters, 1989). Each side has a part to play and each side realizes that the emotions are not genuine. But the experience of emotional labour is most strong when employees are directed to express emotions that contradict their inner feelings (Putnam and Mumby, 1993), and such cases also require management to exert extra effort to enforce these directives.

In some instances, such as nursing or human service work, it is obvious that part of the job involves emotional labour as an accepted, legitimate and integral part of the task definition. In these cases, the issue of 'caring for the caregivers', how the needs of people who must deal with emotional situations on a daily basis can be provided for, is likely to become central (Kahn, 1993 – see the case above).

In other instances, emotional labour might be viewed as a less legitimate demand made on the worker. The issue of emotional labour has been investigated with regard to casino card-dealers (Enarson, 1993), flight attendants (Hochschild, 1983) and corporate actors in general who are seen as having to comply with obligatory emotions and their representations (Flam, 1990). The use of emotional labour in the performance of one's job and the way that employees deal with it has also been studied with investigative detectives (Stenross and Kleinman, 1989), bill collectors (Sutton, 1991) and service workers (Ashforth and Humphrey, 1993).

Morris and Feldman (1996) suggest that emotional labour can best be conceptualized in terms of four variables:

- *frequency* of appropriate emotional display – the more often a work role requires socially appropriate emotional displays, the greater the organization's demands for regulated displays of emotion;
- *attentiveness* to required display rules, including both the duration and intensity of emotional display – the more attentiveness to display rules required, the more psychological energy and physical effort (labour) the job will demand;
- *variety* of emotions required to be displayed – the greater the variety, in terms of positive, negative and neutral emotional displays, the greater the emotional labour;
- emotional *dissonance* generated as the result of having to display organizationally desired emotions not genuinely felt – when true feelings have to be concealed, there is more emotional labour.

There is some disagreement about the consequences of emotional labour. These outcomes can be looked at on both individual and organizational levels. Beginning with effects on the service provider (which, of course, are also linked at some point to organizational outcomes), Hochschild (1983) reported negative outcomes for psychological well-being as a result of alienation from one's true feelings – a consequence of treating the mind and the body as separate entities. The outcomes of emotional labour, when not seen as a 'part the actor is playing', can be harmful. Emotional labour is sometimes seen as marginalizing the personal and relational nature of emotions (Putnam and Mumby, 1993), and may lead to emotive dissonance – strain caused by displaying emotions that are not felt – and self-alienation – the loss of the sense of one's real self (Ashforth, and Humphrey, 1993; Hochschild, 1983; Stenross and Kleinman, 1989; Sutton, 1991). When stress is experienced, it can lead to feelings of emotional numbness and burnout (Van Maanen and Kunda, 1989). Trouble can also occur when the part can no longer be discarded after work – when it begins to merge with the self (Fineman, 1993). Negative effects on task effectiveness include absenteeism, substance abuse (Hochschild, 1983) and raising customer expectations that cannot be met thereby resulting in customer alienation (Ashforth and Humphrey, 1993).

But not all of the research on emotional labour has come up with straightforward negative consequences. Stress is not always a foregone conclusion. It may or may not be experienced as a result of the gap between felt emotion and required emotional display, and may be influenced by the importance of the emotion, the status of the target and whether it is an acceptable or unacceptable emotion that is being 'faked' (Putnam and Mumby, 1993; Rafaeli and Sutton, 1987; Stenross and Kleinman, 1989; Van Maanen and Kunda, 1989).

There may also be benefits to emotional labour. It may make interactions more predictable and help employees avoid potentially embarrassing interpersonal problems and may help them to cognitively distance themselves from unpleasant situations (Ashforth and Humphrey, 1993). In these cases, stress should be decreased and satisfaction increased, rather than the other way round – an outcome supported by Wharton (1993) in a study done with employees of a bank and a teaching hospital. Ashforth and Humphrey (1993) also point out that although behaviour is constrained by the rules, there is usually some personal latitude remaining about how to enact the behaviour and, in such cases, self-expression and personalization of the role may be facilitated. Identification with the role or its norms and values may moderate the negative effects of emotional labour for the employee and turn emotional labour into something enjoyable that works to enhance well-being.

The issue of emotional labour can be compared to the issue of self-expression versus self-presentation – two motives for choosing particular behaviours. Self-expression conveys what we believe our true self to be and allows others to form accurate impressions of us and what we are like. Self-presentation involves choosing behaviours that are intended to create a desired impression, usually in order to gain power, influence or approval (Jones and Pittman, 1982). Research shows that most people prefer to enter social situations that allow them to act in a way consistent with their self-concept – to engage in self-expression (Snyder and Gangestad, 1982). Emotional labour blocks self-expression and can lead

to a discrepancy between what is experienced and what is expected –
and it is this discrepancy that is common to the negative effects on the
worker (Ashforth and Humphrey, 1993).

If we put all of these issues together, it can be seen that even surface
acting may lead to a felt inner emotion because of the effect of behaviour
on the interpretation of felt emotion. Deep acting may lead employees to
lose touch with their 'real self' or lose the ability to distance themselves
from their position (Van Maanen and Kunda, 1989). Self-presenters
influence not just their audience – they influence themselves as well
(Gergen, 1965; Jones et al., 1981; Schlenker, 1985). Or in Goffman's (1959)
terms, the mask may become the face.

In terms of the framework we are using in this book, emotional labour
takes a component of meaning and turns it into a resource. It takes
something from the level of the biological entity and transforms it into a
property of the organization. If we wanted to be really nasty, could we
call it 'stealing'?

Between Two Worlds – Home and Work

In the last section we saw that employees do not leave their emotions at
home when they come to work. In this section, we will also see that the
problems they face in their private life cannot be isolated from their work
life. Wortman et al. (1991) reported that over 75 per cent of married
female professionals in a US study reported experiencing conflict
between work and family responsibilities every day. An Australian study
showed that 52 per cent of the mothers and 31 per cent of the fathers had
taken some time off to care for sick children during the year (Vandenheuvel, 1993). Work affects things not only on the job and within the
organization, but also employees' lives, including interactions within the
family (Menaghan, 1991; Price, 1985; Zedeck et al., 1988), once they exit
the organization's gates. Work–family relations are affected by characteristics of both of these life spheres (Voydanoff, 1987, 1988). For both men
and women, family life is usually the most important aspect of general
life satisfaction and together with job satisfaction it is a significant
predictor of general life satisfaction (Barnett and Baruch, 1987; Gutek
et al., 1988).

The realization that home and work cannot be completely divorced
from each other is growing, particularly when the issue of women comes
up, whether because of their position as primary caregiver in the family
or as part of a dual-earner family. Female employees are more likely than
male employees to be primary caregivers to the elderly and employees
around 40 years of age are also likely to have childcare responsibilities.
There are more and more women who work outside the home, more
single-parent families and more dual-career couples. So why isn't this
section included in a chapter called 'Women'? Because work–family

issues are not exclusively women's issues. Men also have legitimate desires, needs and expectations to participate fully in the lives of their family and community. Therefore, although the impetus for many of the 'family-responsive' policies that we will see here originally came from the increasing numbers of women in the workforce, we would be doing everyone an injustice if we looked at these issues only from that perspective.

The popular press is also chiming in on this issue. A recent *Newsweek* article (Shapiro, 1997) is bound to worry some working parents by pointing out the small amount of time that parents spend with their children, even if it *is* 'quality time'. And the article also makes the point that this is not a women's issue – it's a family issue. While acknowledging the difficulties that exist in cutting down on work hours, it is seen as a possibility in many cases – especially at the higher end of the pay scale. As Lewis (1996: 2) puts it: 'Increasingly then, the workforce is composed of women and men with responsibilities for both the care and the economic support of families, who seek a balance between their work and private lives.'

The workplace is lagging behind societal changes. In most cases, work is still organized around a traditional model of a single breadwinner (usually male) who is supported by his spouse. But changes in the workforce, the nature of families and work itself (such as telecommuting) have made this model largely obsolete. Even in cases where there are 'family-friendly' policies, they are usually 'mother-friendly' and are aimed primarily at enabling women with young children to combine work with childcare. Lotte Bailyn, a professor at the Sloan School of Management at MIT is quoted in *Newsweek* (Shapiro, 1997) as saying that family-friendly benefits are under-utilized even where they exist because the men rarely ask for them and the women may find themselves on 'mommy-tracks' if they do. In some situations, policies may exist but because there are unwritten assumptions about work and how it should be done, exploiting alternative work arrangements may result in stunting one's career (see the case of the engineers at the end of this chapter).

The question also arises about whether policies should focus only on the 'family' or other life aspects as well (Lewis, 1996). In a similar vein, we will refer to these initiatives as work/life policies in the hope that they will eventually be aimed at enabling a more balanced life for the individual (including issues such as study and leisure) without necessarily concentrating on the narrow aspect of 'family'.

Work–family or work/life integration issues are of concern to employees, employers, society and governments. Employers are increasingly becoming aware that their ability to attract and retain the workforce they want may depend on their ability to create work conditions that minimize the interference of work and home life with each other (Kraut, 1990; Rosen, 1991). More and more companies are prominently advertising their policies in their Internet recruiting notices. American examples include Chevron, Hewlett Packard, Johnson and Johnson and SC Johnson Wax among many others. Offering assistance signals concern for employees and positively influences attachment to organization (Grover and Crooker, 1995). Here we can see some examples of 'organizational interventions' to reducing stress that were mentioned earlier.

Organizations make choices – strategic choices – and these are based on their perceptions of environmental contexts and what must be done to adapt to these contexts (Child, 1972). Milliken et al. (1990) argue that an organization's recognition of environmental changes related to work–family issues depends on their external visibility (e.g. media coverage) and an organization's exposure to work–family pressures. Exposure to demands is heightened by a high proportion of employees with family demands – for example, a workforce composed mainly of women with small children.

Recognition of these issues is one thing, but the next step is the interpretation of the importance of these issues for the organization. There are four considerations that may influence the importance of work–family issues and organizational responsiveness: organizational assessment of employee needs, organizational values, workforce characteristics and organizational performance (Milliken et al., 1990). If visibility or demand is high there is more likelihood that organizations will respond to work–family pressures in order to enhance external legitimacy and respond to internal constituencies (Goodstein, 1994). Organizations are more likely to be responsive to work–family issues when there is an expectation of benefits, or a significant impact on productivity (Goodstein, 1994; Morgan and Milliken, 1993), and there is growing evidence that the major beneficiary of these programmes may be the employers (Gonyea and Googins, 1996). Accordingly, there are also suggestions that the issue should be reframed from one of employee benefits to one of a strategic business concern. In the USA it was also found that larger organizations were more likely than smaller ones to respond to pressure for employer involvement in work–family issues (Goodstein, 1994). It is assumed that this is because their size and visibility puts them under greater pressure to maintain social legitimacy. But it may also be that there is more organizational slack or more resources that can be directed in that direction or specialized human resources staff who call attention to these issues (Morgan and Milliken, 1993).

In general, organizational responses to non-work can be classified into three groups (Kirchmeyer, 1995):

- *separation* – employers act as if the non-work world of the employees does not exist;
- *integration* – employers treat work and non-work as related worlds that affect one another and attempt to reduce the gap between them;

- *respect* – employers acknowledge and value the employees' non-work worlds and commit to support it.

It was found that lowered organizational commitment was associated with a separation approach while integration and respect were positively associated with organizational commitment. Respect was the most effective response type and involved the employers providing resources for workers to fulfil non-work responsibilities by themselves.

Kirchmeyer (1995) used the concepts of boundary flexibility and boundary permeability to assess organizational practices addressing work/non-work issues. Flexibility refers to the extent to which time and location are moveable between domains. Permeability is the extent to which psychological concerns of one domain enter the physical locations of the others.

Workplaces can contribute to the provision of practical family care either by actively supporting activities that ease parental burdens, providing services or economic support, or by granting employees influence over work and working hours so that they can provide the necessary care themselves (Holt and Thaulow, 1996). According to Holt and Thaulow (1996) the first method is more prevalent in countries where welfare state services are less well developed and where women are still seeking full integration into the workforce (the UK, Germany and the USA for example), while the second is found more in societies where women have achieved a central position in both the labour market and the political system and the welfare state is well developed (for example, Denmark).

The first approach will rarely affect the work itself or its organization. It may be economically demanding for employers and often requires collaboration with external parties. The second approach costs employers almost nothing but will often affect the division and organization of work within the enterprise (Holt and Thaulow, 1996).

The question of responsibility differs from country to country. The USA represents an individualistic country that stresses freedom of individual choice and a corresponding lack of federally mandated policies. During the 1980s and 1990s, social and political forces in the USA put a lot of environmental pressure on organizations to assume responsibility for providing human services programmes such as childcare (Goodstein, 1994). Today, the interest of the US government in work/life issues can be seen on the Internet. The United States Department of Labour maintains a WWW site on the Internet called the Corporate Citizenship Resource Center (see Internet Appendix) where, among other things, companies are invited to profile their family-friendly policies. The development of work/life policies has also not been uniform throughout Europe and is at least partly affected by cultural differences in attitudes towards employment, the value placed on family life and the individual's sense of entitlement (Harker, 1996). In some countries, such as

Denmark, provision of childcare services is seen as a public responsibility while UK policy sees it as a private matter to be solved by individuals (Holt and Thaulow, 1996; Moss, 1996). In some cases, the impetus in Europe has come from the staff of multinational companies who seek benefits equal to those of their counterparts in other countries (Harker, 1996).

Raabe (1996) proposes that further progress in reconciling work and non-work must move away from the concept of standard work and career paths towards a pluralism of work and career options. She contrasts standard and pluralistic paradigms of work and careers. The assumptions of the standard paradigm are:

1 quantity of work time is directly correlated with quantity and quality of work – long hours of work are necessary for maximum effectiveness and productivity especially for professional and managerial work;
2 long hours of work in continuous standard careers are necessary indicators of high work and career commitments;
3 people need to be available at workplaces and work in standard, predictable ways to achieve productive work;
4 effective managers are always available for consultation, problem solving, facilitation, coordination and control, and, therefore, they need to work long hours in order to manage effectively;
5 standard work and career structures are necessary for optimal work productivity and profitability.

The assumptions of the pluralistic paradigm are:

1 standard work and career arrangements are social, historical constructions and therefore can be reconstructed in alternative forms;
2 what was appropriate and effective in the past may not be necessary or optimal under present conditions especially in less routinized post-industrial work;
3 presence at work and time involved are inadequate and unnecessary indicators of interest, motivation and accomplishment;
4 in many work situations the quality and management of work time are more important to task accomplishment than the quantity of time;
5 non-work activities can contribute to work productivity;
6 work can be redesigned into functional equivalents, or improvements, of standard configurations;
7 variety and flexibility in work arrangements are manageable and compatible with work productivity;
8 all of the above are applicable to professional and managerial work as well.

Supporting evidence for most of these propositions is found in examples from the former West Germany and the USA (Raabe, 1996). A project at the Xerox Corporation showed the positive effects of what were initially work–family initiatives on issues such as effectiveness, productivity and customer satisfaction as well as on work–family integration (Fletcher and Rapoport, 1996).

The main arguments that have been proposed for implementing work/life policies are equal opportunities, quality of life and business rationales – arguments that are interdependent rather than mutually exclusive (Lewis, 1996). In presenting each set of arguments, they will be arrayed beginning with the more narrow ones and proceeding to the broader ones.

Equal opportunity, diversity and gender equality – these rationales can take a number of forms ranging from the most basic and progressing through a commitment to encourage equal division of labour in the home as well.

- To give men and women equal access to paid work;
- to achieve equal representation of women and men at all organizational levels;
- to allow work to be adapted for family reasons and to value the resulting diversity of patterns as equal to traditional work patterns;
- to challenge and modify organizational practices based on an assumed separation between work and family lives so as to empower women and men to make optimal contributions in both areas;
- to make women's and men's family and work roles equally visible, legitimate and valued.

Quality of life: stress and well-being – these arguments rest on the assumption that multiple roles in work and family can create stress. The multiplicity of roles can be a source of satisfaction and protection against stress in some cases, but it can also be a source of strain, such as overload and conflict, which are associated with negative consequences for the individual and the organization.

- To adapt organizational structures and policies to enable people to manage multiple demands in work and home spheres with maximum satisfaction and minimum stress;
- to reduce stress at work and minimize the potential negative impact of work on families and families on work;
- to develop organizational cultures that respect people's overall identities and encourage balanced commitments.

Business – these arguments draw on both groups presented above but emphasize business, or bottom-line, advantages. Recognizing the connectedness between work and personal life is seen as a strategic business adaptation. This is the most widely used rationale.

- To reduce stress and strengthen equal opportunities in so far as this action will enhance the performance of the organization;
- to work towards solutions to work and family issues that are mutually beneficial to all stakeholders.

Programmes such as childcare or eldercare are usually supported because it is believed that they contribute to the employees being at work and working productively (Lambert, 1993). Other flexible work arrangements such as job sharing, part-time work, compressed work weeks, and so on, are less standard and have often been connected with less pay or benefits, poorer conditions and career limitations and are often not available for upper-level professionals and managers (Raabe, 1996). Below is a brief look at some of these work/life policies and their developments.

Flexible working arrangements – these include short-term contract work, annual hours (instead of weekly hours), job sharing, telecommuting and part-time work. The traditional working day (9 a.m.–5 p.m.) and working week is becoming more of a rarity in Europe than 'atypical' work. There is growing use of short-term contracts and casual employment. Many of these arrangements are accompanied by a lack of employment rights, lower pay and instability of employment (Harker, 1996).

Leave arrangements – this is the most commonly adopted form of support for working parents. In all European countries women have the right to a period of leave after giving birth and some employers offer enhanced maternity conditions such as extended leave or additional maternity pay. Here are some examples taken from Bohlen (1996). In Italy, mothers are required to take leave two months before and three months after childbirth. For risky pregnancies, appropriate medical certification allows for leave during the entire nine months. During pregnancy leave, most women receive full salaries – 80 per cent paid by the state and 20 per cent by the employer. In Germany, women are entitled to fully paid leave six weeks before and eight weeks after childbirth for single births. In the case of multiple births, leave is extended to 12 weeks after delivery. In the USA, benefits vary greatly between organizations. The 1993 Family and Medical Leave Act which covers workers at companies with 50 or more employees entitles mothers and fathers to 12 weeks of unpaid leave to care for a new baby (biological or adopted). In most large companies women get six to eight weeks of paid maternity leave but this is part of the benefits of disability insurance plans, not national policy. Other leave arrangements can include paid leave for child illnesses. In France, all women in the public sector, and some men and women in the private sector, are entitled to 12 days leave a year to care for a sick child (Harker, 1996).

Some countries also allow leave for fathers, thus recognizing the father's rights and responsibilities to his family. A recent change in maternal leave laws in Israel allows the father to take the second half of the three-month leave instead of the mother. It is too soon to tell whether Israeli fathers will exercise this right, but in Europe statutory leave programmes are usually taken advantage of by women even when both parents are entitled to them. The Scandinavian countries offer non-transferable rights to mothers and fathers and the experience there suggests that such an arrangement encourages a higher rate of usage by men (Harker, 1996).

Employer-supported childcare – employer involvement in childcare typically takes one of three forms: providing fully or partially subsidized on-site childcare; financing external childcare expenses; or providing information and referral services. These arrangements are often found when there are other creative benefits, and a workforce composed of a large proportion of women and employees of child-bearing age. The purpose of employer-supported childcare is to reduce absenteeism and aid in recruiting and retaining employees, improving public relations, social responsibility and meeting employee demands. Barriers are cost, liability, licensing and space (Auerbach, 1990). As with leave, employer-sponsored childcare is likely to be a function of national statutory provision. In the UK where statutory childcare provision is low, there were about 500 employer-sponsored nurseries, according to a study done by Working for Childcare (cited in Harker, 1996).

Other possible arrangements are partnership schemes between the employer and other partners such as a local authority. This is becoming an increasingly popular idea in Holland and has resulted in a decrease in workplace provision of childcare, but an increase in the number of employer-subsidized places (Hogg and Harker, 1992). Childcare allowances or vouchers are uncommon in European countries other than the UK (Harker, 1996). In Italy, as opposed to the generous policy with relation to maternity leave, there are fewer options open for caring for children after they are born. Public day care or nursery schools for children under the age of three are rare in most regions (Bohlen, 1996).

Women using employer-sponsored childcare services report lower levels of job stress and higher levels of job satisfaction (Raber, 1994). Reporting on the results of three US national surveys of employers providing childcare services, Rhodes and Steers (1990) found lowered absenteeism was a clear benefit of such a programme. In one study 72 per cent of the employers had lowered absenteeism and, in another, 53 per cent. In the third study lower absenteeism was ranked as one of the top three benefits of the programme.

SC Johnson Wax (SC Johnson Wax, 1996a, 1996b)

SC Johnson Wax is a leading Wisconsin-based US manufacturer of products for the home, personal care and insect control. It is a company with a long history of providing for employee welfare and was cited for nine consecutive years (1988–96) as one of the '100 Best Companies for Working Mothers' in a survey conducted by *Working Mother* magazine. The company was founded in 1886 and in 1900 it started offering its employees paid vacations – an almost unheard of benefit at the time. In 1985 they began providing childcare services to employees and a childcare centre accredited by the National Association for Education of Young Children was built in 1991. More than 500 children from birth to 14 are served by the centre whose programmes include year-round before- and after-school care, full- and part-time care for newborns through to kindergarten, and summer day camp from June to August. The centre's services are offered across all three work shifts.

Some of the other work/life policies include flexitime, job sharing and childbirth leave. The Work/Life group, an employee volunteer organization started in 1993, makes sure that the company addresses employees' work/family needs throughout the stages of their lives. There are also programmes and seminars directed at fathers and fathering.

Eldercare – life spans all around the world are increasing. Besides the new business opportunities that this fact opens for organizations, it also presents them with a new reality: some proportion of their employees are bound to be concerned with caring for elderly parents. Policies and programmes include flexible work schedules and information services and are more likely to be offered by larger employers with higher proportions of women that also tend to offer general policies meeting family concerns (Liebig, 1993).

Flexible working hours – flexitime programmes give employees some discretion over their working hours although typically there is a common core of hours (for example, 10 a.m.–12 p.m.) when employees must work. The story on the possible benefits of flexible scheduling is unclear. Work/life policies, especially flexible scheduling, have positive effects on employee perceptions of control over work and family issues. These perceptions of control are associated with lower levels of family–work conflict, job dissatisfaction, depression, somatic complaints and blood cholesterol. This shows that organizations can take steps to increase employees' control over family responsibilities and this control may help them better manage the conflicting demands of work and family (Thomas and Ganster, 1995). Dalton and Mesch (1990) also showed that absenteeism is reduced but that turnover is unaffected. On the other hand, Christensen and Staines (1990) concluded that no compelling case is made for benefits of flexitime to employers in terms of effectiveness, membership or attitudes. It does help solve some work/family conflicts, but fewer than hoped. Holt and Thaulow (1996) comment that the positive results of flexitime are ambiguous. There are studies that show positive effects on stress reduction, studies that show no significant influences on easing transitions between home and work, and those that show that parents working with flexitime experience *more* stress than other parents (although there is also no evidence that these people would be *less* stressed working fixed hours).

In some instances flexitime is used to meet workplace needs rather than family needs. Thaulow (cited in Holt and Thaulow, 1996) found that it is often used by employees to stay longer at work when this is required. However, in general, experience with flexitime is still more positive than negative.

Holt and Thaulow (1996) also point out that not all flexible work arrangements are formal. Informal agreements can also allow for flexible working hours. These agreements can take the form of agreements between colleagues or between colleagues and immediate supervisors. They may include permission to leave early or come in late, swapping of shifts and, of course, positions in which there is little requirement for accounting for hours worked to someone else. In return for such consideration, there is often an unwritten contract that the employee will put in an extra effort when the work requires. These informal arrangements, as many other things in society, depend on a norm of reciprocity.

The Work/Family Balance of Engineers (Perlow, 1995)

Thirty engineers, male and female, in the design and manufacturing unit of a Fortune 100 company were the focus of the study. Three barriers to work/family balance were identified through interviews and observations.

Firstly, *to be seen as working, one must be seen at work.* Example: A female engineering manager with three small children asked to spend one day a week working from home. She thought things were working well but she was passed over for promotion six months later and, after three more months, assigned to a different unit (not in a managerial position – a not uncommon move in the company). In this new position she dealt with material that could not be taken home – a hidden message about the arrangement. When ranked for the annual raise, she fell in the bottom 20 per cent, although previously she had been considered a top employee. There are other examples in the company of people being more productive when working at alternative times and locations, but in each case only work at the office is rewarded. The alternatives clash with managers' assumptions about how and where work is best done.

Secondly, *'face time' is a critical component in evaluation of work.* Not only does work have to be done at the workplace but one has to be at work for extended periods of time to demonstrate commitment. Example: A young male engineer had to leave work at 4.30 p.m. three days a week because of his wife's work. His manager suggested an alternative work schedule (Saturday instead of Monday) which resulted in increased productivity and meeting his next deadline ahead of schedule. When the rest of the team had to start working on Saturday to meet the deadline, he was seen as slacking off, since they increased their 'face time' and he did not (even though there was no need for him to work an extra day). In this company, if work is completed early, one is not necessarily seen as a top performer and rewarded for doing more in less time. Rather, the quality and difficulty of the work are questioned. The assumption is that if you finish early, you must not have had enough work to do in the first place.

Thirdly, *to succeed, work is always expected to be the top priority.* Along with being at work and putting in extra time when the organization decides they should, the engineers are also expected to maintain this high level of presence at work at all times. Such a demand requires sacrifices in home life and sometimes led to engineers leaving the organization.

For the engineers in this organization, physical presence at work is critical for success. Productivity is not enough and engineers who are present but not working as efficiently are given the benefit of the doubt as opposed to the 'absent' but productive ones. Presence and output are rewarded with no attention to how the work gets done. The engineers generally work alone until they run into a hurdle and then start looking for the person or the thing that can help them get past it. This method of work results in recurring spontaneous interruptions and a sense of perpetual crisis leading to the assumption that physical presence is necessary.

In this organization, work is driven by a need to meet short-term deadlines rather than strategically thinking about long-term goals. As a result, in this type of organization, work/life policies offer only very short-term solutions. Those workers who take advantage of flexible arrangements will not be able to satisfy the organization's demand for presence and will find their careers hindered.

People – Some Final Words

We began this chapter talking about identity. Each of the sections deals with identity in a different way. Emotional labour separates our different identities and does not allow us to fully express ourselves or requires us to adopt a different expression. Work/life policies try to allow for the accommodation of different identities while maintaining some degree of distance between them so that they do not interfere with each other. Issues of stress and coping show some of the problems that can occur if we cannot separate our work and our life identities at least partially – if we 'take our work stresses home'. However, it also shows the power of integration of some of our identities – of integrating our identities that allow us social support with our work identity.

Organizations exist for a purpose and that purpose is usually framed in terms of creating value for stakeholders. Although employees are also considered stakeholders, their claim is traditionally considered to be less than that of the 'money people' – the owners (whoever that may be in any particular case). As we mentioned in the introduction, every organization must maintain four functions in order to survive. In terms of functional analysis, this chapter can be looked at as follows. People are organizational resources. The organization has to acquire them and use them properly. If they are misused, the outcomes will probably be negative for both the individual and the organization. Although it might be nice to think that organizations create policies such as work/life programmes because of some inner sense of responsibility, in most cases (although there *are* exceptions) these are created in order to allow the human resources to function at full effectiveness.

Organizations adopt work/life policies in order to allow them to better utilize their human resources. On the other hand, with emotional labour, people are looked upon *only* as resources without taking their complete being into account. Taking control of the employees' emotions and using them to their own benefit is one of the ways in which some organizations try to attain their goals. The question becomes is it a legitimate effort and is it an effective one? The answer is definitely not an absolute 'yes'.

It should not be assumed by the discussion in this chapter that most organizational acts and their consequences are negative. Employee perceptions of being valued and cared about by the organization have a positive relationship with conscientiousness, involvement, innovation and attendance (Eisenberger et al., 1990). Processes that enable the individual to integrate his various identities without submerging them totally within each other, and that allow the person a fair degree of self-expression, will probably result in healthier employees and organizations.

2

GENDER

There are men in our organizations and there are women; however, men and women do not always work in the same organization. The physical organization may be the same but the real organization they perceive and react to and that perceives and reacts to them can be very different. This view is shared by Fine et al. (1990) who present results showing that men, women and people of colour do not share a common organizational life but, rather, each organizes its experiences in a different way. Reality is not absolute and it is the reality that we construct that is important. The topic of women and work is one which merits special attention, if only because there is so much connected with it that needs to be examined, understood and possibly changed.

As Morgan (1986: 178) states:

> It often makes a great deal of difference if you're a man or a woman! Many organizations are dominated by gender-related values that bias organizational life in favor of one sex over another. Thus . . . organizations often segment opportunity structures and job markets in ways that enable men to achieve positions of prestige and power more easily than women, and often operate in ways that produce gender-related biases in the way organizational reality is created and sustained on a day-to-day basis. This is most obvious in situations of open discrimination and various forms of sexual harassment, but often pervades the culture of an organization in a way that is much less visible.

The subject of women in organizations can be looked at from many angles: women as workers, women as managers, special concerns of women such as health effects of new technologies, sexual politics and harassment in the workplace, and women's reactions to stress and coping. Are men and women at work different? Do managers and subordinates relate to them differently? Are men and women experiencing the same reality? Do organizations have to organize themselves differently in order to attract and retain talented women? These are some of the issues we will look at in this chapter. Most of the authors who have written about women in organizations did not have a functional analysis framework in mind. Where possible, their work will be reframed within that perspective.

There is a lot of material to be found on the subject of women in organizations and it is a topic which obviously has not lost its relevance even though it has been under discussion for many years. Why women? Because, when the issue of gender comes up, the focus is on femaleness. 'Femaleness is in varying degrees a problem primarily for women, and secondarily for men. Maleness remains embedded in the organizational culture context and as such is not experienced as problematic' (Sheppard, 1989: 144).

Work and Gender

We cannot separate our social identity from our sex and gender. They are basic parts of that identity. Gutek (1985) has identified three significant influences of gender in the workplace:

- *sex segregation of work* – most of the employed women in the USA work in clerical work or less prestigious professions, and their work is less diverse than that of men;
- *differences in power, status, and prestige* – men typically hold jobs with more of these characteristics;
- *work conditions and personal characteristics that emphasize the effect of gender* – women's jobs usually have more pleasant working conditions and emphasize appearance more than men's.

In other words, women are looked at as a resource, men have the power, and there are broader situational factors which work towards strengthening or enhancing these differences.

In some countries, gender segregation has occurred along sectoral lines. For example, in the social welfare states of Western Europe and Israel, the creation of large public-service bureaucracies has provided a major channel for women to move into management but has created gender segregation, with women managers concentrated in the public sector and men in the private sector (Izraeli and Adler, 1994).

This gender segregation has several outcomes which can be arranged within the cybernetic hierarchy from the lowest to the highest:

Resources: stereotyped skills for men and women
Goal-attainment: differential access to power
Integration (roles): the expectation that only men or only women will fill
    certain jobs
Meaning: limited work experiences in working with the opposite sex and
    a subsequent reliance on stereotypes.

Before proceeding with the discussion on the differences between men and women, it is necessary to make sure our terminology is clear. *Sex* is biological, determined by characteristics such as reproductive organs and chromosomal composition. *Gender* is a term which is used in a social context. It refers to characteristics, abilities or interests that are arbitrarily assigned to the two sexes, characteristics resulting from social expectations, training and experience. Ely (1995) views gender as a dynamic social construction whose meaning, significance and consequences vary as a function of the power differences reflected in the sex composition across the levels of an organization's hierarchy. Sex characteristics are biologically innate while gender characteristics are learned. Studying sex differences focuses on how males and females actually differ. A study of gender differences focuses on how people think males and females differ.

Reviews of the literature have found that sex differences play only a small role in the workplace (Powell, 1988). What seems to be more important are gender differences. In work situations people are constantly undergoing evaluation of one kind or another. They are evaluated for suitability for positions by recruiters, for performance and promotion by superiors, for leadership by subordinates and for contributions by work group members. Evaluation is based on beliefs about the other and, when there is little reliable information to go on, often these beliefs are based on stereotypes, including gender stereotypes.

Stereotypes are perceived as facts – what we know or believe. They are implicit knowledge: knowledge about the world that is not in our consciousness at the moment but which we unconsciously use when the situation requires. They are both descriptive and prescriptive. That is, they not only describe, but also shape the way we believe things should be, our expectations (Bem, 1981).

Gender stereotypes can have serious consequences for women and their work. Effects have been found for the evaluation of intellectual products, salaries, hiring and promotion opportunities, evaluations of performance, authority and leadership, access to resources and power, perceived causes of success and failure, and modes of interaction in face-to-face situations (Haslett et al., 1993). These effects are powerful enough in and of themselves but the effects do not stop with the immediate result. Most of them have longer-term, more important implications. For example, if a man's failure is attributed to external causes and a woman's failure to a lack of ability, then men and women with identical performance records will face different evaluations and future occupational opportunities for advancement. Studies have repeatedly shown that evaluators rate men's applications for professional and managerial positions higher than identical applications from women (Fidell, 1975; Gutek and Stevens, 1979).

Although males and females have the same occupational aspirations, their expectations more closely reflect the existing sex segregation of occupations (Powell, 1988). Even male and female college students, who are doing equally well in college and who have equal commitments to work roles and value family life, hold gender stereotypes. They expect that women would play a more prominent role in the family and men a stronger role in the workplace. They did not anticipate symmetrical relationships in which both men and women share household and work responsibilities (Spade and Reese, 1991).

Why do gender role stereotypes persist? Much of our behaviour is shaped by the demands of the roles we play. Many of the high-status jobs calling for leadership ability are preferentially assigned to men. It is men we see filling those jobs and displaying role-appropriate traits and behaviours, and, therefore, those behaviours or traits appear to be 'masculine' ones. When we characterize a person as having a personality trait that corresponds to his or her behaviour, this is a correspondent inference. When this inference follows the initial interpretation of a behaviour, it completes a first impression – the initial cognitive representation of what the other person is like (Trope, 1986). Sometimes these inferences are justified (Jones and Davis, 1965), but at other times they are not. The correspondence bias (also known as the fundamental attribution error) is the tendency to make correspondent inferences even when they are not justified and when other possible causes of the behaviour exist. In this case, the role defines the person and the implications are wide. Secretaries are seen as submissive and managers as decisive. Guess which is the woman? The process is the opposite of what we expect it to be:

> In short, our stereotypes, reflecting our implicit cultural belief system, tell us that sex, being male or female, determines which personality traits we will inevitably possess, and that those personality traits then determine which occupations and status levels are 'suitable' for us. In contrast, research shows that our sex actually determines social expectations for 'suitable' jobs, roles, and statuses, and these 'sex-appropriate' jobs, roles, and statuses then determine which particular 'personality traits' we will develop. (Haslett et al., 1993: 48)

Status and roles in organizations have been traditionally gendered – certain positions are seen as more appropriate for being filled by men or women. This may be a trend which is starting to be broken today but there is a long way to go before work will be gender-neutral. It is more common for women to enter new jobs requiring new skills than it is for them to enter 'male territory' (Wajcman, 1991b). But just to remain accurate, do not assume it is only women who suffer from barriers barring entrance into certain roles. For example, the Israeli army refused to let a male inductee serve as a nurse even though he had three years of training, a bachelors of nursing degree and full registration. Instead, with the explanation that nursing is 'recognized by the IDF [Israel Defence

Forces] as an occupation for female soldiers', he was sent to be a quartermaster (Collins, 1997).

The problem is not just which jobs men or women receive. Stemming from the genderization of work is a gender-based power structure which, as part of our culture, is mainly taken for granted. Questions will start to be raised but only when more women and men cross the lines and assume positions traditionally held by the other.

The Gender Gap in Management and the Professions

Izraeli and Adler (1994) point out that the global picture of women in management is encouraging, but not yet positive. The studies in their book cover 21 countries and in each country, changing societal patterns have lead to significant increases in the number of women managers. However, in each country, there are similar stories about men controlling the centres of political and economic power and of management as primarily a male-controlled profession. In all of the countries, women still face many barriers such as the stereotypical perceptions mentioned earlier, discrimination, limited access to resources, and so on.

Although the number of women in management is steadily increasing, there are still major differences in the percentage of men and women in these positions, and the movement of women into top executive positions is even slower. The apparent barrier to advancement to the highest levels of the organization known as the glass ceiling is not only a North American effect, it occurs in many countries (Izraeli and Adler, 1994) and has not been greatly affected by women's increased access and commitment to higher education, careers in management, or equal opportunity legislation. As Izraeli and Adler look back on their previous, more optimistic book, *Women in Management Worldwide* (Adler and Izraeli, 1988), they state:

> Our earlier work, as well as that of others, had failed to appreciate the important distinction between entry into management and upward mobility within management. We implicitly assumed that the movement of women managers into the executive level involved similar dynamics to those of women's initial entry into management. We were perhaps overly impressed with the thin trickle of extraordinary women, operating under exceptional circumstances in each country, who had succeeded in breaking through the glass ceiling to assume senior executive positions. The reality however, is that the executive suite has remained highly resistant to women's entry. (1994: 7)

Access to senior positions is also related to access to executive recruiting channels which tend to differ from managerial recruiting channels. Among other things, it involves belonging to the proper networks. In Israel, for example, the near total exclusion of women from the senior ranks of the military and from combat positions, with the corresponding lack of experiences that are considered crucial in Israel for managing large, complex organizations, also excludes them from the executive networks. On the other hand, towards the end of 1997, El-Al, the Israel national airline, announced that for the first time it would be opening up candidacy for pilot positions to women, effectively cancelling its prior requirement that all of the airline's pilots had to have previous careers as air force pilots. Since, until 1997, women were not allowed to enter air force pilot training programmes, *de facto*, they could not become airline pilots for El-Al. Maybe things are starting to change but, if so, the change will probably be very slow.

According to Izraeli and Adler (1994), at least four perspectives are needed to understand the organizational reality that women in management face and the barriers that limit their advancement. Once again, it is possible to examine these perspectives in light of functional analysis (see Table 2.1). One point jumps out from the table – when a resource perspective is used, women are the ones who have to change. That is, a resource is pliable, changeable, and if we cannot use the resource we have, or make it into one we want, we will exchange it for another.

Broadly, the question of the glass ceiling phenomenon has come down to an issue of whether it is perpetuated by organizational factors or by individuals. Blum et al. (1994) found that although beliefs and attitudes about appropriate roles and job assignments for women affect women's management careers, there are also contextual aspects of organizations (existing social structures, personnel and compensation practices, and industry type) associated with gender stratification across organizations. These are macro-characteristics which reflect organizational efforts to adapt to external forces in order to survive and which constrain the dispositions of individual members who have the power to place employees in management positions (Davis-Blake and Pfeffer, 1989). A commonly held view that men, not women, should be managers in a particular organization can lead to the denial of promotion for women regardless of the views of individual decision-makers (Dipboye, 1987).

Another source of support for this position comes from Freedman (1990). On the basis of interviews with women in management positions, he has concluded that the scarcity of women in top management positions is due to structural obstacles and subtle, but persistent, discrimination. Policies and practices of many corporate organizations in the USA still assume the presence of a full-time wife at home tending to the domestic needs of the male employee.

O'Leary and Ickovics (1992) feel that the glass ceiling phenomenon can largely be attributed to sex-role stereotypes which affect interactions within workplace groups, especially when the sex ratio is unequal. The proportion of high status women in an organization can also affect stereotyping of sex roles. The number of female authority role models can make a difference on the effects of gender stereotypes. When there are more, they are evaluated more positively by both supervisors and subordinates (Haslett et al., 1993).

Table 2.1 *Perspectives on organizational reality*

Perspective	Function	The 'organizational reality'	Solution
Individual-level differences between men and women	*Resources*	Men and women are different. The norm for effective managerial performance is based on characteristics and behaviours of males. Women's limited representation in managerial ranks is explained by actual or perceived divergence from these male-based norms.	Women have to change, to 'fit in'.
Power's influence in the organization	*Goal-attainment*	Arrangements that offer privileges to men have persisted because those individuals and groups with a vested interest in the existing situation have the power to prevent its change.	The interests of the most powerful members of the organization must change. The personal and organizational advantages of having more women in executive ranks must be realized.
Organizational context	*Integration*	Organizations are essentially gender-neutral. Characteristics of organizations such as women's underrepresentation in managerial roles, uneven representation in other roles and greater male access to resources, power and rewards shape attitudes and behaviour more than personality characteristics. Tokenism explains difficulties that lone women in senior positions experience.	Organizations have to eliminate barriers and provide incentives for increasing the number of women managers.
Institutionalized discrimination	*Meaning*	Gender discrimination is embedded in managers' basic assumptions about society and organizational life. The significance of gender permeates all aspects of organizational life. Established, taken-for-granted understandings about organizations have built-in assumptions about gender and these are what explain women's underrepresentation, under-utilization and skewed distribution in management.	Both women and men managers have to acknowledge the discrimination and then senior management has to be committed to changing the situation in the entire organization.

Another possibility is that men and women are provided with different developmental opportunities throughout their careers. Both field and laboratory research indicates that women and men may have different opportunities for learning on the job. Managers are less willing to take risks with women or put them in highly visible positions. A US study by Ohlott et al. (1994) found no differences in the opportunities that men and women receive to handle new and different responsibilities and that they have equal opportunities to start new ventures and turn around businesses in trouble. However, they found that men and women differ in terms of the criticality, visibility and breadth of their responsibilities and in the degree to which they interact externally. That is, while men and women may be promoted to similar levels, women may not be getting key assignments such as those involving international relations or negotiations. Career paths may be similar but the responsibilities offered may not be the same. At the next level of advancement, the woman may be eliminated because she did not have the chance to show what she could do when faced with higher-level challenges. As a result, she may be perceived as less qualified than the equal-level male. This phenomenon is more troubling than overt exclusion because it represents a more subtle, and difficult to uncover, source of discrimination.

A similar problem, albeit with key differences, has also been found in other parts of the world. As a result of cultural orientations, the exclusion of women from transfers to branch offices far away from home, and the resulting lack of the range of experience needed for promotion to a managerial position, is seen as being one of the barriers to women advancing in management in Japan (Steinhoff and Tanaka, 1994).

Mentorship is often crucial to advancement in an organization and research evidence shows that it is even more crucial to women's success than to men's (Burke and McKeen, 1990; Morrison et al., 1987). Female managers have greater difficulty finding mentors than male managers do, at least partly owing to the fact that people like to mentor people similar to themselves and there are fewer female top executives. Male mentors might not know how to deal with women in roles other than mother, daughter, wife or lover. The concerns that women have at this stage of their career development are different from those of men and, therefore, even if she finds a mentor, his suggested strategies might not be appropriate. Thus lower-level male mangers have an advantage in achieving career success (Ragins, 1989; Roche, 1979).

Women and Work

So, *do* men and women at work differ or not? In newly formed groups, men are seen as more competent and task-oriented than women. The women are perceived as the 'social' specialists. The differences seem to result from members' beliefs in gender stereotypes but, unsurprisingly, the sex differences in task versus social roles tend to disappear once group members have experience of working with each other (Meeker and Weitzel-O'Neill, 1977; Piliavin and Martin, 1978; Wood and Karten, 1986). Sex differences in task-oriented groups have typically been found in laboratory studies that have strangers working together on a task. These differences tend to disappear when group members know each other better. In strange situations, men and women tend to adopt stereotypical roles but discard them when the situation is more familiar or when they have more information about other members (Powell, 1988).

Sex-role stereotypes are also apparent when women enter non-traditional, blue-collar occupations (Swerdlow, 1989) and the workers seem to develop patterns of accommodation which allow them to accept women as co-workers without relinquishing their beliefs about male superiority. But, again, familiarity makes a difference. The longer male firefighters worked with female firefighters, the more positive their evaluation of them (Craig and Jacobs, 1985).

Other differences found between men and women in workplaces include the workplace disputes they experience and the way they are resolved (Gwartney-Gibbs and Lach, 1991, 1994), characteristic behaviours used to achieve goals (Lipman-Blumen, 1992), their desires for and perceptions of what they receive from the job (Savery, 1990), and the work values rated most important by men and women working in clerical jobs (Mason, 1994).

The way women and men are treated also differs. Supervision for women depends heavily on their occupational status, while for men, it is their ability (Miller, 1992). Is there a gender bias in performance appraisal? Perception of performance is not a totally objective thing. Part of the evaluation rests on the apparent demands of the job and it has been found that, when job descriptions are manipulated experimentally, those jobs which are alleged to be held by women are judged to be easier irrespective of the actual skills or behaviour they require (Deaux, 1984). Ashkanasy (1994) found that gender bias affects supervisors' responses to subordinate behaviour only when behavioural outcomes conform to expectations. Maurer and Taylor (1994) found that while the sex of the ratee may have no effect on ratings, perceived masculinity/femininity of the ratee may have an effect and attitudes held by raters regarding women in the relevant occupation may moderate this effect. However, it must be mentioned that both of these studies were done with college students, not supervisors responsible for rating their own employees.

Differential treatment also extends to pay. Wage gaps still exist between men and women. In 1986 the average wage for full-time female workers was 70 per cent of that of male workers (Powell, 1988). The gap is largely the result of low wages in female-intensive occupations. In 1994, Norwegian women were the best paid European women, earning 86 per cent of what men received, while Spanish women got 70 per cent and Irish women 69 per cent (Sullivan, 1995). According to the International Labour Organization (ILO), women in rich and poor countries around the world work longer hours but are paid 25 per cent less than men doing the same job (Reuter, 1996). There *are* women who earn more than their husbands. According to US Department of Labor statistics, 29 per cent of working wives (10.2 million women) earn more than their husbands (Clark, 1996), and with upper-income women the numbers are higher. This may sound encouraging, but the issue is highlighted in a business magazine like *Fortune* because the subject is problematic. According to one of the interviewees in the article, women who earn more than their husbands are a 'silent sisterhood'. It is something that is not talked about inside or outside the home. Until unequal pay in the 'wrong direction' is a subject that people can feel comfortable talking about, we may still need chapters titled 'Gender in Organizations'.

Women in the Kibbutz – A Case of Gender Segregation and its Implications

Several Israeli kibbutzim (communal settlements – plural of kibbutz) are moving away from their socialist roots and the motto of 'from each according to ability, to each according to his needs' to a system of differential salaries. One of the main questions which has not received adequate attention and which must be answered is 'what will differential pay mean to women in the kibbutz?'

The kibbutz has never been, and will probably never be, a society in which men and women do the same work and participate to the same extent in the power structure of the community. From the beginning of the kibbutz movement, the vast majority of the men worked in production branches, the women in services. The move from communal sleeping arrangements for children to family-based sleeping also served to limit opportunities for women. Now they also had to be at home in the morning to get the children off to school or day care and home at night to watch over them. Women who want to go back to school or take high-level positions inside or outside the kibbutz find themselves with both logistical and social barriers to overcome.

The economic crisis which the kibbutz movement has had to deal with over the last decade has strengthened the status of those who hold economic offices and provide the community's income – mainly men. At the same time, the positions of those connected with the value and ideological sides of the kibbutz (education for example) have weakened. Services are looked at as money wasters. Work branches are encouraged, or ordered, to economize and more and more of the services which were once communal, for example certain meals, are moving back into the private home. The burden, once again, falls mainly on the woman. As a form of recompense, most women work shorter work days than the men do. In their daily life this may make things easier but, in the long run, it means that there are many jobs from which kibbutz women are effectively excluded. It can be said that women on the outside also take care of home and children, but there are many alternatives for middle-class women 'out there', such as hiring cleaning or cooking help, which are not available 'in here'.

The new motto of the kibbutz is 'the member has to be responsible for his or her income'. This transition will have the effect of increasing the discrimination of women in at least three ways (Lipshitz, 1995) or in relation to three system levels:

- *The external society.* Outside the kibbutz, most women do not receive equal pay for equal work. Differential kibbutz salaries will also let this distortion move into the community.
- *The kibbutz.* Most female members work in services and childcare. When the salary scales of the external world are copied on to the kibbutz system, the same discrimination that exists outside will come through the front gate. Most of these types of work provide low wages.
- *The home.* The confinement of the female member to her home also makes it difficult for her to supplement her income by overtime work even if it is available in a work branch in which she can work.

For married women, with two wage earners in the family, the situation may not be as bad as for unmarried women who will be dependent only on their own sources of income.

If the plans go through, the proposed solutions include a form of affirmative action – giving priority to women in technical and higher education so that they can get to a more balanced employment picture. Economic education is also vital so that women can take a respected place in the decision-making bodies of the kibbutz and its branches.

However, to avoid any misunderstanding, the discrimination of women of the kibbutz is not the outcome of a male conspiracy. The women also bear a lot of the responsibility. They were willing participants in many of the events that led to the present situation and it can only be hoped that they will wake up in time to prevent its predicted undesirable outcomes.

Women as Managers

Once women have reached management positions the problems are not solved. Sheppard (1989) found that women managers feel ambivalent about their positions – full of success and accomplishment alongside feelings of discomfort and caution. Her respondents felt that being a woman in a man's world demanded that they handle – or manage – their gender in particular ways. They felt the need for constant vigilance in order not to run the risk of not being taken seriously, not being heard and not receiving necessary information. The strategies they use range from accepting the status quo of male dominance to challenging it. Two strategies are the more common one of *blending in* and the less commonly used one of *claiming a rightful place*. Blending in consists of 'a very careful management of being "feminine enough" (i.e. in terms of appearance, self-presentation, etc.) so that conventional rules and expectations of gender behaviour can be maintained by men in the situation, while simultaneously being "businesslike enough" (i.e. rational, competent, instrumental, impersonal – in other words, stereotypically masculine) so that the issue of gender and sexuality are apparently minimized in the work context' (Sheppard, 1989: 146). Women who used the 'rightful place' strategy feel less concern for making the men feel comfortable.

Hood and Koberg (1994) suggest that like other marginal persons, it is possible for women to acculturate to the organization without being assimilated into it.

As mentioned before, stereotyping also depends on the ratio of women to men or men to women. Tokenism in the workplace still exists as shown, for example, by differences between the experiences of male and female lawyers (MacCorquodale and Jensen, 1993). Kanter (1977) defines skewed groups as those with membership ratios (based on a particular characteristic) ranging from 85:15 to almost 100:0. This is often representative of the representation between men and women in management. The underrepresented members are called *tokens* and the overrepresented, *dominants*. They are usually categorized on the basis of some easily recognizable trait such as sex, age or race. This characterization carries with it a set of assumptions about personal traits and expected behaviour. The outcomes of being a token are often detrimental to performance. They include:

- *performance pressures* – the result of attention that other members do not receive simply because they are different;
- *exaggerated differences between tokens and dominants* – their presence makes dominants more aware of what they have in common while simultaneously posing a threat to that commonality;
- *dominants have a tendency to stereotype tokens thus often distorting or misperceiving their characteristics* – stereotyping consequently forces the tokens to play limited roles.

Therefore, in terms of functional analysis, being a token has effects on all four of the functions: meaning, integration, goal-attainment and resources.

Women are more visible because they are underrepresented. The basics of person perception tells us that this makes both the actor and the observer more acutely aware of what is going on and gives the actor a greater feeling of vulnerability.

There are many ways in which organizations can show women that they are not 'full-fledged members'. As an example, access to organizational networks may be rooted in male-centred extra-curricular activities (Mills, 1989) and the language used may be male-oriented metaphors (Riley, 1983). However, tokenism can be at least partially overcome by building power bases – for example, on the basis of special areas of expertise which are vital to group performance. And, in fact, women managers are perceived by subordinates as more likely to be high on expert power than male managers (Ragins and Sundstrom, 1990). This may be one way for women, who lack easy and open access to organizationally based forms of power, to gain influence. Developing a sense for the political aspect of organizations can also aid tokens in learning how to have the greatest impact on decisions being made in the group.

In addition, becoming good communicators can make them more influential.

The debate is still raging over whether men and women managers differ in style and whether they bring different personal qualities to their work. Grant (1988) and Loden (1985) argue that they do and that it is worthwhile to the organizations to place greater emphasis on female qualities such as cooperation, nurturance and affiliation rather than trying to force women into the male model. Rosner (1990) labelled women's leadership style as 'interactive leadership' because it actively promotes positive interactions with subordinates by encouraging participation, excitement about work and a sharing of power and information.

These views of male/female differences in leadership and management mirror traditional gender stereotypes, and occur because of what Nieva and Gutek (1981) refer to as 'sex-role spillover'. However, there is still disagreement about their applicability to managers. Powell (1995) points out four possible points of view about the relationship between stereotypes and management:

- *no difference* – women pursuing managerial careers reject the feminine stereotype and have goals, motives, personalities and behaviours similar to those of men in managerial careers;
- *stereotypical differences favouring men* – male and female managers differ, as predicted by gender stereotypes, as a result of early socialization experiences that leave men better suited to being managers;
- *stereotypical differences favouring women* – male and female managers differ as predicted by gender stereotypes as a result of early socialization experiences that leave women better suited to being managers today;
- *non-stereotypical differences* – male and female managers differ in ways opposite to gender stereotypes because women managers have had to be exceptional to compensate for early socialization experiences.

A closer look at Powell's categorization reveals that more than the relationship between stereotypes and behavioural differences is at play here. His classification of these four points of view overlooks the possibly important factor of whether the manager accepts or rejects the stereotype in order to play the managerial role (see Table 2.2). As we can see, these different points of view, when looked at together, show that to be accepted as a manager, women have to actively reject the stereotype in two out of three situations while men have to do so only once. Without consciously taking any value stance about who makes a 'better manager', there is still the implication that 'male is better'.

Leadership studies show a mixed result. Sex differences are found in the laboratory but field research in natural work settings finds little or no difference in how male and female leaders actually behave (Osborn and

Table 2.2 *Managerial behaviour and stereotype acceptance*

	Managerial behaviour		
Gender of manager	Different for men and women – congruent with stereotype	Different for men and women – incongruent with stereotype	No difference
Male	Acceptance of stereotype – stereotypical differences favour men	Rejection of stereotype – behaviour opposite to stereotype	Acceptance of stereotype
Female	Acceptance of stereotype – stereotypical differences favour women	Rejection of stereotype – behaviour opposite to stereotype	Rejection of stereotype

Vicars, 1976; Powell, 1988). One exception is that women tend to be more participative or democratic than men (Eagley and Johnson, 1990). Women and men are similar in terms of style, philosophy, motivation, ability and so on. They seem to do the same things in the same ways. Those sex differences which are found are probably the result of the different organizational realities that each sex faces rather than innate sex differences. Differences might be attributable to the fewer resources that are available to women managers, their lower self-confidence, behavioural responses to expectations from others, or perceptive differences in evaluating women's leadership behaviour because of assumptions about what 'effective leadership' behaviour is – that is, 'masculine leadership'. The specific image of the ideal manager varies across cultures but, in all places studied, it corresponds to the characteristics that the particular culture primarily associates with men (Izraeli and Adler, 1994). The assumption that the behaviour and styles of men are what define 'good leadership' leads us to assume that something different is not as good (Hennig and Jardim, 1977). The common and known becomes defined as the desired and accepted. This perspective might even explain the 'democratic nature' finding. Women who adopt stereotypically male leadership styles (autocratic, directive) may be more negatively evaluated. Therefore, the freedom of choice about leadership styles may be more limited for women.

A leadership position implies power but power is a transactional factor, not an absolute one. It is part of a relationship. Power is the ability to exert a degree of control over people, things and events but it also means acceptance of that power by the other side. When the influence strategies of men and women are studied, it is found that they use the same strategies with the same frequency but only under a specific condition – when they have equal access to power and equal self-confidence (Instone et al., 1983). And as we have seen, this is a situation which often does not exist in reality. Women are often not given the same power and acceptance that is automatically given to men in similar positions and with similar qualifications (Kanter, 1977).

What about reactions of subordinates? As late as 1985, a survey done by the Harvard Business Review showed that 47 per cent of male executives reported that they would feel comfortable working for a woman (Sutton and Moore, 1985). While this may sound encouraging, it still means that over one-half of male executives reported that they *would not* feel comfortable working for a woman. In this case, as in many others, laboratory studies and field study results differ. In the laboratory, it was typically found that both female and male managers are judged more favourably when their behaviour is stereotypical. From that we could assume that effective managerial behaviour for men and women differs. But in studies of actual managers and subordinates, it is usually found that subordinates respond similarly to both types of managers (Powell, 1988).

There is one point on which men and women managers will never be identical. Pregnancy is a status which clearly calls attention to a woman's uniqueness. There is a widespread belief that women will eventually leave to have children and that pregnancy leads to organizational wastage. This view is also present in a country such as Israel where its irrationality is plain to see. Israel is a country which allows three months paid maternity leave, but it is also a country where the majority of men do at least one month of reserve army duty once a year, *every* year, until at least the age of 45. Simple arithmetic will tell us who is causing more work disruption.

Nonetheless, there is no escaping the fact that pregnancy is seen as a threat to a woman's organizational power and position. A laboratory study with graduate students showed more negative impressions of and less satisfaction from a pregnant manager. More social conversations were also initiated with her than with a non-pregnant female manager and the reactions were the same for male and female subjects (Corse, 1990). But once again, the results have to be looked at with caution. Laboratory findings may not have much connection with what actually goes on in organizations.

Women and their Technology

Modern technology, especially computer technology, is changing a lot of work relationships. It is changing the relationship between organizations and their customers and suppliers, workers and their technology, organization of work itself, the relationship of workers to the production process and the structure of the labour force. The first issue is beyond the scope of this chapter and here we will be concerned only with those issues relating to employees and their technologies.

Under the heading of women and their technology, there are at least two issues to be looked at: women's health concerns and effects on work and career.

Health Issues

Ever since the introduction of visual display units (VDUs) into the workplace, there has been concern over the possible health and safety hazards that they pose. Skeletal problems are well known, including symptoms such as lower-back strain, 'tennis elbow' and neck aches, as is eye strain, with or without headaches, and potentially more serious problems such as repetitive strain injury (RSI). These are issues which affect men and women alike, although the greater percentage of women in clerical work possibly makes them more interested in the problems and possible solutions.

One type of potential health risk has particular effects on women, however – the effects of VDU work on reproduction and possible hazards to pregnancy and fetuses. Bramwell and Davidson (1992) reviewed studies of possible reproduction hazards and concluded that no evidence of an effect is found. They determine that if there is an increased risk from VDUs, it may be a result of the stress that is associated with VDU work, rather than a direct effect of the technology. That stress may be a result of the fact that VDUs allow a much higher degree of control over clerical work than existed before. Measurements of all types are possible – from the number of key strokes per minute to mistakes made. An increased feeling of 'being watched' all the time along with increased productivity demands, possible reduction in the number of clerical workers employed, and so on, can lead to increased stress. The effects of that stress, as indicated in Chapter 1, can be detrimental to both physical and mental health.

Certain problems, therefore, appear to be directly connected to the technology itself, but others are the result of the managerial and supervisory practices that have followed its introduction. Although both issues need attention, readers of this volume are probably in a better position to deal with the latter.

Effects on Work and Career

As we will see more fully in the next chapter, depending on which point of view you take, the new technologies can be seen as increasing or decreasing the dehumanizing aspects of work. What is clear is that work as we know it is rapidly changing. New technology can open many opportunities for women but it can also leave basic conditions unchanged, or worse, create a new prison for women. Among hourly production workers, women's expectations about the likely effects of new technology were more pessimistic than men's and the gender differences persisted when other demographic variables and characteristics of the employee's current job were controlled (Hackett et al., 1991).

The design of new technology is not value-free. There are many choices that have to be made along the way and these choices are influenced by values, power considerations and goals. The very flexibility of the new technologies allows for a greater deal of managerial discretion and choice about job design and organizational arrangements (Albin and Applebaum, 1988), and the way in which it affects the nature of work is bound to rest on existing relationships, including power relationships.

The way women are stereotyped can affect the way male research and development workers think and, ultimately, the way technology is designed. Helmers and Buhr (1994) describe how gender images become embedded in machines and use the development of the typewriter to show the negative results of this process. Wajcman (1991a, 1991b) points out that although new technologies may disrupt established patterns of sex-typing and open opportunities for changing the sexual division of labour, these may be forestalled by male power. Women may get their chance at other jobs if employers may approach technological change from a position that seeks to replace expensive male workers with lower-paid female workers. So has their position improved or not? The design and use of technology itself can lock women into an inferior position in the labour market. Liff (1993) notes that information technology changes in the office have affected the content and experience of women's work, but have basically left the boundaries of gendered occupations undisturbed.

Clerical work is one area which has been greatly transformed by computer technologies. In most advanced industrial economies, clerical work is mainly done by women, and in the USA, a lot of it is done by women employed on a temporary basis (Callaghan and Hartmann, 1992; Gottfried, 1991). The introduction of computer and communications technologies in clerical work is a change in resources that carries with it a change in embedded functions as well as meaning. At least three broad issues connected to its effects can be examined (Albin and Applebaum, 1988):

Resources: extent of contextual knowledge requirements (knowledge of the firm's products, production processes, procedures, regulatory environment)
Goal-attainment: fragmentation versus integration of tasks
Integration: entry and mobility characteristics of jobs

When computerization first entered the office, organizations approached it in a Tayloristic fashion – by fragmenting the work. This increased productivity but devalued workers' skills, made tasks repetitive and distanced the workers from a feeling of responsibility and commitment to the organization and its work. As experience with the technologies increased, their potential for integrating work processes began to be recognized. By using the technology to decentralize communications, decision making and control, and reducing functional specialization and hierarchical processes, costs could be reduced and efficiency increased. Multi-skilled, multi-activity clerical positions were created resulting in 'para-professionalization of clerical work' (Albin and Applebaum, 1988: 144). But, unfortunately, this is not the case everywhere and many organizations are still closely following Tayloristic principles when automating their offices. When this is accompanied by uncoupling work processes and, at times, geographical separation of different stages of it, there is very little chance for a clerical worker to rise beyond the low level of becoming one of the few clerical supervisors. They cannot acquire additional skills and have no avenues for upward mobility.

There is also a fear that computerized office work will lead to the 'paperless office' and a large reduction in the number of office jobs. The design of work for those few who remain is a question. Will it be increasingly fragmented and standardized and placed under the control of the machine or will routine work be left to the machine and the office worker freed to do more skilled and satisfying work? In short, it is not the machinery itself which will cause the difference, but the choices made about how it is implemented.

As Wajcman (1991b: 31) observes:

Although the effects of particular technologies must vary in different contexts, it has become clear that the overall tendency is for technology-led changes to operate within and reinforce preexisting differences in the patterns of work. Technological change thus tends to further advantage those who already have recognized skills and a degree of control over their work tasks.

For example, Webster (1990) found that automation served to entrench the inequalities already existing between typists and secretaries in Britain.

Until women are fully represented in the decision-making bodies, managerial staff and design teams, there is no guarantee that the new technologies will be used to enable their development and advancement and not turn them into automated extensions of the machines.

Women and Stress

Although stress in general was covered in the first chapter, women also have to deal with a unique set of stressors that men typically do not encounter and they show different ways of interpreting and coping with them (Offermann and Armitage, 1993). These stressors include discrimination, sexual harassment, stereotyping, conflicting demands of home and work, social isolation and a lack of institutional support. For this reason, here we will briefly look at stress issues unique to women.

Burke (1996) mentions that most of the research on stress and health among managers and professionals has been done on men. However, managerial work is stressful for everyone. Offermann and Armitage

(1993) categorize stressors experienced by women managers at three system levels:

1 *the person* – stressors originating with the woman herself (self-esteem, personal control);
2 *the organization* – stressors originating in organizations (on-the-job support, sexual harassment, tokenism, sex discrimination, 'old boy' networks);
3 *the society* – stressors stemming from society at large (work–family interface, discrimination, attitudes about women in management, support).

The stress experienced by women managers comes from a combination of these sources.

Research using female subjects has shown that those with higher occupational levels and more demanding jobs are more prone to type-A behaviour (high levels of competitiveness, time urgency, irritability) and show the same symptoms of stress as male managers (Kelly and Houston, 1985). Like men, female managers who are more committed to their jobs are more likely to exhibit type-A behaviour, but as opposed to men, they show the same positive relationship between a high need for power and type-A behaviour (Hood and Chusmir, 1986). Davidson and Cooper (1992) report that women managers scored higher on both stressors and stress outcomes than male mangers and reported more type-A behaviour as well. They experience more pressure at work and more of this pressure comes from external sources as opposed to the pressure on the men which came from internal sources (Davidson and Cooper, 1986). The pattern is similar when other countries are looked at. For example, in India, female executives also experience more stress than males (Beena and Poduval, 1992).

One of the most common sources of occupational stress is role conflict and women are often subject to a special type of role conflict more than men are – the work/home conflict. As might be suspected, a substantial proportion of managerial women report experiencing conflict between their work and family lives (Greenglass, 1985), conflict which has negative effects on well-being in both spheres (Burke and Greenglass, 1987). The conflict can take two forms (Greenhaus and Parasuraman, 1994):

• time-based conflict – the time devoted to one role makes it difficult to fill the requirements of the other role;
• strain-based conflict – strain produced in one role spills over into the other role.

Of course, this is not a conflict restricted to managerial or professional women but, for these women, the demands may be even greater because they are likely to be in dual-career relationships which place heavy demands on both parties (Gilbert, 1993). However, it has also been found that the impact of a dual career is greater for women than for men (Lewis, 1994; White et al., 1992). Organizations have a great, but not the only, role to play in enabling women (and men) to cope better with home/work conflicts. This subject was addressed in the previous chapter.

The ways in which men and women react to experienced stress may also be different. Male managers are more likely to express physical ill-health whereas stress-related illness in women is more likely to manifest itself as psychological illness (Cooper and Melhuish, 1984). Type-A behaviour was more predictive of both cardiovascular risk and poor physical and psychological health in women than it was in men, even though men scored higher on more work stressors than the women did.

But work stress is not limited to managerial women. Female clerical workers' bosses may be agents of extreme stress, especially bosses who are unsupportive, do not delegate responsibility, are inconsistent and uncoordinated, and who emotionally and sexually harass subordinates (Balshem, 1988).

An investigation of the Canadian military showed considerably different levels of burnout and psychosomatic symptoms between men and women. Work environments into which women were only recently introduced were felt to be impoverished in terms of support systems and women found them lacking in coping resources. Supportive collegial relationships were also found to be of more salience to women than to men (Leiter et al., 1994).

The picture is not all negative, however. Women who work outside the home generally enjoy better health than women who work at home (McDaniel, 1993).

Sexual Issues in the Workplace

The sexualization of the workplace can include both sexual harassment and sex discrimination or, as MacKinnon (1979) believes, sexual harassment should be viewed as a *form* of sex discrimination.

Discrimination can be overt or subtle and can be judged across five dimensions (Benokraitis and Feagin, 1986):

- structural or situational
- cumulative or episodic
- deliberate or accidental
- public or private
- formal or informal.

Definitive definitions of what constitutes sexual harassment do not exist but there are several key elements which appear again and again

(Powell, 1988). Harassing behaviour is regarded as unwelcome and unsolicited and it can be either verbal or physical. As a result, individual definitions become overwhelmingly important and these definitions are influenced by both personal and situational elements. Three general models have been proposed to explain sexual harassment (Powell, 1988). Listed in system order these are:

1 *Natural/biological model.* Sexual harassment has everything to do with sexuality. Sexual aggressiveness towards others is the outcome of biological necessity and, therefore, it is not surprising to find its expression in work settings, as well as other settings.
2 *Organizational model.* Certain organizational characteristics prepare the way for sexual harassment. These include the hierarchical structure of organizations, a confusion of leisure and work norms activated by overtime or business trips, and access to grievance procedures and mobility.
3 *Sociocultural model.* Sexual harassment is an expression of power and hostility. There is very little connection between it and sexuality. People with the least amount of power (usually women) are most likely to be harassed.

DiTomaso (1989) researched workers in three types of organizations: a heavy manufacturing firm, a service firm and a public agency. She found that women who transcend their traditional subordinate role to men by working in 'male' jobs or otherwise challenging male authority are most likely to become conscious of the sexualization of the workplace as represented by both sexual harassment and sexual discrimination. Snizek and Neil (1992) found many women who claimed promotional discrimination (37 per cent) in a large Australian government research organization, and even more (41 per cent) who alleged that they experienced day-to-day discrimination.

Sexual overtures in the workplace may be the product of an organization's cultures and norms, not only the product of an individual's private predilections (Gutek, 1989), although the inclination is to think otherwise. As a result, predicted responses to harassment commonly revolve around 'telling the perpetrator to stop', even though this is usually not done in cases of actual harassment. The hesitancy can result from fear of retaliation, a feeling of powerlessness to enforce complaints and a general discomfort stemming from the relative organizational positions of the victim and the victimizer. 'When people see sexual behaviour in the workplace, they attribute it solely to individuals' wishes and actions and ignore the influences of hierarchy, work roles or organizational norms' (Gutek, 1989: 59).

The only way for an organization to rid itself of occurrences of sexual harassment is to apply sanctions and embed the refusal to tolerate it in the culture of the organization. Cultural change is a difficult thing, but a continual display of a lack of willingness to ignore sexual harassment is a definite first step.

Gender – Some Final Words

Looking at the issue of gender in organizations in terms of the four functions that must be fulfilled for the system to survive, we arrive at the following:

Resources. The question of resources can be looked at from two directions. Women are an under-utilized resource in the organization and the organization is not contributing as much to the women as it might. As long as they are relegated to certain positions they cannot fulfil their own developmental potential and cannot contribute their maximum to the organization. In many cases, they are not paid adequately or fairly for their work, are not accorded their proper status, or are in gender-segregated jobs, and are, therefore, also being deprived of resources.

Goal-attainment. One of the ways that an organization attains its goals is through proper use of its resources and technologies. The fragmentation of clerical work is not an effective use of those technologies and resources. The realization that women can also be effective leaders is a step in the right direction.

Integration. Women will be fully integrated into the organization only when structural and organizational level policies and culture change enough to permit them to do so. The glass ceiling has to be demolished. Organizational policies have to clearly show that sexual harassment will not be tolerated. The special sources of stress which women experience have to be acknowledged and improved ways of coping offered.

Meaning. Under the function of 'meaning' there are two questions which need to be addressed. First, what is the meaning of 'women in organizations'? The meaning is now in a time of transition. The old meanings and stereotypes are slowly being broken down, in some areas of the world more slowly than in others. The new meanings which are being created are moving in the direction of acknowledging the differences between men and women, of seeing that they are less than previously thought and, at the same time, realizing that the organization can only benefit from the differences where they exist. Second, how are women contributing to the meaning of 'organization'? For the moment we are mainly looking at how women can fit into a male-defined entity. Will an increasing number of women in positions of power and influence in organizations redefine what we mean and expect from organizations? Except for some exploration from the direction of feminist research (which is beyond the scope of this chapter), this direction of inquiry seems to remain an open question.

We have focused mainly on women when discussing hopefully, the reasons for that have become obvious. Us women who are treated as the 'outsider' and it is they and the o tions for which they work who have to make conscious decisions n let all of this talent and ability be wasted.

LIVERPOOL JOHN MOORES UNIVERSITY
LEARNING SERVICES

gender but,
ally, it is
ganiza-
t to

Examples of flexibility and its impact can be seen in many organizational spheres:

- Human service agencies that manage to survive under fiscal restraints are those which are flexible and able to adapt to customer or client needs. The rational model of management doesn't work (Mordock, 1989).
- Automobile plants with flexible production using team-based work systems, high-commitment HR practices and low buffers consistently outperformed mass production-based plants (MacDuffie, 1995).
- Japanese and German manufacturers are more successful than their counterparts in Britain and France in achieving organizational flexibility. Achieving this flexibility depends on trust and cooperation which developed in Germany and Japan after the Second World War through an institutionalized system of labour-management consultation (Lorenz, 1992).

The need for flexibility is undisputed. But what is it and what does having 'it' actually mean?

There are many types of flexibility and they can be classified according to the cybernetic hierarchy. For example:

R: physical flexibility – where do we work?
R: temporal flexibility – when do we work?
R: technological flexibility – what do our machines do?
G: employment flexibility – who are our employees?/who is our employer?
I: career flexibility – what is our career or careers?
I: functional flexibility – what do we do?
I: relationship flexibility – virtual groups and organizations cutting across time and space.

As we will see, most of the discussion about flexibility has focused on functions connected to resources and integration with some attention to goal-attainment. Creativity, another form of flexibility which is more intimately connected to the fourth function, meaning, is given its own chapter in this book. In this chapter we'll look at types of flexibility both from the organizational and individual level.

Life Pattern Flexibility

The career is coming under attack from both employers and employees. Organizations are telling their employees in subtle and not-so-subtle ways that they can no longer depend on receiving job security and upward mobility in return for hard work, good performance and commitment. This message comes from organizational changes such as downsizing (which shatters security and trust), delayering and high-involvement work teams (which remove the upward steps to career mobility), decentralizing (which restricts possibilities for advancement through lateral moves) and reorganization (which upsets career plans). Employees, partially as a reaction to this message, and partially as a result of value changes, are also no longer as willing to become 'company men (or women)'. There is more emphasis on lifelong learning and development and less need to lock into a single career identity. As Douglas Hall states: 'the organizational career is dead, while the protean career is alive and flourishing' (1996: 8).

A career has traditionally been defined as a steady progression towards positions of increasing authority and responsibility and success has been measured in terms of position in an organizational hierarchy. It assumes the existence of an internal labour market (Herriot and Pemberton, 1996). If this is no longer the case, then different ways of defining career success must be developed, as well as different approaches to career management and development in organizations.

The features of the new career contract as depicted by Hall (1996) can be arranged in terms of the cybernetic hierarchy we have been using:

Resources – *continuous learning and sources of development*. Career will be viewed as a series of short learning stages rather than being measured by chronological age and life stages. Development will come less from formal training programmes and more from continuous learning resulting from work challenges and relationships with other people in the work environment.

Goal-attainment – *profile for success*. Demand in the labour market will shift from those with 'know-how' to those with 'learn-how' and employability will replace job security in importance. Employees and employers will expect that 'whole people' come to work, not just the 'work' person.

Integration – *protean careers*. A career that is driven by the person, not the organization, and that will be reinvented by the person, as the person or the environment changes.

Meaning – *psychological success*. The old career goal was vertical success gained only by ascending along the organizational pyramid. The new career goal is psychological success, which can be achieved in an infinite number of ways.

This type of career requires a high level of self-awareness and personal responsibility. It gives the individual a lot of autonomy, an experience at the same time both exciting and frightening. Since the new career is basically a continuous learning process, the person must develop self-knowledge and adaptability and learn how to learn. New strategies and competencies will have to be learned since the old ones will no longer adequately serve us. According to Fletcher (1996), the main form of learning will be collaborative, rather than individual, and the recognition of diversity as a source of learning will be invaluable.

Brousseau et al. (1996) identify four patterns of career experience that differ in terms of direction and frequency of movement within and across different kinds of work over time and the motives lying behind each pattern. As we can see in Table 3.1, each pattern can also be associated with a different functional emphasis.

In the past, a time of relatively stable external environments, employees with expert and linear careers had the advantage. Now things have changed. As organizations and environments become more turbulent, employees with transitory and spiral careers are more comfortable and accepted. They are prepared to move and adapt flexibly to changing circumstances – exactly what many organizations need today. The experts can no longer count on job security and the linear progressers can not count on climbing up a ladder that has had most of its rungs removed. In other words, an emphasis on resources and goal-attainment will probably not leave the individual in a very good position, whereas those workers more comfortable with stressing individual integration and meaning will be better able to manage in the new environment.

Table 3.1   *Patterns of career experience*

	Expert	Linear	Transitory	Spiral
Direction of movement	Little movement	Upward	Lateral	Lateral
Duration of stay in one field	Life	Variable	3–5 years	7–10 years
Key motives	Expertise, security	Power, achievement	Variety, independence	Personal growth, creativity
Functional emphasis	Resources	Goal-attainment	Integration	Meaning

Career transition can be the result of voluntary or involuntary factors. Job loss can have powerful negative effects on psychological and physical health. Sudden and unexpected job loss can lead to stress (and its accompanying symptoms and effects), discouragement and self-doubt. However, if constructively coped with, it can also be a time of gaining new awareness and for setting new career directions. People who manage the transition from one career to another, whether within the same organization or by moving to another, are characterized by flexibility in response to changing circumstances, information-seeking behaviour and a willingness to go outside of known territory (Pliner, 1990).

But not everyone changes careers. Sometimes even when it seems that the individual has made a 'career error' and is unhappy with the choice made, there is no move to look for a new career. Why do employees stay with occupations they do not identify with?

Career entrenchment is the tendency to stay in a vocation because of investments, psychological preservation and a perception that there are few career opportunities (Carson and Carson, 1997). People who change careers are likely to forfeit financial investments (retirement benefits, holidays, etc.), as well as educational credentials and career specific skills. Investments that were initially perceived as helpful to career development become seen as expenses. Career changes are also likely to involve disruptions in self-identity, interpersonal relationships and social status.

The dynamics of career entrenchment are as follows (Carson and Carson, 1997):

1 *Choice*. A career choice is made based on interests, opportunities and preferences.
2 *Investment*. Investments of money and sustained effort to achieve success are made.
3 *Evaluation*. Periodic evaluations of the fit between needs and goals and the opportunities offered to fulfil them. If congruence is perceived, investment continues. If incongruence is perceived, career change may occur if past investments were low. If they were high, rationalization of investments to achieve psychological preservation may occur.

Psychological preservation is likely to occur under three conditions:

• when individuals, under their own volition, publicly select sub-optimal careers over more fitting alternatives;
• when individuals believe that persistence in a course of action will increase the likelihood of need fulfilment – as tenure lengthens, rationalization efforts grow as people try to convince themselves that career success is within reach;

- if career change requires additional investments in time, effort and money – if these are beyond the individual's capacity, they may try to defend against the change by focusing on the soundness of the original career choice and flaws of the alternative.

4 *Rationalization.* If successful, active reinvestment may occur. If unsuccessful, a search for an alternative career may begin with resulting career change if there is desire, willingness and opportunity. These factors will probably diminish as time passes.

   When time and energy are spent in justifying past career investments, that same time and energy are not spent in scanning the environment for other career possibilities. The resulting perception is that there are few options. There may also be fewer options because of a deterioration of ability, age discrimination or job-specific skills.

   The individual's propensity for risk taking may also affect the ability to recognize alternatives. People who can tolerate risk are more likely to avoid career entrenchment than those averse to risk taking. Learning, applying and testing new skills and the accompanying chance of failure are ever present in career changes. Career mobility may also be limited by situational factors such as dual-career marriages.

5 *Entrenchment.* Resource allocation, justification of investments and perceived constriction of career options result in career entrenchment. Entrenchment does not necessarily mean dissatisfaction. Satisfaction with or reconciliation to the situation may result in further career investment. Dissatisfied individuals will engage in coping strategies to manage stress associated with entrenchment. These strategies include exit (leaving – most rational but least used because, by definition, those entrenched do not change jobs), voice (actively and constructively trying to improve conditions), loyalty (passively but optimistically waiting for conditions to improve) and neglect (passively allowing conditions to deteriorate which may be accompanied by focusing energy on noncareer activities).

One of the problems of career change may be related to Schein's (1996) concept of the career anchor – a person's self-concept consisting of self-perceived talents and abilities, basic values and the evolved sense of motives and needs as they pertain to the career. Career anchors evolve as one gains occupational and life experience, but once the self-concept has been formed it acts as a stabilizing force – the values and motives the person will not give up if forced to make a choice.

We often become aware of our career anchors only when forced to confront our self-image – when making or considering making or accepting a change in some aspect of our career. People with different anchors will probably have different reactions and experiences in the changing career world (Schein, 1996). The eight anchor categories

Schein's research identified, their corresponding place in the cybernetic hierarchy and the possible impact of the changing workplace are presented in Table 3.2.

Schein's original research resulted in identifying the first five categories which divide very nicely into the four levels of the cybernetic hierarchy. Security/stability and autonomy/independence, both of which fall under integration since they refer to the individual's relationship with the organization, are polar opposites. In the first case, one is dependent on the organization and apparently does not have enough faith in oneself, while in the second case, there is so much faith in oneself that there is no need to rely on any one organization. Follow-up studies in the 1980s led him to add the last three categories (Schein, 1996) – all of which fall under the heading of meaning. Obviously, people's motivations and needs and values are changing. Some of these changes may be in reaction to a changing organizational reality, while others will force the organizations to change in order to accommodate them.

New organizational forms are developing which also have impacts on careers. Organizations such as Nike, Motorola and Novell developed a network form of organization (Allred et al., 1996). Network organizations link independent firms to provide critical expertise needed for specific projects or products. Rather than having a single organization perform all of the steps needed, organizations providing complementary services (for example, research, marketing or design) are networked to provide the most efficient service at each stage. In many cases, the relationships are long term and control mechanisms are replaced by trust. Network organizations are flatter than traditional organizations and rely more heavily on partner relationships to conduct their business.

Because of these features, managers in network organizations must develop collaborative knowledge and abilities in order to enhance their employability (Allred et al., 1996). These skills include:

- *referral skills* – the ability to analyse a problem and prescribe a solution with the network firm and across its partners, so when a problem is recognized the best member to address it must be identified and the problem referred to the proper location;
- *partnering skills* – the capacity to conceptualize, negotiate and implement mutually beneficial outcomes;
- *relationship skills* – giving high priority to the needs and preferences of key customers and partners.

According to Nicholson (1996) the most far-reaching changes to careers are coming from the transformations of work and organization created by information technology, and some observers of the career issue have referred to the arrival of the 'boundaryless career' as the electronic

Table 3.2 *Career anchors in a changing world*

Anchor	Motivation	Functional hierarchy	Future issues
Technical/functional competence	Primary consideration is actual work content	Resources	Knowledge and skill are becoming increasingly important but knowledge and skills become obsolete today at a very rapid pace. To remain technically competent means constant learning and updating, and the questions are 'whose responsibility is it' and 'who will bear the cost'?
General managerial competence	Holding and exercising managerial responsibility	Goal-attainment	Managerial career ladders may become less clear and status may be defined more by skills than hierarchical position. General management may cease to be a position and become more of a process skill needed in all roles. These people will need to re-examine what their real motivation is, e.g. power, responsibility, task accomplishment.
Security/stability	Long-term work life stability and security	Integration	Because of the shift from employment security to employability security, these people will probably experience the most severe problems. This person's base of security has to move from dependence on an organization to dependence on oneself.
Autonomy/independence	Maintaining independence and freedom	Integration	High congruence with new organizational policies. The necessary self-reliance is already part of their nature.
Entrepreneurial creativity	A desire to create something entirely of their own making	Meaning	A premium is placed on creativity today and increasing mobility makes it easier for this person to go to the place in the real or virtual world which is most open to his or her ideas.
Lifestyle	Career as part of a larger life system	Meaning	These people are often in dual-career situations and have to merge two careers and two sets of family and personal concerns into a coherent overall pattern. Organizations will have to consider how to maintain support systems for these social units.
Service/dedication to a cause	Desire to do something meaningful in a larger context as well as maintain an adequate income	Meaning	The number of people in this anchor is increasing as a result of changing values and a consciousness of large-scale problems. And the larger context is increasing in size as information technology makes more of the world and its problems accessible and visible.
Pure challenge	Overcoming impossible odds, solving unsolved problems and winning out over competitors	Meaning	Must be willing to be active learners since there will be many challenges to be met but their nature will be changing rapidly with technological change.

transfer of materials, ideas and operations breaks down boundaries of units, organizations and even the separation between home and work. Jones and DeFillippi (1996) compared bounded and boundaryless careers and industry knowledge and self-knowledge. Boundaryless careers are found in industries based on project-based organizing, individual performance and collaboration among highly skilled professionals. They use the example of the film industry, and predict that in the future we are likely to find similar examples in advertisement, medicine, computer software, law and similar industries.

The six necessary career competencies, their definition according to the functional structure we have been using and their meanings in traditional and boundaryless career are shown in Table 3.3. When we look at this table, we see that the emphasis has been placed on three functions – meaning, integration, and resources – which need to be mastered before the work can be done. The missing function – goal-attainment – here refers to the actual doing of the work.

As a result of characteristics of the boundaryless career, the competencies, challenges, strategies and implications of navigating a boundaryless career are different, in part, from those necessary for traditional career styles.

Industry Knowledge

Meaning – *knowing what*. There is a high degree of uncertainty in industries with boundaryless careers because of new technologies, globalizing markets and rapid shifts in consumer preferences. The major challenge is to deal with this uncertainty – to remain employed, reduce income variability, manage the shift between periods of activity and unemployment, deal with time pressures during employment periods and manage one's reputation to increase job opportunities.

Strategies for gaining knowledge about the criteria for success in order to understand what projects and roles best develop one's reputation and create future job opportunities include a career path of horizontal, upward movement – horizontal across firms and upward in terms of roles and project status. This is basically the spiral pattern mentioned earlier (Brousseau et al., 1996). The loyalty is to the profession or industry rather than to a single organization.

Integration – *knowing when*. The first challenge is knowing when to stay in a role or function before it limits one's opportunities. Staying too long makes it more difficult to move because other people's expectations limit what they allow you to do. A second challenge is knowing when to stretch current skills to exploit established skills. The third challenge is knowing when to go through the window of opportunity before it closes.

Resources – *knowing where*. The multiple paths for entrance, training and advancement within a career system can be a source of freedom and

Table 3.3 *Career competencies for traditional and boundaryless careers*

Competency	Function	Traditional career	Boundaryless career
Industry knowledge			
Knowing what (type of career system one is entering) Understanding the industry's opportunities, threats and requirements for career success	Meaning	Understanding the firm's specific practices, jobs, roles and culture	Understanding the industry
Knowing when (to stay or leave and employment situation) Timing and choice of activities within one's career	Integration	Dictated largely by the employer who decides when role transitions should occur	Pacing and timing of a career become more difficult since advancement does not imply hierarchical movement up a ladder and may depend on differing definitions of career success
Knowing where (to gain entrance, training, and advancement) The geographical, spatial or cultural boundaries for entrance, training and advancement within a career system	Resources	Controlled by the firm	Question of where to enter is difficult since boundaries are diffuse and there are many viable paths into a career
Self-knowledge			
Knowing why (one is pursuing a particular career) Understanding one's motives, interests and meanings	Meaning	Often taken from the organization and defined by the employer	Individual's identities, interests and meanings are grounded in roles and statuses based in occupations, professions and industries
Knowing with whom (to initiate contracts and relationships) Creating social capital by gaining access to those who provide opportunities and important resources	Integration	Social capital defined by connections to key stakeholders within the firm	Social capital oriented across firms with more varied options for relationships
Knowing how (to perform the tasks and roles needed for capturing opportunities) Skills and talents needed for competent performance	Resources	Firm-specific experiences play a large role in the development of skills and roles making the employee less valuable to other employers each year	Transferability of skills and experiences across employers is valued

a source of anxiety and the responsibility is on the individuals, not the firms. Challenges include where to gain training and experience, remaining in the industry and advancing in it. In the boundaryless career training does not guarantee entrance and once one enters, there is no promise of remaining and advancing.

Self-knowledge

Meaning – *knowing why.* The boundaryless career system challenges people to improvise outside concerns around the unpredictability of periods of project activity often followed by periods of involuntary unemployment. It demands greater self-direction and motivation since steady work is uncertain. Greater sacrifices are often required in personal life and therefore there must be clarity about the career as one's primary focus.

The strategies chosen depend on whether career or balance is the primary focus. Boundaryless careers permeate and often overtake one's life, thus they require a clear sense of one's personal values and career goals. They are best suited for those who highly value a career and want it to be a central and defining feature of their life.

Integration – *knowing whom.* The importance of building strong social capital resources may lead to treating all social interactions as means to personal ends.

Resources – *knowing how.* The skills that are needed for many boundary-less careers are both technical and collaborative skills. Increased training, especially across functions, as well as the development of unique and valued skills and training may help preserve employability and contribute to career success.

Today, everyone has to view him- or herself as a temporary employee. Restructuring, re-engineering, re-organization – in many cases these are all buzz-words for the creation of unemployment. And the unemployment picture, mainly in Europe, is getting worse. The latest victims of the cuts are white-collar workers who thought they were immune – that getting fired or being made 'redundant' was something that only happened to blue-collar workers. In 1996 the German automobile industry predicted that it would lose 100,000 jobs during the next four years (Branegan, 1996). At the beginning of 1996, the American communications giant AT&T announced that it would be letting 13 per cent (40,000) of its employees go – most by the end of the year (Church, 1996). AT&T used to be viewed as an organization with a lifelong commitment to its employees – no more. At the same time, the USA is better at job creation than Japan or Europe (Hirsh, 1995).

In an attempt to combat some of the unemployment, some countries and organizations are looking towards job sharing. In effect, this means that people agree to work fewer hours and bring home less pay so that other people can work as well. Other 'solutions' are found in temporary and part-time employment.

Employment Flexibility

In the USA, 20 per cent of new jobs created between 1991 and 1993 were temporary jobs (Feldman et al., 1994). Traditionally, temporary employees were viewed as replacements for permanent employees who were absent temporarily for reasons such as illness or vacation. Today, temporary employees are viewed as a critical part of the personnel strategies of many organizations and there are some positions which are staffed *only* by temporary employees. It has been suggested that the temporary workforce has allowed organizations to maintain a degree of job security for groups of core employees by increasing insecurity among non-core personnel (Magnum et al., 1985).

Under the name 'contingency workers', Fierman (1994) includes part-timers, freelancers, subcontractors and independent professionals. These categories represent people hired by companies to cope with unexpected or temporary challenges. The numbers of contingency workers is steadily growing, although how fast and by how much is disputable. For young people, low-commitment contingent work has traditionally been a way to explore career opportunities. For older workers who are forced into contingent jobs involuntarily, they can be quite stressful. For some employees, temporary work is a way to find a permanent job.

There are some important differences between part-time and temporary workers. In some sense, a career path for temporary employees may closely resemble the previously described boundaryless career paths but, in some cases, temporary workers are increasingly working full-time as replacements for permanent workers (Smith, 1993). Part-time employees are usually considered 'permanent workers' who work less than a full work-week. However, along with part-time employment there may also be poorer benefits, lower pay, less opportunity for advancement and more uncertain lives. This was basically the cause of the 1997 teamsters' strike at UPS in the USA – a much publicized, 'landmark' strike.

As with temporary employees, there are basically two reasons that people give for becoming part-time workers (Feldman and Doerpinghaus, 1992):

- *voluntary* – a compromise between the desire to have a career and the desire to have a family or needing or wanting the flexibility for other reasons;

- *involuntary* – a stop-gap measure for those unable to find permanent employment.

There are three reasons typically given by organizations for using temporary employees and all of them are basically concerned with the resources function:

- *Cutting costs.* Temporary employees typically do not receive the same wages or benefits as permanent employees. Often the organization does not engage in training temporary employees and uses people trained elsewhere. Recruiting and testing costs may also be saved as some employers view the temporary employment period as a selection tool for hiring permanent employees as needed.
- *Avoiding restrictions and consequences.* The use of temporary employees can avoid the negative consequences of having to fire workers when they are no longer needed and all the attendant legal and emotional outcomes associated with that practice. Hiring temporary workers may also allow the organization to effectively establish a multi-tiered wage system without having to deal with perceptions of wage inequality among the permanent workers. Either lower-paying jobs or high-paying activities (such as consulting) may be done in this way.
- *Increasing flexibility.* Temporary workers allow organizations to deal with fluctuations in demand for output without negatively affecting the permanent workforce. They can also allow for greater flexibility in distributing the workforce by sending them to different parts of the organization to meet changing demands. Job descriptions and union restrictions may not enable the organization to do this with permanent workers. Temporary workers may also bring highly specialized skills that are necessary to the organization's functioning but which are infrequently or unpredictably needed.

When hiring part-time workers covered by collective agreements, the two most important reasons were flexibility in scheduling work and employees' preferences for part-time work (Zeytinoglu, 1992). Savings in wages and benefits were of minor importance in such cases.

Smith (1993) refers to enabling and restrictive strategies of flexibility. With enabling strategies, organizations upgrade labour processes and nurture long-term relationships with a core workforce. Downgrading of the employment relationship and deskilling of work processes is what occurs when restrictive strategies are used. The workforce is hired and fired as demands change.

The flexibility demanded by organizations which leads to the use of contingent employees can clash with another fact of organizational life. Competitive advantage doesn't depend only on flexibility. It depends on

retaining a highly trained, motivated, creative and empowered workforce – objectives that are hard to meet with non-permanent employment. Or, to put it in our terms, when the organization focuses only on
the resource level, and ignores the others, the outcomes are fairly certain
to be detrimental in the long run.

Functional Flexibility

One of the most basic components of organizational flexibility is increasing the skills of the workforce. In organizations with a long tradition of
rigid divisions of labour and adversarial labour–management relations,
this may be a tough obstacle to overcome. One possible alternative is
offered by Cappelli and Sherer (1989) who propose defining union
boundaries on the basis of employment (having the contract apply to
specific workers) rather than on the basis of tasks performed (applying the contract to job titles). They feel that this system would provide greater autonomy for workers, as well as greater flexibility. The
researchers provide survey results showing that the system is preferred
by workers who feel constrained by traditional union contracts.

At the most extreme but opposite level from the small, rigid, division
of labour and narrow job descriptions, we find what could be called a
'job-free organization'. In place of jobs there are part-time and temporary
work situations. Instead of thinking of organizations structured from
jobs, we start thinking in terms of work needing to be done. In such an
organization there would be no job descriptions except for the most
general one of 'do whatever needs to be done'. Bridges (1994) states that
many organizations are on the way to being 'de-jobbed'. In the state of
our fast-moving economy, Bridges calls jobs 'rigid solutions to elastic
problems'. Needs change constantly and 'the job' is inflexible.

But the question is whether such an organization could survive the
short term in order to get to the long term. Can people who have been
socialized into a 'normal' bureaucratic organization change quickly
enough to self-organize and accept responsibility and accountability for
processes and performance? Or will anarchy and chaos doom the
organization before the learning process moves far enough along? The
concept of organizational rewards will have to change as well. Such a
change requires vision and commitment, total commitment, and such
things are hard to come by and require time. Moving from the job
organization to the post-job organization requires learning. Our organizations today maintain policies, programmes, structures and strategies
that enable people to be more successful as job holders but would ruin
the organization if people did what needs to be done rather than 'doing
their jobs'. Some of the technology useful to an organization trying to
operate in this way is in place – database and networking technology, for
example. What is missing, as usual, is the social and cultural infra-

structure. Rewards, training, hiring and careers are just some of the human resource issues that have to be radically changed.

Pirelli Cables – a Case of Unfulfilled Functional Flexibility (Clark, 1993)

In 1985, the board of Milan-based Pirelli Cables decided to replace its plant in Southampton in England with a new automated manufacturing plant which opened in South Wales in 1987. The factory is a CIM (computer-integrated manufacturing) plant, which basically means that orders input into the business system can be used to generate a production schedule. The schedule is downloaded into the manufacturing system and direct instructions are provided to individual machines through process-control systems. Many operations previously carried out by separate machines are now linked together into a continuous machine process. The plant was conceived as an experiment since there was some concern that the corporation was not keeping pace with advanced production technologies.

The human resource policy that was built for the plant included a participative management style, integrated pay systems, single status, full functional flexibility, skills-based training and elaborate employee involvement mechanisms. The organizational structure was flat and lean, with three levels of management: the divisional manager, three senior functional managers and eight middle/junior managers. It was assumed that the majority of the traditional management functions would be built into the CIM system. The union agreement included a whole range of issues not found in more traditional agreements – in particular, its provisions on flexibility. It was accepted by the union that employees be 'completely flexible' – meaning that they would undertake any tasks within their capability (following appropriate training if needed) and vary shifts and patterns of work to meet operation demands. Non-management employees were hired into one of three generic job titles: producer, maintainer or administrator. But, contractually, each could be required to carry out any function within their capabilities.

Because of the new work system, it was assumed that technical competence or experience were not enough to ensure success. Prospective employees had to have the 'right attitude'. A skills training policy was enacted to enable new employees to achieve greater work flexibility. Completing skill modules resulted in additional pay.

After three years, a modification to full functional flexibility was proposed, and agreed on by employee ballot, and a cap was put on the number of skill modules that could be completed. Each employee would then be assigned primary and secondary areas of responsibility. This change meant that the opportunity to deploy total flexibility was not taken advantage of in practice and was effectively limited by skill module capping. By mid-1990 there had been no flexibility of staff between the three main functions, only within them. Maintenance had the most flexible patterns and administrators the least.

Clark (1993) gives six reasons for abandoning full flexibility:

- '*Horses for courses*'. Many employees were more suited to and interested in certain areas of work rather than others. Producers and shift managers agreed that it was best for staff to work in those areas which best suited their temperament, skills and abilities.

- *Need for specialist knowledge.* Regular work in one area allowed the company to use staff knowledge and experience to produce high-quality work.
- *Interest in 'ownership' of particular work areas.* When employees are allocated duties giving them overall responsibility for a particular area, there is a greater possibility of a commitment to, and achievement of, high-quality work.
- *Training.* Staff were sometimes requested to remain in one position to provide training to newcomers. Continual improvements in the technology and production procedures require constant updating of staff if they are to continue working competently in their secondary areas.
- *Skill retention.* Skills that are not used in practice cannot be utilized adequately.
- *Tight staffing levels.* Pressures to reduce costs were both a reason for and a limitation on, flexibility. Tight staffing levels in maintenance reinforce the need for flexibility but the same pressures among the administrators did not allow staff in one area to be spared for training in an unrelated area.

Although full flexibility was not achieved there is a great difference between work patterns in the CIM plant and those in the corporation's traditional plant that it replaced. The workforce expressed a willingness to be as flexible as required and that agreement is enshrined in the union contract. But, in practice, it turned out that Pirelli does not need full flexibility to do what it wants to do.

The second part of the picture at Pirelli involved self-supervision – a major change in both attitudes towards work and involvement in work. If there is a problem, the employees seek to solve it themselves or in collaboration with other staff. If the work is going well, employees may walk around to find someone who needs help. The combination of self-supervision and functional flexibility has benefits for both management and employees. For management, it is functional in terms of smooth production flows. For employees, it led to increased job satisfaction and interest. This is not to say that there is no criticism. As usual, a minority abused the system leading to low morale. Clark's article ends on a more pessimistic note about the success of the plant. In 1990, the market was hit hard by the recession and, in 1992, several redundancies were announced.

Technological Flexibility

The demands on organizations to be more flexible and the capabilities of the new production and information technologies to meet this demand are leading to more and more technological change in organizations. The main capabilities of micro-electronics based computing technologies are the capture, storage, manipulation and distribution of information. It is these capabilities that account for their use in administrative, service and manufacturing environments.

These technologies have the advantage (and attendant difficulties) of being more than discrete improvements in existing technology. The electric typewriter was an incremental improvement on the manual one. The electronic typewriter, with its memory capabilities, started crossing the line from being a substitute innovation to being a radical innovation, although it was simple to ignore its new capabilities. The next step was the dedicated word processor, but the leap to computers with integrated capabilities to not only type and store documents but also to integrate data from different programs was a move from 'doing the task a little better' to 'doing the task in a radically different way' and to 'doing radically different tasks'. The linking of discrete systems into networks also allowed for group input into projects (on the office side) and integrated manufacturing systems (on the manufacturing side). With networks, people are connected to people and people are connected to data. The flow of information that was once hierarchical can now be direct. And since information is one of the major sources of power, the shared information has to be accompanied by a shared expectation that the information will be used responsibly. That is, it has to be accompanied by trust.

The technological changes are relatively simple to make when compared to the changes required in organizational culture and practices. These changes include skills, work organization, decision making, authority, communications, and so on. The rigid bureaucratic forms of organization are not compatible with the flexible forms of technology which demand networking and decentralization, not rigid hierarchy and a tight division of labour. Teamworking and the need to find compatible systems of rewards are going to have to replace individual motivations and advancement. Bessant (1993) reported that the general trend of organizational changes found in a study of 28 companies using computer-integrated technology shows a theme of integration – that is, the organizational changes reflect the dominant technological trend.

The problem of the managerial and organizational changes necessary to achieve flexibility is not new. It has been discussed many times over the past 15 years (see, for example, Hirschhorn, 1984; Pasmore, 1988; Walton and Susman, 1987).

According to writers such as Bessant (1991) and Piore and Sabel (1982) we are undergoing a paradigm change – a discontinuous shift – similar to what occurred with the development of mass production in the early part of the twentieth century. Because we are in the *middle* of the shift, it is still impossible to tell what the final organizational forms will, or should, look like. As we are coming to realize with most things today, there is probably no 'one best way'. Possibly, even within a single organization, the final form may be a shifting form – one that changes smoothly and fluidly as conditions and demands change – a form designed to sustain continuous change rather than maintain an equilibrium.

One of the capabilities that might most be in demand in the new systems is the ability to self-organize. Self-organization locates the initiative in teams, allowing for coordination without hierarchy (Hackman, 1990). The results are greater flexibility and faster response time because of the elimination of elaborate organizational control mechanisms.

Industrial Technology

The basis of traditional mass production was the use of dedicated machines (machines that can perform only one operation at a time) and the use of dedicated workers (workers who perform standardized tasks). These two components allowed more control (by the organization) over the input–output conversion procedures, and a reduction in uncertainty. Mass production run with the use of fixed automation is characterized by high technical complexity, sequential task interdependence and routine production tasks. This combination makes for a very *inflexible* organization.

Advanced manufacturing technology (AMT) is the result of over 20 years of technological developments that enable manufacturing organizations to become more flexible in their responses to customer needs while continuing to control costs. It consists of innovations in materials (machinery, etc.) and knowledge technology that have drastically changed the work process of traditional mass production organizations. Zammuto and O'Connor state that 'AMT refers to a family of technologies that include computer-assisted design and engineering systems, materials resource planning systems, automated materials handling systems, robotics, computer numerically controlled machines, flexible manufacturing systems, and computer-integrated manufacturing systems' (1992: 701). The common element among all these technologies is the use of computers to store and manipulate data (Dean et al., 1992).

In contrast to the use of dedicated machines, flexible manufacturing technology allows the production of many types of components at little or no extra cost. Each machine in a flexible manufacturing system can perform a variety of operations thereby combining the advantages of small-batch production with the cost-savings of continuous-process production. The key is the use of a system that is computer controlled. Computer-integrated manufacturing (CIM) is a technique by which commands given to the machines by the computer control the change-over from one operation to another (as seen in the Pirelli case). The machines do not have to be physically retooled, saving a lot of time and money. In a CIM system, the computers control feeding the machine with components, assembly and transfer to other machines, and unloading the final product.

But as Zammuto and O'Connor (1992) point out, the literature shows that the benefits gained by companies using AMT are more likely to be productivity improvements, not flexibility improvements. Often there are difficulties in gaining *any* improvements. Implementation problems are common, installations are sometimes abandoned and frequently there is a general feeling that the organization is getting a poor return on its investment. Obviously, it is not only the technology that is at fault here. AMT leads to greater technical complexity, more complex tasks and higher task interdependence. These lead to greater levels of uncertainty and greater effects of errors in the process and their resulting costs. As usual, there is more than one way to deal with these issues (Ettlie, 1986).

It is not the technology itself that determines the outcome – it is what the organization decides to do with it. Firms with a higher AMT level may involve employees more in decision making than firms with lower levels (Gyan-Baffour, 1994), but there are also cases in which programmable technology can be used to decrease worker autonomy and enhance managerial control.

Implementation strategies can be ranged on a continuum from control oriented to flexibility oriented (Zammuto and O'Connor, 1992). Control-oriented strategies push knowledge and access to information upward in the organization, while flexibility-oriented strategies push it downward. A highly mechanistic structure can be developed in which decision making is centralized in middle managers and technical specialists, routine tasks are performed by the technology, employee discretion is reduced and the result is increased managerial control. Coordination and problem solving occur at higher organization levels because the information and expertise are presumed to reside there.

As mentioned before, one of the main ways to complement flexible technology is through a flexible work team (Parthasarthy and Sethi, 1992). This is a group of workers who take on the responsibility for performing all operations needed in a specific stage of the manufacturing process. The keyword is integration rather than differentiation. Flexibility-oriented designs attempt to control uncertainties by resolving problems close to the point of their occurrence – uncertainties are compartmentalized.

Compartmentalization reduces total system disruption because the complex systems are composed of stable subsystems, which are composed of even smaller, stable subsystems. Interdependence across system boundaries may be increased, leading to a need for integrating mechanisms which will permit the necessary mutual adjustment to occur. In the end there is a potential for an organic rather than a mechanistic structure. The characteristics of an organic structure including decentralization – locating expertise and information access at lower levels – create opportunities for continuous organizational learning, a significant subject given its own chapter in this book. Zammuto and O'Connor (1992) propose that these organic structures appear to be the key to gaining flexibility benefits from AMT.

That there is generally little resistance to technical change (for example, Daniel and Millward, 1993; Northcott and Rogers, 1984; Smith, 1988) may seem surprising because of the potential of these technologies to lead to deskilling, loss of employment, enhanced managerial control, and so on. But, again, these changes are not inevitable and the same technology can be used to enhance job content, upgrade employee skills and increase their autonomy.

Findings from the British Workplace Industrial Relations Survey (WIRS) showed that reactions to technical change were consistently and substantially more favourable than reactions to organizational change (changes in work organization or working practices not involving new machinery or equipment) (Daniel and Millward, 1993). The surveys were conducted in 1980, 1984 and 1990 in about 2,000 British workplaces. By 1990, change was more common among non-manual than manual workers. Fifty-five per cent of workplaces experienced technical change among non-manual workers compared to 40 per cent of workplaces with technical change affecting manual workers. Support from manual workers directly affected by conventional technological change (not including micro-electronics) was reported to be 85 per cent. There was slightly less support for technical change that included the introduction of micro-electronic technology, but even that reached the 80 per cent level. Reactions of office workers were even more favourable to both types of technical change. Accounts of strong resistance to technical change were very rare. Although these reports of worker reactions were given by management and, in most cases, by a relevant union representative, they also gain support from behavioural data.

Workers may show support for advanced technological change for several reasons:

R – the new technology is perceived as an important resource. The benefits over the old technology are concrete, manifest and demonstrable. Its advantages in terms of factors such as quality, quantity and ease of operation are easily seen. Not all of these features are perceived by everyone as advantages in cases where trust and the job situation are precarious, but as opposed to the early 1980s, when technology was seen as a threat to jobs, it is now perceived more as increasing job security.

G – the new technology allows both the individual and the organization to come closer to achieving their goals. It represents a competitive advantage and the accompanying hope of greater job security. Employees usually know what technology is being used in their field and they compare what is going on in their organization to what is happening in others. Being a 'technology leader' is both intrinsically satisfying (pride, status) and raises expectations for success in the future.

I – in some ways the new technologies provide for some integration between the worker's 'work life' and his or her 'private life'. The technology is no longer as alien as it was 10 years ago. Many features of the new technology are becoming more familiar to the workers and valued in their home and leisure lives, as personal computers, VCRs and video games are becoming commonplace in many homes. Employees are therefore becoming exposed to the power and advantages (sometimes fun) of advanced technology whether they are drawn to it initially by themselves or whether they are exposed to it by their children. M – the new technology sends messages to the workers about the meaning that the owners give to the organization. Investment in new technology demonstrates the organization's commitment to the future of the workplace. It signals to the workers that their place of employment is regarded as having a future, at least in the medium term. It represents progress and advancement – this may be something to be welcomed or something to be endured but, either way, it is seen as inevitable.

In summary, the introduction of new technology tends to be associated with success. And as this series of studies shows, the technological change, especially the introduction of flexible technology, has a symbolic, as well as functional, aspect and the symbolic importance may have an influence far beyond the actual effect on quality or efficiency.

Information technology

Most of us are probably more used to seeing computer-based information technology in the office rather than on the shop-floor. In this section we'll look at some of the implications of these technologies in non-industrial applications and in particular we'll concentrate on the integration function – the question of roles and role change.

Roles can be defined as constellations of expectations, skills, knowledge and responsibilities that direct and constrain behaviour. Role perception is the role incumbent's view of how one is supposed to act in a given situation and role expectations can be defined as how others believe the role incumbent should act in a given situation.

When information technologies are introduced into an organization, organizational roles may become modified. Gash (1991) presents a model in which human interaction with information technologies create opportunities to penetrate the set of expected behaviours of other functional areas. But it is an *opportunity* and may or may not be exploited.

According to this model, two forces serve as catalysts for the re-definition of organizational roles: first, the desire to increase functional autonomy and reduce obstacles to goal attainment; and, second, a perceived need to respond to perceived changes in environmental demands. Roles are emergent and dynamic rather than static. When interaction patterns between organizational members are altered, roles become redefined (Rothman, 1979). Information technologies require increased, or at least different, knowledge by the users and allow for the alteration of the distribution of technical knowledge in organizations. As users gain this knowledge, their relationship with other role incumbents (such as systems support staff) in the organization changes. For some, acquisition of knowledge may prompt them to take on tasks associated with other functional areas. For example, users may start developing their own applications as the need arises rather than request them from the support staff. The worker thereby permeates the formal and informal boundaries created by differentiation or specialization. Since the boundaries have become more permeable, the role relationships are subsequently altered.

This is less likely to happen when information technologies are used only to automate routine tasks such as the transfer from producing a report manually to producing it via the computer. In such cases the workers are usually not involved in designing or implementing the system and are simply presented with a turn-key operation and showed the basics of using it. Job content and skills do not change greatly, role expectations (except perhaps for increased speed and accuracy expectations) do not change and it is unlikely that role relationships will change.

Flexibility in Time and Space

Virtual teams, virtual organizations, virtual corporations, virtual universities – sometimes it seems as if the future will not be real, it will be virtual reality. Going by names such as distance learning and on-line education, more and more academic institutions are offering degrees to people who will never see their ivy-covered walls. There are obvious advantages to these programmes such as the ability to continue working while studying, combining learning with demands of family life, learning with a geographically and culturally diverse group of students, being able to study where you want without having to uproot yourself and your family and low overhead costs for the institutions.

Virtual corporations are temporary organizations formed by a group of companies that join forces in order to exploit specific opportunities (Byrne et al., 1993). Today there are many tasks that no one company can do alone. The virtual corporation is formed to take advantage of specialized skills and knowledge that cannot be contained in one place. Each participating company contributes its core competency – its area of greatest strength. There are no organization charts or offices and, when the project is done, the corporation vanishes. The advantage is enormous flexibility and the disadvantage is the problem of coordination.

Nohria and Berkley (1994) present characteristics of an ideal type of virtual organization:

1 The disappearance of Weber's material files and their reappearance in flexible and electronic forms by means of information technology. Information becomes easier to manage, reproduce and disseminate – it is no longer a scare resource.
2 The replacement of face-to-face communication with computer-mediated communication as a means of conducting the organiza-

tion's primary activities and an increase in informal face-to-face communication for purposes of maintaining organizational coherence.

3   The transfer of issues of organizational structure from the organization of people to the organization of information and technology, so that the functioning of the organization appears spontaneous and structureless while the functioning of information systems seems all-pervasive and 'magical'.

4   The networking of people from different organizations to the extent that clear external boundaries of the organization become difficult to establish in practice.

5   The transformation of bureaucratic specialization turns into global, cross-functional, computer-mediated jobs. Employees can get a wide-angled view of the organization and greater feelings of independence from the organization because of their importance and knowledge.

What is the relationship between organizational form, technology and people?

If an ideal type of virtual organization is thinkable at the present time, its viability is attributable to the seismic shift we have witnessed in technology in recent decades – a shift marked by the development of such things as personal computers, networked databases, and instant forms of telecommunications such as electronic mail. It is not merely that new technology allows new configurations of people and machines, but that our relationship to technology continuously restructures both our thinking and our discourse. As workplaces witness the proliferation of these new 'modes of information,' people's expectations and projections about organizational life change just as radically, probably more radically, than the existing organizational environment itself. (Nohria and Berkley, 1994: 115)

A virtual team, like other teams, is a group of people who interact on interdependent tasks to achieve common goals. The subject of teams in general will be explored further in Chapter 4. Can virtual work teams who get together only in cyberspace to produce work really be considered teams? According to differentiations made by Katzenbach and Smith (1993), such groups are probably better considered work groups and not true teams. Many of the mechanisms that people use for confirming that they have shared values and beliefs, shared meanings and understandings necessary to building trust, are not verbal. In the virtual group environment we are confined to words and emoticons (those 'faces' composed of keyboard symbols that are supposed to tell us when someone's cutting remark should not be taken seriously – :-) for example). The entire non-verbal range of communication is missing and with it probably goes the possibility of building real teams.

On the other hand, because communication is primarily through written text and graphics, virtual work fosters social equalization – there are few social context cues to signal differences between people on a social or organizational level. People have time to think out their responses and the fastest reactor is not necessarily the one who gets the most attention. The shyer person is heard and the less assertive person is not interrupted. Boundaries are less obvious and, therefore, less divisive, and there is some reduction of status differentials. Electronic communication can disturb the hierarchy because communication is less dependent on irrelevant cues such as gender, status and power. Since the person is unseen, cues such as age, race or physical attractiveness also become irrelevant. All the preceding is true, of course, mainly in circumstances which involve writing, mailing and responding. Use of real time 'chat' and video cameras will change the situation.

The reality of working in virtual teams is different from the reality of face-to-face work, and if accommodation is not made for these differences, virtual teams will probably fail. Members of virtual teams can even occupy different time zones, making synchronous work almost impossible. Successful virtual teams also have to include the same elements necessary for any successful teams – the inclusion of the right people, a defined purpose. In addition, careful attention has to be paid to establishing excellent communication links since there is no possibility for 'accidental' informal communication in the hallway or the coffee room. Trust is very important in a virtual team because the opportunities for misunderstanding are many and those for clearing the air are fewer.

Distance separates people psychologically more than it does geographically. The law of propinquity proposes that the probability of two people communicating is inversely proportional to the distance between them. Allen (1977) found that the probability of weekly communication reaches a low asymptotic level within the first 25 to 30 metres. The problem is not connected entirely to the problem of 'walking' the distance. Krackhardt (1994) notes that there is evidence that this law applies even with the use of modern communication technology.

Nevertheless, electronic communication in its many forms can also be used to unite a group of people geographically separated into a powerful group. Pliskin et al. (1997) describe a strike of Israeli academic staff members which continued for more than two months. During that period, email was used as a major means of communication between the strikers and is credited with playing a major role in the success of the strike. Specifically, email helped the strikers maintain their unity both through raising morale and by offering practical advice. It closed the communications gap between the strikers and their representatives and created a feeling of closeness, as well as facilitating the negotiation process by allowing the strikers to express their support or rejection of possible solutions. The World Wide Web is also being used to distribute information, create sympathy and generate support for other labour issues. For example, it was used to publicize and discuss the Safeway (supermarket chain) and the UPS strikes in the USA in 1997. The Internet can also be turned into an Intranet – a private Web site usually internal to an organization.

Telecommuting

Advanced technology and changing attitudes towards work have made it possible for some employees to work outside the confines of traditional offices. The place they choose may be their home, the beach or almost anywhere they can use a computer. Telecommuting is most suited to jobs that involve information handling and demand little face-to-face interaction. For example, a computer programmer working on a customer problem line is a perfect candidate for telecommuting.

Working in the company of others has many benefits – structure, social interaction, discipline. In many respects, the office is a community. We learn social skills from dealing with people we are going to have to see again. Working at home means having the discipline to manage yourself and requires a significant amount of emotional maturity and self-discipline.

There are benefits to both the employee and the employer from telecommuting. When voluntary, it may give those who choose it more flexibility to manage their lives. It does not mean there will no longer be a need for childcare where it was needed before. Employees save time, energy and nervous tension by not travelling to and from work and getting caught in traffic jams. They also save money on things such as transportation, parking, car maintenance, clothing and eating out. There may be feelings of greater autonomy and ownership of their work and a greater sense of responsibility and commitment.

Sometimes, however, telecommuting is not voluntary (see the Chiat/ Day example below). Companies may institute it to cut down on real-estate costs for example. In such cases, working at home may lead to feelings of being left out, cut off from the informal interactions and the knowledge that is picked up in the hallways and coffee rooms. There may also be fears that loss of 'face-time' may adversely affect careers. Is the appropriate saying in this situation 'out of sight, out of mind' or 'absence makes the heart grow fonder'?

On the employer side, the benefits can include more productive time from employees because of fewer interruptions from co-workers and no recovery time after long commutes. A study of telecommuting done by British Telecom and reported on in *Fortune* (1995) found that the average telecommuter puts in 11 per cent more hours than his counterpart in the office. It is also easier to retain skills and knowledge within the organization rather than losing them when, for example, employees relocate for some reason. This advantage may become a more and more significant factor with the increase in dual-career couples. Telecommuting can enable one partner to be mobile without negatively affecting the career of the other. Disabled employees with valuable skills can be hired without having to invest in costly renovations.

In Israel, telecommuting consists mainly of freelance workers or independent consultants. Few full-time employees work on this basis. When it does occur, it is often viewed as a temporary measure to allow employees otherwise unable to come into the office the opportunity to continue working. But it is assumed that when the baby is old enough or the broken leg heals, the employee will return to his former arrangements (Sommer, 1996). One Israeli experiment that got a lot of advance publicity was run by Bezeq, the national telephone company. The experiment involved three information operators in the southern part of the country. Bezeq installed equipment in their homes so that information requests could be handled from there. The experiment died a quiet death after only a few months, but not before it starred as a short comedy episode on one of the country's satirical programmes.

The reaction of the public to any type of working from the home can also be a problem. A newspaper article (Sommer, 1996) reported on women who had started a business working at home but finally moved into a storefront because other people did not see them as working. 'When you are a woman working from home, people assume that you are not really working and they don't hesitate to demand your time, asking you to lead class trips or volunteer for committees. When we opened the store, people congratulated Eudice and me. We officially became working people.'

Many problems still remain unsettled in regard to telecommuting; for example, health and safety issues. If an employer is responsible for providing a safe workplace for employees, what responsibilities and authority does it have over the employee's home working site? Does the company have to provide or ensure that the employee has a fire extinguisher handy? Maintenance and repair – who is responsible for the state of the equipment? Evaluation is another issue. When employees are evaluated and paid according to the amount of work produced, there is no problem. But salaried employees who finish their work would usually involve themselves in something else if they are in an office setting. At home, the temptation might be to watch television. Another point is blurred boundaries. As opposed to the 'normal' situation in which work and home involve separate locations, times of day, dress, and modes of behaviour, telecommuting can lead to a condition in which there is no clear-cut shut-off of the work day. People literally 'take their work home with them', which can lead to feelings of stress and tension.

In most cases, it appears that telecommuting works best not when it is a replacement for the office, but when it is an adjunct to it. It is probably more appropriate for people more established in their career who are confident in their abilities.

Chiat/Day Advertising Agency – Venice California (Jaroff, 1995)

The staff of the Chiat/Day advertising agency in Venice, California, work in what is still considered by most people to be a very unusual organization. The difference is noticeable from the moment you step inside the headquarters building – there are no executive offices, no cubicles for the secretaries, no filing cabinets. What you find are couches, portable phones and lockers familiar to every American high-school student. The staff can work where they please and many of them telecommute. They maintain contact by cellular phone, pager, fax, computer and modem.

This is what is known as the virtual office. The transformation from the conventional office to the virtual office was sudden and took just six months.

Employees who choose to go into the 'office' stop at a desk in the lobby to pick up a portable phone and laptop computer. The phone can be programmed with the extension of the particular employee. They then head for one of the open areas which resemble a living-room setting and plug into the modem jack. Practically the only enclosed spaces in the building are several 'strategic business units' (what most of us would probably call conference rooms) which can be used for the occasional meetings of working groups.

Personal stationery and files are stored in the employees' private lockers but, aside from these, it is a paperless organization. Email and voice-mail are used to send and receive messages. Documents are stored in electronic 'filing cabinets'.

But what is the psychological cost of this move? The loss of human interaction necessary for creativity and social relationships, physical status symbols? The virtual office is still in its infancy and the balance sheet of costs and benefits has yet to be totally calculated. But although slow moving, it is moving and other organizations such as CKS (a California advertising group) and Ernst and Young (America's second largest accounting firm) are moving in that direction, although not yet as completely as Chiat/Day.

So if the workers are in favour of it, and we know how to design organizations in order to achieve the maximum flexibility benefits from it, what's the problem?

The problem seems to be culture. There are about as many definitions of organizational culture as there are writers on organizational culture. The approach we will adopt here rests on the premise that the full meaning of things results from interpretation. Culture is treated as a set of cognitions shared by members of a social unit. These cognitions are acquired through social learning and socialization processes that expose the individuals to a variety of culture-bearing elements, including observable activities and interactions, communicated information and material artifacts.

Culture is a social construction that both reduces ambiguity and facilitates social interaction. However, since members of an established culture see it as an objective reality, not, for the most part, as a social construction, culture may become a set of blinders limiting the alternatives that people perceive as well as the variables with which they must deal.

Culture has two basic components:

- *its substance* – the networks of meanings maintained in its ideologies, norms and values;
- *its forms* – the practices by which these meanings are expressed, affirmed and communicated to members.

Organizational culture will be explored further in Chapter 5, but for now it is sufficient to note that it can have an impact on factors related to technology implementation success, such as involvement (Giordano, 1988), trust (Hildebrandt, 1988) and commitment (Walton, 1989). All of these factors lead to extended commitment both by employers and employees. Each side is willing to go one step further to ensure the welfare and success of the other.

Structure is also related to technology implementation and influenced by organizational culture. Organization designs are a matter of choice and one of the factors influencing that choice is values. The competing values model (Quinn, 1988) was used by Zammuto and Krakower (1991) to examine the relationship between organizations' competing values profiles and several organizational characteristics. The competing values model proposes two axes reflecting different value orientations combining into a four-cell model of value systems with each cell having a different means–end emphasis.

One axis is a flexibility–control dimension showing preferences about structuring. A flexibility orientation emphasizes decentralization and differentiation; a control orientation emphasizes centralization and integration. The other axis represents an internal–external focus dimension. The internal orientation emphasizes the maintenance of the organizations socio-technical system; the external orientation emphasizes improvement of the organization's competitive position in the environment.

Zammuto and Krakower (1991) found that the flexibility–control dimension was related to different patterns of coordination and control. Using these outcomes and those of other researchers, Zammuto and O'Connor (1992) predict that organizations having a culture emphasizing control orientation would be likely to have a mechanistic structure and a resulting AMT implementation failure or, with less likelihood, productivity gains. Those organizations emphasizing flexibility-oriented values would have an organic structure. Because organic structure facilitates AMT implementation, implementation failure is considered less likely and the most probable outcomes are predicted to be productivity and flexibility gains. The more likely scenario is a mixed case – cultures that combine flexibility and control-oriented values and structures that have both mechanistic and organic characteristics, with predicted results also falling somewhere in the middle range.

It is also important to realize that culture not only affects the implementation of the technology; the technology is also an artefact of the culture. The same sense-making processes that go on when workers try to understand their organization go on when they try to make sense of their technology. The technology is more than a functional piece of equipment. It has meanings for members that go beyond its actual performance. In this sense, the computerization of work is also a symbolic process that requires symbolic understanding – what is the *meaning* of the technology and technological change (Prasad, 1992; Shulman et al., 1990). Symbols are not stable but are constructed and dynamically interpreted by organizational members (Feldman and March, 1981) and, therefore, have an impact on organizational processes.

Flexibility – Some Final Words

In this chapter we have seen that discussions about flexibility have covered mainly three of the functional emphases: resources, goal-attainment and integration. We have seen people and technology looked at mainly as resources to be used by the organization in achieving its goals. But we have also seen that if the issues of integration and meaning are ignored, those resources will not function to their full potential.

The resources function dealt with issues such as the use of technology and gaining greater effectiveness from employees through physical and temporal flexibility. From the viewpoint of the organization, goal-attainment involves the use of new categories of employees – contingency employees and employees who will pass through a number of careers during their working lifetime. The presence of employees whose commitment to themselves is probably greater than their commitment to the organization will require the organization to deal with issues of integration in new ways.

People and organizations have to learn new roles. As opposed to the not-so-distant past, more decisions and responsibilities for life and career planning now fall on the individual rather than the organization. These problems will be compounded by information technologies and electronic communication which allow groups, teams and even organizations to form and reform as the need arises without the need for physical reorganization. Relationships are more transient and, again, this might result in moving the focus from the organization to the individual. For people working at a physical remove from the organization, more self-discipline is required, together with a strong sense of purpose of what they are doing and why they are doing it. Here we have come to the issue of meaning – culture.

This less developed function – meaning – also has great importance and cannot be ignored. Issues of meaning which need to be explored in the future include:

- what is the meaning of work and a career?
- what is the organization telling me when it makes a technological change?
- what kind of organizational culture, if any, can people develop who interact only electronically?

The bottom line is that, from this point of view, the individual is responsible for fulfilling these four functions in the 'flexible world'. The organization which does not recognize this and tries to continue running in the traditional ways in the face of all of these changes will find itself in a difficult position, as will individuals who do not recognize these same changes. In the next chapter, we will look at a more extreme form of flexible organization – self-organization.

4

GROUPS

We discover by reading many articles about work groups and texts on group dynamics and team building that few of the authors distinguish between groups, teams, crews and other ways of performing collective task-oriented behaviour by small sets of people. However, articles and texts on team building usually list the characteristics of effective teams and suggest some of the goals of team building. After considering some of these definitions, characteristics and goals, we will propose a perspective based on functional theory that may help sort out the differences between groups, teams and crews. We then review the literature on the role of groups in organizations in the light of this perspective.

Groups and What They Do

In a classic text on group dynamics, Cartwright and Zander (1968) listed a number of attributes of individuals in interaction. The larger the number of attributes and the greater their strength, the closer the set of individuals would be come to being a 'full-fledged' group:

1 they engage in frequent interaction;
2 they define themselves as members of a group;
3 they are defined by others as belonging to the group;
4 they share norms concerning matters of common interest;
5 they participate in a system of interlocking roles;
6 they identify with one another as a result of having set up the same model–object or ideals in their superego;
7 they find the group rewarding;
8 they pursue promotively interdependent goals;
9 they have a collective perception of their identity;
10 they tend to act in a unitary manner toward the environment.

Shaw (1981), after reviewing 80 different definitions of a group, provided a much simpler definition: 'A group is defined as two or more persons who are interacting with one another in such a manner that each

Table 4.1   *Cartwright and Zander's group attributes and group functions*

Function	Group attributes
Meaning	2 Define selves as members
	3 Defined by others as belonging
	6 Have some model–object or ideals
	9 Have a collective perception of identity
Integration	5 Have a system of interlocking roles
Goal-attainment	4 Share norms concerning matters of common interest
	8 Pursue promotively interdependent goals

person influences and is influenced by each other person'. This definition is too general for our purposes since it leaves open how people are influencing one another and to what end. Also the definition only considers the group in isolation and not how it might relate to a larger organization and to the social and physical environment.

We pause to look over Cartwright and Zander's list in the light of functional analysis. We subscribe to the definition that a fully functioning group, in terms of functional theory (Effrat, 1968; Hare, 1982; Parsons, 1961), is one whose members are committed to a set of values that define the overall pattern of activity (meaning), have accumulated or generated the resources necessary for the task at hand (resources), have worked out an appropriate form of role differentiation and developed a sufficient level of morale for the task (integration), and have sufficient control in the form of leadership to coordinate the use of resources by the members playing their roles in the interest of the group's values to attain specific goals (goal-attainment) (See Table 4.1.).

With the advent of so many means of electronic communication and the 'virtual group' and the 'virtual organization,' the first item, on Cartwright and Zander's list, concerning interaction, need not be face to face. However, interaction as a concept is 'content free'. Unless the interaction deals with the basic functions of a group, the group will not continue to exist. Items 2, 3, 6 and 9 all relate to the first function of 'values that define an overall pattern of activity'. Items 2 and 9 appear to be essentially the same.

No item on the list has to do with accumulating or generating resources. One reason for this is that much of social psychology is based on the study of groups of second-year university students with discussion tasks that require few resources. Another reason is that the organizational consultants, who write the applied texts and articles, are not called in if there is a problem with resources or technical equipment. They are only called if there is a problem with a group or organization concerning their commitment to the basic values and goals of the group/ organization, a problem of group/organization role conflict or low morale, or if the coordination of the activity through centralized or distributed leadership is not working properly. Thus the item of resources rarely appears on their lists.

Item 5, about interlocking roles, refers to the third function of appropriate role differentiation. Although there are norms associated with each functional area, item 4 indicates 'norms concerning matters of common interest', suggesting that the item refers to the leadership or goal-attainment function. Item 8 falls into the same category.

Item 7 would require more evidence of the type of reward, since rewards can relate to any of the four functions. Some persons belong to a group because they like the overall purpose of the group, some because it provides resources that they need, some because it allows them to play a role that they enjoy or they like the other group members, regardless of what they are doing, and some because the group product is one that they value. Item 10, the relationship to the environment, was not included in early discussions of the four functions. However, if by 'environment' we mean the social environment of other groups and organizations, as well as the physical environment, then, as with the item 'rewards', we will need to consider which function of the environment the group members are acting toward.

Functions within Functions

It may be sufficient for some levels of analysis to note the success the group or organization has in fulfilling each of the four functions. However, if there is a failure at any point, it may be desirable to look more closely at the activity in a functional area to see just where the problem lies, since to fulfil each function four sub-functions are necessary.

The easiest example to begin with is in the functional area of producing resources. When a group needs a new piece of equipment, first it is necessary to have a concept of the type of equipment (meaning within the resources area). Then tools and special materials may be required to make the new product and new skills by group members (resources within the resources area). Next group members' roles may need to be adjusted to match the production requirements for the new resource (integration within the resources area). Finally the new item is produced (goal-attainment within the resources area).

Burningham and West (1995) provide enough detail of processes within groups to be able to identify the four sub-functions within the functional areas. They do not describe the phases within phases in the production of resources, but they do describe in some detail the phases within phases in the other three functional areas, except, of course, they do not label them using our terminology. Here we will reproduce their descriptions, leaving aside a word-for-word translation of their terms, but providing some summary remarks.

Vision (meaning): 'Vision is an idea of a valued outcome that represents a higher order goal and motivating force at work.' Work groups with clearly defined objectives are more likely to develop new goal-appropriate methods of working because their efforts have focus and direction. Vision has four parts: clarity (readily understandable), visionary nature (describes a valued outcome that engenders commitment), attainability (practical likelihood of achieving goals) and sharedness (the vision gains acceptance).

Participatory safety (integration): 'Participativeness and safety are characterized as a single psychological construct in which the contingencies are such that involvement in decision making is motivated and reinforced while occurring in an environment that is perceived as interpersonally non-threatening.' The more group members participate in decision making through having influence, interacting and sharing information, the more likely they are to invest in the outcomes of those decisions and to offer new and improved ways of working.

Task orientation (goal-attainment): 'A shared concern with excellence and quality of task performance in relation to shared vision or outcomes, characterized by evaluations, modifications, control systems, and critical appraisals.'

The description of vision includes the sub-functions of meaning (visionary nature), integration (sharedness) and goal-attainment (attainability), but does not refer to the resources necessary to derive the vision. Participative safety focuses on the sub-function of integration, namely participation in decision making. The process is very similar to that of the process of achieving 'consensus' as described by Leavitt (1972) and others as an ideal method of making group decisions. The description of task orientation is the only one that alludes to the sub-function of skill of group members in that skills must be present to achieve quality of task performance.

To these three functional areas, Burningham and West (1995) added *support for innovation*, defined as the expectation, approval and practical support of attempts to introduce new and improved ways of doing things in the work environment. In their research on groups in an oil company, they found that all three aspects of group activity were positively related to group innovativeness.

Types of Groups

In texts on organizational behaviour, one often finds the effective group described as a 'team' and instructions given for 'team building' (Francis and Young, 1979; Patten, 1988). Some use the term *group* and *team* interchangeably. Guzzo and Dickson (1996), in their review of research on performance and effectiveness of teams in organizations, suggest that teams usually involve more commitment. In everyday and in scientific usage, *group* is the most general term. However, group is also used to refer to a set of individuals who have some characteristic in common without actually meeting each other. This is the sense in which the term *nominal group* is used in social psychology. In dictionaries *team* and *crew* refer to particular types of groups (cf. Simpson and Weiner, 1989). The term *team* usually refers to sports groups, and *crew* typically refers to a group of persons managing some form of technology (stage crews, film crews), especially forms of transportation such as boats, aircraft or spacecraft (Hare, 1992b, 1993).

Using the functional (MIGR) cybernetic hierarchy, it is possible to make some distinctions between different types of groups. Crews of boats, planes or spacecraft can be placed at the bottom of the cybernetic hierarchy (R level), since their function is bound to a particular type of equipment or technology. They are equipment or technology driven. Change the technology and you change the nature of the crew. Aircrews are an example, where large amounts of information about the conditions of the plane and the weather must be processed in a short period of time in addition to controlling parts of the equipment used in take-off, flight and landing (Foushee, 1984). Ginnett (1993) notes the aspects of aircrew roles for a Boeing 727 that are fixed because of the placement of their seats in the cockpit. The captain sits in the left seat where he tests all emergency warning devices and is the only one who can taxi the aircraft since the nose gear steering wheel is located on the left side of the cockpit. The first officer, in the right seat, starts the engines and communicates with the tower. The flight engineer, in a seat that faces sideways facing a panel that allows him to monitor and control the various subsystems aboard the aircraft, is the only one who can reach the auxiliary power unit. For a smaller or larger aircraft the relationship of roles to equipment will be different.

As an example of the dependence of a crew on its technology, Hutchins (1990) describes the navigators on large ships who work with specialized tools. He observes that the tools do not amplify the cognitive abilities of the crew members, but instead transform normally difficult cognitive tasks into easy ones. The nature of the tools affects the division of labour among the crew members and the techniques by which they coordinate their work activities. When navigation errors are made, there is an opportunity for instruction in the use of the equipment based on the novice's 'need to know' (Seifert and Hutchins, 1992).

Moving up, at the G level are work groups in business, manufacturing, health and education. These groups are bound to a product, an object or the care or education of a person. They are product driven. Change the nature of the product or the service provided and the group must be reorganized.

At the I level would be sports teams that are rule driven. They produce nothing. However, the playing field is usually swarming with referees to ensure that the game is played within the rules. Change the rules and you have a new game (Kew, 1987).

LIVERPOOL JOHN MOORES UNIVERSITY
LEARNING SERVICES

At the top of the hierarchy, at the M level, are scientific research and development groups. They are not bound by existing equipment, products or rules. They are discovery driven. Their task is to develop new concepts and to discover new relationships between old or new concepts. Wolpert and Richards (1988: 9), writing about 'a passion for science', suggest that 'perhaps it is, above all, the thrill of ideas that binds scientists together, it is the passion that drives them and enables them to survive'.

In research and development groups, as in groups in general, status hierarchies develop which are based in part on the external status characteristics of group members (Cohen and Zhou, 1991). While most of the external characteristics reflect a group member's past performance, and therefore may be relevant for the group's current activity, gender also has an independent effect on group status, with males generally being accorded higher status.

Status in a group may affect a member's opportunities to have innovative contributions accepted or to learn necessary skills. In a study of a research and development unit in a high-technology manufacturing company, Brooks (1994) identified group learning tasks. She then noted that organizational structures made it difficult for low-power members to carry out the learning tasks. Unequal former power among employees was seen to have a critical influence on the success or failure of learning groups.

Integration and Role Differentiation

In addition to sorting groups, teams and crews by functional specialty (MIGR), they can be classified according to the amount of integration and role differentiation required. Although some merge the two characteristics (cf. Dyer, 1987), they can be kept separate for at least a two-by-two table of types of group that are either high or low on each characteristic. Olmsted made this type of distinction for types of group leadership in his analysis of group activity (Olmsted, 1959; see also Olmsted and Hare, 1978: 14). Sundstrom and Altman (1989: 185) have also used this double dichotomy in their typology of work groups.

Sports teams provide the simplest example of this type of classification. Golf teams are low on both integration and role differentiation. Each member of a golf team plays the game alone, without any coordination with other players. The skills required of each player are exactly the same. Synchronized swimming teams are high on integration but low on differentiation. The various swimming routines of the team members require a high degree of coordination, but each swimmer does the same stroke or manoeuvre. Track teams are low on integration but high on differentiation. Each track event (running, jumping, shotput, etc.) is an individual event (with the exception of relay races), but each requires a different set of skills. Football teams (American type) are high on the need for both integration and differentiation. The positions and moves of each player in relation to every other player on the team are carefully rehearsed before each game and the skills and physical characteristics of the team members differ according to their position on the team.

Each type of group requires a different leader style, a different mix of task and social–emotional activities, and thus different solutions to the four functional problems. A golf coach is primarily concerned with the 'task ability' of each player since the players do not function together. The swimming coach is also concerned primarily with skill, with some attention to social relationships since the team members must present a unified activity. The concerns of the track coach are similar to those of the golf coach, except that a greater number of different skills are involved. The football coach must give attention to both task and social–emotional concerns since the team must not only work well together in their different roles but also compete directly and physically with an opposing team on the playing field whose objective is to disrupt their activity. For some groups, the main function of the members is to support the activity of the central person, such as the surgeon in a surgical team or the pilot in an airplane.

Group Development

The introduction to this volume included a one-paragraph description of the phases in group development. Here we provide more details of the process. In the functional theory that we have outlined, the members of a group or organization first agree on an overall definition of the situation (meaning), then secure or develop resources necessary for specific goals (resources), develop a set of roles and a level of morale sufficient for the task (integration), and coordinate the resources and roles in specific goal-related activity (goal-attainment). At this stage, setting deadlines is especially important. These phases are followed, eventually, by a terminal phase which is similar to the first (meaning) in which the group members reassess the meaning of the activity as they go their separate ways (Hare, 1993).

If this outline of development is true, then why are there so many conflicting approaches? There are theories of group development that describe apparently different orders of development (cf. Bales and Strodtbeck, 1951; Bennis and Shepard, 1956; Schutz, 1958; Tuckman, 1965). Some researchers maintain that there is no normal sequence of phases (Gersick, 1988), while others argue that there is no evidence for any phases in group development (Cissna, 1984), although there may be continual growth as a group becomes more cohesive and better able to handle the task (Barker, 1991). The apparent conflict in theories results from the fact that what you observe depends on your general theory of group process, and especially on the characteristics of the individuals who form the group and the task in which they are engaged. Tasks vary in the extent to which they require commitment to a well-defined purpose, specialized skills, role differentiation and coordination. (For a summary of some of these theories, see Hare, 1973, 1976, 1992a, and Hare and Davies, 1994.)

An example of a theory that emphasizes the variability in groups is that of McGrath (1991). In his theory that focuses on time, interaction and performance, he identifies four modes of group activity that coincide with the four RGIM functions:

Mode I: inception and acceptance of a project (goal choice) [meaning]
Mode II: solution of technical issues (means choice) [resources]
Mode III: resolution of conflict, i.e. political issues (policy choice) [integration]
Mode IV: execution of the performance of the project (goal-attainment) [goal-attainment].

For each mode McGrath indicates the type of activity required to meet the production goals of the group, to provide for the well-being of the group and to give support to the individual members. He notes that if the solution to the problems in any one of the modes is in hand, then the group may skip this mode.

It is rare to observe a group that is actually starting in square one. For the laboratory groups in university observation rooms, before the observation begins the experimenter has already selected the task, provided the necessary information or equipment in the form of case studies or puzzle parts and indicated that there is, or is not, a leader in the group. Thus what is observed is mainly the process of moving through the sub-functions in the fourth phase of goal-attainment. For 'real life' groups, such as the cockpit crew of an aeroplane, observers may express surprise that they do not observe a developmental sequence of 'forming, storming, norming, and performing' (Tuckman, 1965, based on observations of therapy groups) in the few minutes during which the cockpit crew moves from individual introductions to a team capable of performing interdependent work (Ginnett, 1993).

To explain this, Ginnett uses Hackman's concept of a pre-existing 'shell' that predefines what is expected of the team. The shell includes context and design factors, but also a set of expectations about the roles of each individual in the crew. The mechanism of the shell allowed the crew to develop so quickly (Ginnett, 1993). From a functional perspective, the 'shell' is clearly a name for the result of activity in the first three phases of group development. For Ginnett's cockpit crew, the observation only began after the crew members had been well trained for their roles and indeed had been members of previous functioning crews before the one that Ginnett observed.

Some groups never get started because the members cannot agree on an overall definition of the situation, and others become stuck or abort at some phase (Kuypers et al., 1986). After surveying a variety of work groups, Hackman (1990) identified a number of mistakes that designers and leaders of work groups sometimes make. He called these errors 'trip wires' because they could bring the group to a halt. These trip wires and the functional area that they influence are as follows:

1   specify challenging team objectives, but skimp on organizational supports (resources);
2   assume that members have all the competence they need to work well as a team (resources);
3   fall off the authority balance beam (goal-attainment);
4   call the performing unit a team but really manage members as individuals (integration);
5   assemble a large group of people, tell them in general terms what needs to be accomplished and let them 'work out detail' (meaning).

Individuals may also drop out of the group at each phase. Persons who agree with the overall goals may feel that the resources are inadequate. Those who accept the goals and judge that the resources are sufficient may not care for the role they are assigned. In this case, since they are already committed to the overall purpose and agree that the resources are adequate and that the only thing left is to get on with the task, the disaffected ones may band together to create the 'revolution within the revolution' that will most likely occur in the third phase.

Is it really that simple? No, again. For a finer-grain analysis one can identify four sub-phases within each phase (the functions within functions discussed above), which can be shown to be related to Shambaugh's (1978) observations concerning phases in the accumulation of group culture and emotionality (Hare, 1982).

Unfortunately this is not the whole story. For a comprehensive analysis of development in a formal group one would also need to note the development of individual members and informal subgroups over the same period, as well as relations between the small group and other groups in the same organization or network (Burlingame et al., 1984). The classic Western Electric studies (Roethlisberger and Dickson, 1939) provide ample evidence that the activities of informal groups in a relay assembly test room (Hare, 1967) or bank wiring room (Homans, 1950) may or may not support the activity required by the formal work group.

Effective Groups

By now you probably have the idea that an effective group is one that can solve the four basic problems of meaning, resources, integration and goal-attainment. However, the literature on groups in organizations suggests some additional considerations about how to make groups effective. For example, group members need to be committed to the meaning of the group and also to the organization. Part of this commitment is expressed through communication, so that is the relationship we first consider. Training can help, norms need to be enforced and leadership makes a difference, especially when it is distributed over all group members and the groups become self-directed. In the next few pages of this chapter, we will take up each of these topics in turn.

Commitment and Communication

While it is customary to focus on the commitment of the group members to the values and goals of the whole group, Becker and Billings (1993) note that the focus of commitment is related to such individual variables as the intent to quit, job satisfaction, pro-social organizational behaviour and certain demographic and contextual variables. Research based on responses of employees suggests four types of commitment: the locally committed, who are attached to their supervisor and work group; the globally committed, who are attached to the top management of the organization; the committed, who are attached to both local and global foci; and the uncommitted, who are attached to neither.

Ancona and Caldwell (1992) report somewhat similar distinctions concerning the level in the organizational hierarchy to which new-product groups in high-technology companies direct their communications. The groups engage in upward communication aimed at moulding the views of top management (meaning), horizontal communication with other groups to coordinate the work and obtain feedback (integration and goal-attainment) and horizontal communication outside the organization for a general scanning of the technical and market environment (resources). The groups develop distinct strategies toward their environment: some specialize in particular external activities, some in multiple external activities and some remain isolated from the environment.

Ancona and Caldwell (1992) also investigated the impact of diversity on communication and group performance in the new-product groups. Both functional and tenure diversity had distinct effects. The greater the functional diversity, the more the group members communicated outside the group's boundaries; and the more external communication, the higher the managerial ratings of innovation. Diversity also affected internal group processes, such as clarifying group goals and setting priorities. In turn, this clarity was associated with high group ratings of overall performance. However, the direct effect of diversity was that it impeded performance. Although it might bring more creativity to problem solving and product development, it could impede implementation

because there was less capability for group work than with homogeneous groups.

One organization which seems to appreciate the power of communication to produce commitment is Hallmark Cards. As can be seen in the
following case, communication plays a large role in its organizational
culture. Although that may seem obvious in the case of an organization
that produces greeting cards, nevertheless, Hallmark seems to have
given the commitment processes a lot of thought. The Hallmark case also
shows points dealing with creativity and work/life policies.

A Commitment-building Company – Hallmark Cards (Flynn, 1996)

Hallmark Cards Inc. is a company familiar to most Americans as a producer
of a wide assortment of products such as greeting cards, gift wrap and items
for parties. It is the largest greeting card manufacturer in the world. The
company was founded in 1910 by Joyce Hall and to this day continues to
be a family-run business although, through a profit-sharing programme,
employees now own one-third of it.

Hallmark is obviously doing something right. Talented people are attracted
to the company and, once they are in, tend to remain there. There are
thousands of employees who are members of the Quarter Century Club –
people who have spent 25 years or more with the company. Club members
are recognized with a big party each year. The company is non-unionized
and recent attempts to bring in a union failed because employees did not
show enough interest in changing anything about the organization.

There is a strong commitment to people at Hallmark and a number of
commitment-building mechanisms. Here are some examples:

Policy flexibility. Human resource policies are guidelines more than strict
rules. The director of employee relations and staffing often interprets them
on a case-to-case basis because, as he explains: 'Doing that gives us a
great deal of flexibility. It helps our employees and shows we care about
them individually.'

Job termination. Anyone employed for at least two years cannot be
terminated until the director of employee relations and staffing has reviewed
the situation. Firing an employee with an additional five years of tenure
means that the employee's division vice-president must also review the
decision.

No lay-off history. Hallmark is one of the few major American companies
that has never laid off any employees (Levering and Moskowitz, 1993). Lay-
offs are viewed as unethical by members of the founding family. Employees
at sites that are low on work have several options: they can take time off
without pay and keep their benefits intact, move to other work units that
need extra help, or do some community service while continuing to draw
their usual salary.

Open communications. When employees talk to their managers, the
managers listen. Division heads walk through the factory and just talk to
people. There is a daily newsletter (Noon News), a newsletter targeted at
managers (Directions) and computer-monitored signboards throughout the
headquarters building. In the CEO forums held about 10 times a year, the
president and CEO meet with a group of about 50 workers, chosen

randomly by divisions, for 90 minutes. Hallmark Corporate Town Hall meetings were instituted in 1995 and were planned to be held quarterly with three meetings in one day and 400 employees attending each. The president and CEO open the meeting with a report on some company topic and then the floor is open for discussion.

Performance recognition. When a department exceeds in something, there is always some form of recognition, such as gift certificates or tickets to ball games.

Family-friendly environment. There are three main areas – family care assistance, counselling and education, and alternative work arrangements.

- Family care assistance. These programmes are designed to help employees make care arrangements so that they can come to work both physically and mentally. Family Care Choices is a service designed to help employees locate care for their children, family members with disabilities and aging parents. Moment's Notice is an emergency back-up care and sick-child care programme which is run through an agreement with a nearby school.
- Counselling and education. The message sent by the company is that Hallmark helps those who help themselves. Many of the counselling and education programmes are linked to family situations. A child behavioural specialist is on-site twice a week to provide personal advice (partially subsidized by the company) to parents seeking guidance. Lunch and Learn seminars held twice a month deal with family topics such as elder-care issues, parenting, parental leave and so on. Free parenting workshops are also held quarterly on Saturday, to allow both parents to attend. The Personal Assistance Program pays the cost for up to four sessions with a psychologist and bereaved employees can enter a company counselling and support group which serves as an informal network.
- Alternative work arrangements. For over 10 years the company has offered part-time schedules for anyone who thinks they are needed. But that is not the end of the story. Hallmark also has a strong commitment to keeping part-timers fully integrated into the workforce. Several unit directors are former part-timers and as of 1996, one director was still working on that schedule.

Diversity efforts. The Corporate Diversity Council (CDC) was formed in 1993 and is composed of senior management from every company division. It identified nine initiatives and programmes, an ideal state for each, the present state of each and the necessary steps to close the gap along with assigned accountability, completion dates and effectiveness measures.

Creativity. Executives are put through a simulation in which they must design a line of greeting cards so that they can better appreciate the frustrations felt by the creative staff (Johns, 1996). Re-engineering efforts resulted in bringing together writers, artists and designers who were previously separated by great distances, to work on developing new cards (Greenberg and Baron, 1997).

Building Productive Groups (Training)

Group effectiveness is interdependent with organizational context, boundaries and group development. Sundstrom et al. (1990) list the key factors as: (a) organizational culture; (b) technology and task design; (c) mission clarity; (d) autonomy; (e) rewards; (f) performance feedback; (g) training/consultation; and (h) physical environment. Note that these are the familiar functions with the addition of physical environment. Group boundaries may mediate the impact of organizational context on group development.

To promote effective groups, May and Schwoerer (1994a) encourage managers to provide for successful job experiences, social modelling, verbal encouragement and interpreting the stress or anxiety experienced during job performance. They especially emphasize the need for activities in the integrative area by providing groups with training that leads to open communication and relationship building among members, and in the resource/skill areas, by matching the team's complexity and uncertainty with members' skills to reduce the stress experienced by employees.

To provide data for stress management, May and Schwoerer (1994b) recommend using a survey of physical symptoms, cumulative trauma disorders (such as the carpel tunnel syndrome), observations, video tapes and employee interviews about their jobs, tools and pain experienced at work. Sokol and Aiello (1993) add that it is helpful to make the intact work unit the target for stress-management training.

Maintaining Productivity

Enforcing the norms in a group can be done in several different ways. In a study of the management of events in Japan, Britain and the USA, Smith et al. (1994) compared the effectiveness of five sources of guidance that were used to manage both routine and non-routine events: (1) company policy manuals; (2) unwritten but accepted departmental policy; (3) advice from a superior; (4) advice from other experienced workers; and (5) workers' own experience. Country- or organization-specific factors were more important predictors of effectiveness than uniform guidance policies. In Japan, frequent reference to supervisors and manuals was associated with productivity and cooperation. In US and British companies, employees placed more importance on using their own experiences.

Group Leadership

Steckler and Fondas (1995) offer a 'diagnostic tool' to identify problems that a group leader may face. They suggest that once difficulties have been identified, the organization will know which human resources practices will be useful as levers of change. Their 'framework' has two categories. The first identifies three types of critical relationships the leader (or any other member) has at work: with one's self, with higher-and lower-level employees, and with peers. We would make this four, by keeping separate relationships with lower-level employees and those with higher-level employees, since a person who is comfortable dealing with subordinates may have difficulty taking orders from a superior.

For their second category, they list three types of workplace problems: behavioural or process skills (resources), psychological reactions to his or her role (integration) and job-design features (goal-attainment). Again, we would note that there are four necessary functions and add meaning. However for the group leader, the overall definition of the work has usually been set by the organization, with the possible exception of some of the work by research and development groups, so the fourth function may not be evident.

Lipman-Blumen (1996) presents a model of 'connective leadership', based on 20 years of research on the characteristic ways in which leaders accomplish their goals. She finds 'connective' leaders distinctive in several ways. First on her list is that they join their vision to others (meaning). They are on a lifelong journey seeking the meaning of their own lives and invite their constituents to join them in the dedication to enterprises that provide opportunities for ennobling themselves. She also lists functions in the integration area (conflict resolution, developing networks and coalitions) and the goal-attainment area (groom other leaders, help others accomplish their goals).

When Mael and Aldkerks (1993) examine the relationship between 'cohesion among members of a platoon leadership' and various other organizational factors, they are referring to the platoon leader and the non-commissioned officers who make up the platoon leadership. In military usage, in the USA, a combat 'team' can have hundreds of members. Thus, when we read about cohesion in a light infantry platoon, we need to keep in mind that a platoon may be composed of four squads of about 12 members each, making a total of over 40 members. However, their findings can apply to smaller groups since there is often more than one leadership function even in relatively small groups. Mael and Aldkerks find that having a set of leaders that is perceived as cohesive by the members of the group is helpful all round. Perceptions of cohesive-ness among the leaders were found to be related to group cohesion, organizational identification, job involvement, task motivation, career intent and perception of unit effectiveness. The platoons with a high perceived cohesion among the leaders also performed better in simulated combat.

Self-managing Work Groups

Self-managing groups, often referred to as self-directed work teams, have been introduced into the workplace to foster worker empowerment, to reduce levels of management and to foster cooperation and creativity. One aspect of self-managing groups involved in manufacturing was a higher quality of the exchange relationships between members, compared with more traditional work groups (Seers et al., 1995). In common with other studies of self-managing groups, these self-managing groups were found to be more cohesive and higher on job satisfaction. The quality of the relationships may be one factor contributing to group effectiveness. In a telecommunications company, self-managing groups, performing customer service, technical support, administrative support and managerial functions were more effective than comparable traditionally managed groups that performed the same type of work (Cohen and Ledford, 1994).

In the literature there is a general assertion that self-directed work groups can 'empower' employees and in turn improve quality of performance. However, each group member does not have to be competent in all aspects of the task since other members can compensate for an individual's areas of deficiency.

National culture may have an effect on the ease or difficulty in introducing team-based work. Kirkman and Shapiro (1997) caution US organizations that wish to use self-managing work teams in their foreign affiliates since there may be cultural values that interfere with team work and especially self-managed teams. Three cultural values that may inhibit working in teams are the perceived distance between the American values and those of the target culture, an emphasis on individualism rather than collectivism and the perceived fairness of team-based pay. Four cultural values that may create problems for self-management of teams include the perceived difference in values with the USA, the power distance (the extent to which a society accepts the fact that power in institutions and organizations is distributed unequally), a 'doing' versus 'being' orientation and 'determinism' versus 'free will'.

Organizational Forms

The discussion of teams in organizations leads us into a discussion of alternative organizational forms since many organizations in the not too distant future will probably become more and more team based owing to the complexities they have to deal with. Changes occurring today in organizations are part of a long-term shift based on two characteristics – the use of influence rather than power and a greater capacity for human accomplishment (Heckscher, 1994).

First we will look at the bureaucracy and some of its problems and proposed alternatives. The first alternatives are 'ideal types', existing in theory only. Afterwards we will 'backtrack' and take a look at some existing, team-based organizational forms.

The Bureaucratic Organization

Modern organizations can be characterized by bureaucracy (Clegg, 1990), and bureaucracy can be characterized by rule-based specification of authority and the limits of that authority, specification of a hierarchy of authority, supervision of the exercise of authority, the continuous and ongoing nature of administrative activities, differentiation of person from office, specialization of work activities based on expertise and documents as bases for official business (Weber, 1947).

Scott and Hart (1989) see the goals and values of modern organizations as being based on an 'organization imperative' which assumes that good for the individual can only arise from the modern organization and, therefore, all behaviour of organizational members must be directed towards enhancing organizational health. Managers are legitimate authority figures who require power to maintain organization well-being and to provide a fair distribution of benefits, social and organizational. Managers 'come first', they are morally superior and have no moral concerns beyond improving the functioning of the organizational system. Employees have the job of making certain that events happen as the supervisor want them to.

Some problems with bureaucracy are problems of *badly managed* bureaucracy and others are problems *inherent* in the bureaucratic model (Heckscher, 1994). The first set of problems is relatively easily fixed by better management within the system. It is the latter problems which call for an alternative model and on which Heckscher focuses.

Heckscher (1994) calls bureaucratic segmentation the 'fundamental problem' of bureaucracy. This is the principle that people are responsible only for their own job. Work is divided into pieces and different individuals are accountable for these different pieces. Moving outside the boundaries causes trouble and confusion. Tightening up the boundaries is one way of improving bureaucratic management but this segmentation has undesirable consequences.

One consequence is that intelligence is wasted. There can never be a complete match between redefined jobs, training, aptitudes and abilities. There is a lot of personal capacity that goes to waste when only the top of the organization has all the information needed to make decisions about the whole system and when that is the only place where strategy questions are considered.

A second consequence is ineffective control of the informal organization. As we all know, 'working to rule' or 'going by the book' is a sure way to incapacitate a system. The hidden, informal systems are what allow work to be done or stop it from being done. In the bureaucracy, there is little attempt to control the informal politics.

The third consequence is ineffective management of change and adaptation over time. The evolution of bureaucracies occurs in a bumpy fashion – routine punctuated by intense periods of revolution from above. When irrationalities of the system come to light, the top levels try to rebalance it. However, effective organizational change cannot usually be managed by a single person since it has its own dynamic which must come into play. Many people working together and trying to improve the whole system over a period of time is not a part of the bureaucratic structure.

The Post-bureaucratic, Interactive Organization

Based on these shortcomings of bureaucracy, Heckscher proposes as the desired change:

> . . . *an organization in which everyone takes responsibility for the success of the whole.* If that happens, then the basic notion of regulating relations among people by *separating* them into specific redefined functions must be abandoned. The problem is to create a system in which people can enter into relations that are determined by problems rather than predetermined by the structure. Thus, organization control must center not on the management of tasks but the management of relationships; in effect, 'politics' must be brought into the open. (1994: 24; original emphasis)

He proposes calling this new post-bureaucratic organization the 'interactive' type of organization because dialogue, rather than one-way communications, plays a central role. Rather than hierarchy and authority, there is consensus – the result of involving those concerned with a given issue in discussion, information gathering and development of agreement. He proposes that the best way to develop strategy is to use the full intelligence of all through a social process of discussion.

His description of the interactive type of organization is as follows:

1 Consensus is created through institutionalized dialogue.
2 Dialogue is defined by the use of influence rather than power.
3 Influence depends initially on trust – the belief that all members are seeking mutual benefit rather than personal gain. The main source of trust is interdependence which is an understanding that what each of us receives depends on combining the performances of all.
4 Because of this interdependence as the main integrator, there is a strong emphasis on organizational mission. Key objectives have to be understood by all.
5 There is widespread sharing of information about strategy and a strengthening of consciousness about the connection between individual jobs and the mission.
6 The focus on mission is supplemented by principles for action which are periodically discussed and reviewed.
7 'Who decides' is determined by the nature of the problem and processes are needed for deciding how to decide.

8 Influence relationships are wide and diverse but may also be shallow and more specific, leading to a sense of isolation and loneliness.
9 For the influence system to function, peer evaluation must be thorough and open so that people know each other's strengths and weaknesses.
10 Boundaries are relatively open and there is no expectation that employees will spend their entire career in one organization. Openness is also seen in alliances and joint ventures between organizations.
11 Equity can be a problem because the organization can no longer rely on objectivity and equality of treatment. There is an effort to reduce rules and pressure to recognize the variety of individual performances. A possible solution is the development of public standards of performance which are openly discussed and negotiated with individual employees.
12 There is an expectation of constant change and a need for flexibility in defining time frames for different tasks.

As opposed to the Weberian model which proposes rational-legal legitimation of orders (orders are accepted as valid if they conform to the rules defining appropriate power given to a particular office), in the interactive organization, legitimate decisions must be justified by the agreement or consent of those who are affected by them and those who can contribute knowledge to them. This is the idea of consensual legitimacy. Not every decision has to go through a consensus process but decisions have to be made according to principles developed through such a process. Bureaucratic hierarchy may continue as a structural option but it is under the control of consensual mechanisms.

Heckscher (1994) sees post-bureaucratic organization not as a real system, but as an ideal type drawn from examples of organizations that seem deliberately to violate bureaucratic principles such as Saturn Corporation, GE-Canada and Shell-Sarnia. Other examples can be found in autonomous teams, participatory planning processes, cross-functional product development teams, and so on. Teamwork and networks – these are the phenomena we are seeing here. In many cases, we see them within the bureaucracy but Heckscher (1994: 18) believes that these mechanisms 'can be extrapolated to a full and distinct form of organization with greater capacity than bureaucracy itself'.

Doing 'whatever needs to be done', collaborating beyond assigned roles, is a feature of the post-bureaucratic organization. As Donnellon and Scully (1994: 87) put it: 'A post-bureaucratic organization may require a kind of trust in what is best in human nature and also send a signal that trust, cooperation, and sharing are not ideals too abstract for a social order.'

But the interactive, post-bureaucratic organization is not without its problems (Gordon, 1994). Some of these problems are based on the evidence that organizations that exceed the size of a face-to-face interactive group tend to break into subgroups which leads to in-group/out-group biases and prejudice (Turner et al., 1987). When there are subgroups there is competition which, overall, has detrimental effects on organizational efficiency and morale. Bureaucracy has the effect of countering these tendencies toward inefficiency since resource allocation decisions are made by people higher up in the hierarchy who do not share the group's social identity and who act according to professional norms (Gordon, 1994). Assuming that those at the top of a bureaucratic organization are interested in overall organizational efficiency, Gordon (1994: 200) proposes that the post-bureaucratic organization 'would relinquish the efficiencies and even the sense of administrative fairness that bureaucracy has achieved and mire itself in intergroup competition and politically driven resource allocation'.

Instead of returning to advocating the bureaucracy, or moving to advocate the interactive organization, Gordon (1994) proposes a model he calls 'socialized rivalry', a model which he claims channels the processes of in-group bias and out-group prejudice into constructive directions instead of trying to overcome them. The design includes the following features:

1 Work groups compete for organizational resources based on proposals that are dependent on local knowledge and aim at improving efficiency and quality.
2 Work groups have at their disposal a certain amount of management and technical expertise to use in developing their projects.
3 Innovation initiatives are local but evaluation is through an objective board of experts.
4 Compensation is structured so that both the innovative group and the rest of the organization share in productivity increases resulting in a hybrid system between achievement-linked rewards and equal reward.
5 Validation of resource allocation to groups would take place through organizationwide debate and democratic approval of the recommendation of the panel of experts.
6 Career tracks would promote leaders beyond the group to moderate parochialism and narrow self-interest.

According to Gordon, this model would encourage small-group spirit and channel the competitiveness into organizational efficiency and moderate it by an organization-wide perspective. The advantages of small groups such as high motivation, high internal control and discipline, mutual support and cooperation are sustained, while the disadvantages of destructive intergroup competition, conformity, suppression of creativity and individual initiative, and a lack of openness to information or expertise from the outside are avoided. It must be remembered, however, that like the interactive organization, this too is only a proposal, yet to be tried.

Self-organization

Shipper and Manz (1992) suggest an alternative to self-managed groups in which the whole work operation becomes one large empowered group. Everyone is self-managed and can interact directly with everyone else in the system. They describe a company that has 44 plants and over 5,300 associates, which relies on self-developing groups without managers or bosses. Organizational themes found in the company include a culture and norms supporting employee empowerment and success, a lattice organization structure, no bosses or managers, successful associates working without structure or management, and unstructured research and development for increased creativity and innovation.

As mentioned earlier, the challenges of the future (which is already here) are indicating very plainly that we cannot continue to organize the way we have been doing. Organizations will probably have to move much closer to the model of a complex adaptive system. Some of the characteristics of complex adaptive systems (Freedman, 1992; Waldrop, 1992) which are relevant to our discussion include:

- they consist of a network of agents acting in a self-managed way without centralized control;
- the environment in which the agents find themselves is constantly changing and evolving since it is produced by their interactions with other agents;
- organized patterns of behaviour arise from competition and cooperation among the agents producing structures arising from interactions and interdependencies.

The processes in a complex adaptive system are those of mutual adjustment and self-regulation. They are decentralized systems having a bottom-up direction for combining actions rather than top-down centralized control. The structure that emerges is 'not simply an aggregation of individual actions, but has unique properties not possessed by individuals alone' (Drazin and Sandelands, 1992: 233).

This type of organization may be the pinnacle of team-based organization, although it is a particular vision of what 'team-based' means. In this instance, the teams are more like a set of fluid molecules – grouping and regrouping, as the need arises. Self-organization can not be imposed from outside, but operates from within the system itself. Organization is not designed into the parts, but is generated by the interaction of those parts as a whole.

The self-organizing form has implications for organizational learning and creativity, the subjects of the next two chapters. Self-organizing or self-renewing systems are characterized by system resiliency rather than stability (Wheatley, 1994). When the systems have to deal with new information, they reconfigure themselves in the ways needed to do so. As Wheatley states:

Part of their viability comes from their internal capacity to create structures that fit the moment. Neither form nor function alone dictates how the system is constructed. Instead, form and function engage in a fluid process where the system may maintain itself in its present form or evolve to a new order. The system possesses the capacity for spontaneously emerging structures, depending on what is required. It is not locked into any one best form but instead is capable of organizing information in the structure that suits the present need. (1994: 90–1)

Wheatley (1994: 91–4) fluently describes the processes occurring in self-organization and their implications. According to her, an organization can only exist in such a fluid fashion if 'it has access to new information, both about external factors and internal resources', and can process that information with 'high levels of self-awareness, plentiful sensing devices, and a strong capacity for reflection'. Instead of making information fit the existing structure, structure is made to fit the information.

But the structure is not passively changing with each change that occurs. 'As it matures and stabilizes, it becomes more efficient in the use of its resources and better able to exist within its environment. It establishes a basic structure that supports the development of the system. This structure then facilitates an insulation from the environment that protects the system form constant, reactive changes' (1994: 92). Part of the structure can be considered to be the culture that develops and supports self-organization.

In a seemingly paradoxical way, openness to the environment, to information from outside, leads to higher levels of system autonomy and identification. This greater sense of identity leads the system to being less permeable to externally induced change. 'Some fluctuations will always break through, but what comes to dominate the system over time is not environmental influences, but the self-organizing dynamics of the system itself' (1994: 92).

Another principle fundamental to self-organizing systems is self-reference. 'In response to environmental disturbances that signal the need for change, the system changes in a way that remains consistent with itself in that environment. The system is autopoietic, focusing its activities on what is required to maintain its own integrity and self-renewal. As it changes, it does so by referring to itself; whatever future form it takes will be consistent with its already established identity' (1994: 94).

Each element in a system influences other elements directly and/or indirectly. The relationships are 'mutually determining and determined' (Morgan, 1986: 238). The environment is dynamic, formed by acting and reacting, cooperation and competition. As each agent tries to adapt to the others, it changes the environment of the others as well.

Freedom and order coexist and support each other in autonomous systems. 'If we allow autonomy at the local level, letting individuals or units be directed in their decisions by guideposts for organizational self-reference, we can achieve coherence and continuity. Self-organization succeeds when the system supports the independent activity of its members by giving them, quite literally, a strong frame of reference. When it does this, the global system achieves even greater levels of autonomy and integrity' (Wheatley, 1994: 95).

Team-based Organization

Not all alternative organizational forms have to be as extreme as those mentioned above. Organizations that are team-based exist and thrive (see the Whole Foods Market case below). However, moving to a team-based organization or even to team work is often not a simple matter.

Making a transition to teams is often done without a realization of how different team work is from the traditional bureaucratic model of work. Major changes in the division of labour are made in organizations when team work is adopted: tasks are performed by teams, there is cross-training and blurring of job and functional boundaries, flexibility in tasks, possibility of synergistic joint efforts and changes in the manager's role. Often, the 'different' mode of work – team work – is adopted but it is paired with traditional ideas about performance, evaluation and rewards (Donnellon and Scully, 1994). In the bureaucratic organization, the structure of rewards is built on the division of labour. As one moves up the ladder to roles of increasing difficulty and increasing organizational value, rewards increase as well. In the team organization an alternative approach is needed.

The first concern is *what* is rewarded. In many instances, successful performance of tasks in organizations today requires knowledge and experience that are distributed among people. Therefore, it is impossible to accomplish them without using groups or teams. The move to teams usually brings with it an accompanying concern that, without individual accountability, there will be disincentives for maximum individual contributions and added incentive for 'social loafing'.

For managerial and professional employees, an additional complication is that for many, job descriptions include both individual and team tasks (Donnellon and Scully, 1994). The usual procedure is to continue individual performance assessment and rewards. As Donnellon and Scully (1994: 70) note, a possible negative consequence of this process is that 'even if individuals were personally motivated to contribute to the team despite the lack of individual accountability for team outcomes, their individual accountability for other non-team tasks could discourage the diversion of attention and energy to team tasks'. An alternative solution of trying to assess individual contributions to team performance is still tied closely to bureaucratic assumptions that the only things that people will invest in are those they are held individually accountable for. The very attempt to separate out individual contributions is counter-productive to the integrative nature of team work. 'Face work', impression management, withholding information and even outright sabotage of efforts of other team members are strategies that may be employed to ensure that one's individual contribution stands out. Obviously, these are not strategies conducive to optimal team functioning and outcomes.

A second concern is *who* does the assessment. In the traditional bureaucratic organization, the assessment role has typically belonged to the manager who ranks a group of employees and distributes performance ratings and raises. A possible solution in a team setting is for the team, not the manager, to do the assessment. In this way, those who actually observe performance are those who assess it, enabling the use of more concrete, less political criteria and, hopefully, a more reliable result. However, in cross-functional teams, members may receive contradictory messages from the organization which result in dual loyalties (Donnellon and Scully, 1994). One message says the team is accountable for the team task and the other message says that promotion lies along the functional hierarchical path.

Although focusing on the post-bureaucratic organization, Donnellon and Scully (1994) present an alternative approach to performance and reward which may be applicable in any organization given the assumption that some mix of team work and individual work is needed for effectiveness and efficiency. They suggest the following:

Rely on intrinsic motivation (and have an income floor). Unlink the ties between pay and work and head towards a more egalitarian pay system. Enrich jobs to enhance their internal motivation potential by giving teams responsibility for significant tasks and the autonomy to decide how they should be accomplished. Focus on skill development. Use performance evaluation for its feedback and learning function, not for rating and sorting employees.

Celebrate excellence (and have an income ceiling). In the post-bureaucratic organization, expertise becomes a particular form of contribution, not a basis for status and material rewards. Because of the necessary inter-dependence among experts needed for most tasks, teams need excellence in all of their experts, not 'stars'. Many people can be deemed 'excellent' and rewards other than scarce rewards or promotions and very high salaries can come to be valued and used.

Keep the concept of merit out of the language and culture. Attempts to solve problems with merit systems have usually centred on trying to improve the process and remove subjectivity. But obtaining unbiased ratings is impossible and, even if it was possible, making an organization more meritocratic may involve remaining very close to the bureaucratic model. Abandoning the meritocracy scares people and the post-bureaucratic organization may need to change quickly to demonstrate that fair treatment and secure livelihoods are part of it. The change is likely to be difficult since it involves psychological and cultural change – difficult outcomes to achieve.

Donnellon and Scully (1994: 88) sum up some of the transition problems in the following way: 'Paradoxically, the flexibility, trust, and fast adaptation that are supposed to be the *results of* post-bureaucracy may indeed be required *in advance* to move effectively and creatively toward new ideas – such as the complete departure from meritocratic thinking – in the spirit of contribution that the post-bureaucratic organization encourages.'

Whole Foods Market – a Team-based Company (Fishman, 1996; Whole Foods Market, 1997)

'Team member happiness' is the title of one section of the *Declaration of Interdependence* of Whole Foods Market (Whole Foods Market, 1997) – a section that begins with the statement: 'Everyone who works at Whole Foods Market is a Team Member.'

The original Whole Foods Market, the largest natural foods grocer in the USA, opened in Austin, Texas in 1980. Since then, it has expanded throughout the country by opening new stores and acquiring others.

Whole Foods is organized around decentralized team work. The defining unit of activity is the team. Each store is an autonomous profit centre built around an average of 10 self-managed teams (grocery, produce, and so on). Teams have clear performance targets and designated leaders. The team leaders in each store are also a team, the store leaders in each region are a team and the six regional vice-presidents are a team.

It is impossible to disregard the primacy of team work in this organization – all work is team work. Only teams have the power to hire for full-time jobs. Candidate screening is done by store leaders and applicants are recommended for a job on a specific team. But after a 30-day trial period, the candidate must be approved by two-thirds of the team to become a full-time employee.

The company's gainsharing programme is tied to team performance – sales per labour hour. This plan is an incentive to the teams to accept only people they believe will perform. Otherwise, they will feel the results of their incorrect decision in their pocket before long. Pressure for performance comes from team peers, not from headquarters. Teams also make decisions about ordering and pricing – additional factors that determine profitability.

For an organization to operate the way Whole Foods Market does, there must be a free and open flow of information and that is exactly what we find here. The financial system is open – every person in every location has access to it. Along with information on sales and profit margins, salaries and bonuses are listed for each employee by name. Once a year a morale survey of employees is done and the results are also made public within the organization.

There is a lot of competition at Whole Foods – competition against goals and competition against other teams in the store and against similar teams in other stores and regions. Employees tour the other stores on a periodic schedule. The visits combine an opportunity for social interaction with performance audits and feedback sessions. But along with the competition, there is also a realization that everyone is playing the same game on the same side. There is also lateral learning, or what John Mackey (co-founder and CEO) calls 'cross-pollination' – finding out what other teams and stores are doing well and bringing these things into your organization.

Groups – Some Final Words

Following our promise, given in the introduction, to use functional theory to help organize the literature on work groups in organizations, we first note that any group, in order to survive, must provide solutions to four functional problems. There must be an overall meaning of the activity that sets both a direction and boundaries for the work. There must be resources adequate for the task. There must be enough integration in the form of role differentiation and level of morale for the group members to work together. There must be enough coordination of the resources and the integration functions to provide for goal-attainment.

Further, we can 'zoom in' on any of the four functions to note the four sub-functions that are necessary to fulfil each function. In order to achieve the main function, there must be within it some meaning, resources, integration and goal-attainment. Whether within a function or between functions, the expected phases of development move from meaning, to resources, to integration, to goal-attainment. To undertake a new activity, group members may not need to pay much attention to one or more of these functional problems if they have already been dealt with on a previous occasion or the group may need to recycle though a functional area several times before an adequate solution is found.

The most effective groups are those with adequate solutions to each of these problems. In the USA, with its emphasis on sport, the effective groups in organizations are described as 'teams' with courses set out by consultants for 'team building', often including off-site 'outward bound' type activities, complete with T-shirts and other team symbols.

As societies shift from more authoritarian to more democratic modes of group and organizational management, there is a move to 'empower' workers in self-managed teams. In cyber-space where 'virtual teams' and 'virtual organizations' exist that cut across many of the older formal group and organizational boundaries and hierarchical levels, where group members are not physically present in the same setting, self-direction becomes a necessity.

5

LEARNING

In the first part of this book the focus was on the individual in an organizational setting. In Chapter 4, 'Groups', we moved up one system level to consider the problems and the solutions found for them faced by individuals working together in groups. Individuals learn about themselves and how to get along with other individuals. Groups also learn, or more accurately, the individuals in groups learn about their group and about its relationship with other groups. Moving up to the next system level, organizations also learn, but again, it is actually the individuals in the organizations who learn about the structure and processes in their organization and how their organization relates to other organizations, to the larger society and the environment.

Organizational learning is a metaphor (Lovell and Turner, 1988) to focus attention on the ways an organization adapts to its environment. Weick and Westley (1996) quibble with the concept of 'organizational learning'. They classify it as an 'oxymoron', pointing out that organizing and learning are antithetical processes. To learn is to disorganize and increase variety. To organize is to reduce variety. They conclude that people writing about organizations are never sure whether learning is something new or simply warmed-over organizational change. We also note that the literature on organizational learning, organizational (culture) change and organizational creativity covers many of the same variables and the same relationships. In this chapter we begin with ideas about organizational learning and add a discussion of organizational culture, since what is learned in an organization must become part of the culture if it is to have more than a momentary effect. If the change in culture is more than simply moving on to the next phase in ordinary organizational development, and especially if it is more than simply utilizing some device or process taken from another organization, then we begin to think in terms of 'organizational creativity'. Individual, group and organizational creativity will be the subject of the next chapter.

As we summarize books and articles dealing with organization learning, we note, along with Tsang (1997), that the 'prescriptive' suggestions are usually offered by organizational consultants, while the 'descriptive' analyses are written by academics striving for scientific rigour.

What is Organizational Learning?

Organizations are routine based, history dependent and target oriented. Levitt and March (1988), in a review of research on organizational learning, find that organizations learn by encoding inferences learned from history into routines that guide behaviour. Organizations learn from direct experience as well as from the experience of others and develop conceptual frameworks for interpreting their experience. They are able to encode, store and retrieve the lessons of history despite the turnover of personnel and the passage of time. Probst and Buechel (1997: 24) highlight three characteristics of organizational learning:

1   change in organizational knowledge;
2   increase in the range of possible actions;
3   change in intersubjective constructions of reality.

Organizational learning is complicated by the ecological structure of the simultaneously adapting behaviour of other organizations and by the endogenously changing environment.

According to Argyris (1996) and Argyris and Schön (1996), the most effective learning involves a 'double loop'. The first loop consists of learning that takes place within an organization's existing system of values and the action frames in which values are embedded. The second loop involves changes in values and frames and calls for reflective inquiry that cuts across incongruent frames. In their view, the ability of organizations to engage in productive organizational learning is primarily constrained by the inquiry-inhibiting ideas about how things should be done (theories-in-use) that shape the normal patterns of organizational inquiry under conditions of threat or embarrassment. Fiol and Lyles (1985) refer to the first loop as 'adaptation' and reserve the term 'learning' for the second loop.

Not all learning has to be double-loop learning in order to be 'good' learning. The incremental, adaptive type of learning is also needed in order to permit continual improvement and to allow the 'larger' learning to be consolidated. The learning process is often far from being 'neat and clean'. Learning does not always take place in clearly defined linear stages and it is not always planned.

Of course, as noted above, organizations themselves do not learn, but the individuals in the organizations learn as they communicate, learn and change, and this in turn influences organizational learning and change. Individuals learn about themselves (Torres, 1994) and themselves in relationship to others (Lundberg and Brownell, 1993), about the dynamics of the small groups they work in (Glaser, 1992), about the organization and how to be a facilitator for empowerment and self-management, and about the uncertainties and threats in the environment (Clark et al., 1994), which includes other organizations and the market for the products of the organization as well as the physical environment and the natural resources. In their summary of 'key questions in organizational learning', Miner and Mezias (1996) provide a list of sample issues at each of four levels of learning, although they do not include the physical environment and natural resources:

1 *Individuals* – acquisition of new skills, norms and values; effects of experience and ambiguity; individual interpretation.
2 *Groups* – performance feedback; shared understanding; coordinated behaviour.
3 *Organizations* – aspiration level; interplant and intraplant learning; organizational information processing.
4 *Populations of organizations* – shared experience; timing; technological standards; effects of various coping rules.

Another concept that covers all of these aspects of learning is 'global learning' (Srivastva et al., 1993). Organizational learning is required not only for organizations operating within one nation, but also for multinational firms where the complexities of global change need to be considered.

In their 'cultural perspective' on organizational learning, Cook and Yanow (1993) suggest that the result of organizational learning is to be found in the organizational culture which contains the 'know-how' associated with the organization's ability to carry out its collective activities. In a more formal definition, they describe organizational learning as 'the acquiring, sustaining, or changing of intersubjective meanings through the artifactual vehicles of their expression and transmission and the collective actions of the group' (1993: 384). Weick and Westley (1996: 445) endorse Cook and Yanow's definition of organizational learning since they 'avoid the blind spots of "learning" as an achievement verb when they insist that observers pay attention to the acquiring, sustaining and changing of intersubjective meanings. And they also avoid the non-experiential references to whole organizations when they use artifactual vehicles that embody collective know-how as their referent'. These meanings, whether they are acquired by new members or created by existing ones, are maintained though interaction by members of the organization. Of course, if the organizational culture is not conducive to learning by allowing flexibility, innovation, and new insights, then little learning may take place (Fiol and Lyles, 1985) – in fact, not only little learning, but also little creativity, as we shall see in the next chapter on creativity. But learning is not a free ride. There is a cost to learning since it depletes assets that might be used in other organizational activities (Schulz, 1992).

The Learning Process

Bales (1955) outlined seven steps that an individual goes through in making a decision:

1 Observes an event, X.
2 Makes a tentative induction that X belongs to class of objects, O.
3 Deduces a conditional prediction that if the event X belongs to a general class, O, it should be associated with Y.
4 Observes that Y is indeed associated with X.
5 Concludes that X and Y are members of class O.
6 States a premise that all members of class O should be treated in way W.
7 Proposes that X and Y should be treated in way W.

Bales's steps in the decision process can be summarized in three main phases: observing, formulating hypotheses and proposing action. Once the action is taken it is evaluated and the individual has learned that the action was either effective or not effective.

In Western societies individual learning follows the steps in the scientific method. The main objective is to gather information and evaluate it before making a decision (Daft and Huber, 1987). For organizations, knowledge must be acquired, information distributed and interpreted, and added to organizational memory. Huber (1991) identifies five ways in which knowledge can be acquired: (1) drawing on the knowledge available at the organization's birth; (2) learning from experience; (3) learning by observing other organizations; (4) grafting components of other knowledge; and (5) using information about the organization's environment and performance. However, once an individual has reached a decision, some decision rule or process must be introduced to combine individual decisions and reach agreement on a solution acceptable to a group or an organization. The ideal process is one of reaching 'consensus' (Leavitt, 1972) using 'dialogue' (Schein, 1993). Dialogue has as its underlying premise that humans operate most often within shared, living fields of assumptions and constructed embodied meaning and that these fields tend to be unstable, fragmented and incoherent. Isaacs (1993: 24) emphasizes this point by asserting that 'given the nature of global and institutional problems, thinking alone at whatever level of leadership is no longer adequate. . . . Human beings everywhere are being forced to develop their capacity to think together – to develop collaborative thought and coordinated action'. Dialogue establishes a field of genuine meeting and inquiry. Senge (1990) also emphasizes the necessity to have vision, values, integrity and dialogue within four 'disciplines' that are necessary for organizational learning, but adds 'systems thinking' as the fifth discipline. Systems thinking is the ability to identify patterns in the organizational system that control events. Since the patterns in the organizational system that control events are embedded in the organizational culture, individuals who are accustomed to thinking in system terms will have a better chance of understanding and changing the cultural values and thus engaging in the second loop of 'double-loop' learning.

As people learn to perceive, enquire into and allow transformation of the nature and shape of these fields, and in the patterns of individual thinking and acting that inform them, they discover entirely new levels of insight and forge substantive and, at times, dramatic changes in behaviour. As this happens, whole new possibilities for coordinated action develop. Weick and Westley (1996: 456) suggest that these insights are likely to occur at 'learning moments' when a set of conditions occurs that make learning possible: 'As organizing becomes disorganized, the forgotten is remembered, the invisible becomes visible, the silenced becomes heard.' As examples of occasions which juxtapose order and disorder they cite the use of humour, improvisation on a routine and a pocket of order in a setting of chaos.

What must be learned? All aspects of the social system that relate to the activity of the organization need to be understood and evaluated. If new methods are to be introduced, new skills must be learned before the new methods can be used. There may be 'competency traps' if workers feel that they are already competent at a task and thus do not need to learn more, although better methods may exist.

Attewell (1992) provides an example of obstructions to knowledge diffusion from business computing in the USA, drawing on various sources of statistical data. Although the dominant explanation of technology diffusion focuses on influence and information flow, know-how and organizational learning can obstruct the adoption of innovation (which will be discussed further in Chapter 6). Firms may delay in-house adoption of complex technology until they obtain sufficient technical know-how to implement and operate it successfully. In response to these knowledge barriers, new institutions attempt to lower the barriers through consultation, service provision and simplification. As the knowledge barriers are lowered, diffusion speeds up and technology shifts from being provided by outside sources to an in-house provision.

On the other hand, the case of networking in Dutch secondary schools presented below is an example of successful knowledge diffusion and the building of a learning community.

Secondary School Networks in Holland (Veugelers and Zijlstra, 1996)

Organizational learning means not shutting oneself off, being open to information from the outside, to different perspectives. The Upper Secondary Education School Network in Holland is the outcome of a collaborative experience which began in 1988 between the Centre for Professional Development in Education at the University of Amsterdam and 20 schools. The schools learn from each other, analyse each other's practices and develop various programmes. The network idea is widespread in Holland with nearly 70 per cent of the 450 Dutch schools for upper secondary education participating in them. Upper secondary education consists of pre-university education (ages 15–18, a requirement for university entrance) and senior general education (ages 15–17, usually leading to higher vocational education).

The impetus for network development was external – a response to government-required restructuring. As a result of the government reform, the upper secondary education was required to change its methodology to help students become more active learners. In turn, the schools are becoming more autonomous in determining their educational approach and methods. Within regulatory limits, each school may organize as it sees fit. Schools are receiving more responsibility for managing their own finances, task definition and education structuring. They differ in the amount of time they spend teaching, tutoring and counselling, special programmes offered and educational philosophy. Schools are in the process of developing their unique identities.

With all of these changes, the schools must find solutions to a number of challenges. The network approach was formed to emphasize the ability of schools to learn from each other. The idea is not 'copying' but creating a situation in which each school can adapt what it learns to its own particular needs. The functions filled by the network include:

INTERPRETATION OF GOVERNMENT POLICY   Consequences of government policies are not always obvious or clear. Discussion among teachers from different schools provides greater insight into these consequences and possibilities for restructuring education and implementing policy.

INFLUENCING GOVERNMENT POLICIES   The network can also try to influence policy by giving feedback as a group. They can point out things which need adjustment and show the implications of policies for practice. Government representatives may be invited to network meetings to discuss these issues.

LEARNING FROM OTHERS' EXPERIENCES   Besides the more concrete learning that goes on, as teachers present their own practices and reflect on the comments of others they become more aware of the rationale behind their own choices. They must explain how and why they do what they do and therefore, not only learn what others are doing but also have the opportunity to clarify their own thinking for themselves through reflection.

TAPPING INTO EXPERTISE   Network participants come to learn about people in other schools who they can turn to for help or collaboration.

DEVELOPING NEW EDUCATIONAL APPROACHES AND MATERIALS   Subgroups within the network create products that schools can use. These include teaching materials, organizational models, training materials for staff, and so on.

CREATING NEW INITIATIVES The university and the secondary schools have become partners in teacher training, professional development and research.
Through the network, teachers have learned that there are many choices and alternatives. But perhaps even beyond that, the authors note that participating in a network also leads to a broader view of education and the feeling of belonging to an educational community.

Kofman and Senge (1993: 7), writing about 'the heart of learning organizations', assert that it is necessary to build 'communities of commitment' where the commitment is more than commitment to the organizations: 'It encompasses commitment to changes needed in the larger world and to seeing our organizations as vehicles for bringing about such changes'.

In the theory of task and group development outlined in Chapter 4, we noted that, typically, the acquisition of new skills precedes changes in roles. The roles, in turn, are governed by rules. Zhou (1993) examined the rate of rule founding and rule change at an American university by reviewing the minutes of the Academic Council, Faculty Senate and other university publications. Over a period of 90 years, 343 rules were established and 740 changes were made. The rule founding and change followed two distinct processes. Rule founding reflects an organizational response to external crises and shock, while change is regulated by an internal learning process. Once rules are established, they are path dependent, sensitive to agenda setting and adaptive to governmental restraints. The rules become institutionalized over time.

From intensive field observations in four companies – Motorola Corporation, Mutual Investment Corporation, Electricité de France and Fiat Auto Company – Nevis et al. (1995) came to the following conclusions:

All organizations are learning systems. All have formal and informal processes and structures for acquiring, sharing and using knowledge and skills, even those organizations considered poor learners.

Learning conforms to culture. The nature of learning and the way it occurs are determined by the organization's culture or subcultures.

Style varies between learning systems. There are a variety of ways in which organizations create and maximize their learning. Seven bipolar learning orientations can be described and the pattern of learning orientations that make up the organizational learning system will tell a lot about what is learned and where the learning occurs:

1 *Knowledge source* – does the organization develop new ideas internally or look outside the organization for them?
2 *Product-process focus* – does the organization focus on accumulating knowledge about outcomes or about the basic process underlying its products?
3 *Documentation mode* – is knowledge privately or publicly held?
4 *Dissemination mode* – is dissemination formal or informal?

5 *Learning focus* – does the organization focus on single- or double-loop learning?
6 *Value-chain focus* – are learning activities focused more on the internal ('design and make') or the external ('sell and deliver')?
7 *Skill-development focus* – is the focus on development of individuals' skills or team and group skills?

Generic processes facilitate learning. Ten factors that facilitate learning can be identified which are considered generic factors that any learning organization can benefit from regardless of its learning style:

1 *Scanning imperative* – understanding of the environment in which the organization functions.
2 *Performance gap* – perception of a gap between actual and desired states of performance.
3 *Concern for measurement* – effort spent on defining and measuring key factors.
4 *Experimental mind-set* – support for trying new things and accepting the possibility of failure.
5 *Climate of openness* – information accessibility, open communication, perceived benefits of debate and legitimate disagreement.
6 *Continuous education* – ongoing commitment to continuing education for all organizational levels.
7 *Operational variety* – support for variation in strategy, policy, process, structure and personnel.
8 *Multiple advocates* – new ideas and methods put forward by more than one 'champion'.
9 *Involved leadership* – direct, hands-on leadership involvement in vision implementation.
10 *Systems perspective* – perception of the interdependence of organizational variables.

The learning orientations and the facilitating factors can be divided into three stages – knowledge acquisition, dissemination and utilization – plus a fourth integrating area into which falls skill development, involved leadership and systems perspective.

Nevis et al. (1995) see two general directions in which organizations can enhance learning. The first direction involves embracing their existing style and improving its effectiveness. This approach involves selecting two or three facilitating factors to improve on. A second possibility is to change learning orientations. Change may be perceived as an attack on the existing organizational culture and the proposed solution involves moving towards balance between the two poles, rather than moving straight to the opposite pole (for example, instead of moving from initiator to innovator, try to achieve some type of balance between the two).

In a learning organization, failure is not something to be avoided (Sitkin, 1996). Although both individuals and organizations prefer success over failure there can be benefits to failing and liabilities to success. Success encourages the status quo, and if the goal is stability, reliability and short-term performance, success is the foundation upon which to build. As long as conditions do not change, all will be well. But what about the liabilities of success? Sitkin (1996) points out that there are at least four of these:

Complacency. Success tells us that things are going well, that no corrective action is needed and, therefore, there is little motivation to try something new or different.

Risk aversion. The tendency towards complacency is exacerbated because of the way 'blame' is often allocated in organizations. *Not* doing something usually draws less fire than doing something and failing.

Restricted search and attention. Success, even very modest success, leads to little perceived need to alter what is operating adequately, an adherence to old routines and attention only to information which reinforces those routines since there are no cues to show the need to look for new information or new routines.

Homogeneity. Success leads to 'sticking with what works', the same operating procedures and the same type of personnel. Eventually this can lead to homogeneous employees, monolithic organizational cultures and less diverse activity. (In short, inbreeding.)

With all of these limitations of success, maybe failure is what works. Although failure is usually not a desired outcome in and of itself, it is probably a more effective means of learning than success. According to Sitkin (1996), the benefits of modest failure can be characterized as follows:

Attention and the processing of potential problems. Failure doesn't allow us to continue with the status quo without answering a few questions. Therefore, it can draw attention to potential problems and stimulate the search for potential solutions.

Ease of recognition and interpretation. Identification of criteria for ineffectiveness is easier than identification for effectiveness. Failure is a signal that is clear, that shows that this outcome represents a problem.

Stimulating search processes. Large failures are more effective in drawing attention but more modest failures are more effective in translating that attention into search processes. Large failures are threatening and can produce defensive behaviours such as escalation of commitment to prior routines (Staw and Ross, 1987). Small failures are less threatening and may lead to both attention and search.

Motivation to adapt. Failure produces a readiness to learn. There is a clear target and actions taken are usually aimed at correcting an identifiable situation. Actions that fail usually stimulate adapting to new circumstances. In addition, failure can create more willingness to consider new alternatives and reconsider 'traditions' – an 'unfreezing' process.

Risk tolerance. Just as success was mentioned above as bringing risk aversion with it, failure has been associated with increased risk seeking (Kahneman and Tversky, 1979) which, in moderation, is usually associated with increased innovation and ability to adapt to changing circumstances.

Requisite variety. Failure can stimulate experimentation. Experimentation can lead to increased variety in organizational repertoires, and variety is a means of enhancing performance and promoting learning and adaptation (Weick, 1979).

However, not all failures will facilitate learning equally well (Sitkin, 1996). Failures that contribute to learning are those that result from thoughtfully planned actions that have uncertain outcomes and are of modest scale. They are part of a rapid action–failure–action cycle, and occur in domains that are familiar enough to permit effective learning. If these characteristics hold, then we have what Sitkin (1996: 554) calls 'intelligent failure'.

Intelligent failures can be encouraged by certain organizational characteristics such as the removal of procedural constraints on natural experimentation, legitimizing intelligent failure, dealing with natural aversion to failure and building an organization level perspective recognizing the importance of intelligent failures. All of this involves building and supporting an organizational culture that allows and encourages use of intelligent failures rather than 'cover-up' operations when things do not go as expected.

Visions and Vision Statements

Building a shared vision is one of the essential components of a learning organization according to Senge (1990).

What is a vision? No two organizations should have identical visions but each vision should address three core themes that state what the organization stands for and what everyone must focus on. The formula, according to Lipton (1996), is: vision = mission + strategy + culture.

Mission. This variable addresses the question of why an organization exists and why it is in business. A mission must rise above the interests of any single stakeholder group, captivate people and require little or no explanation. It must show why an organization is special and different.

Strategy. The strategy gives the operational logic for what the company hopes to accomplish. It defines the business in which the organization competes and its distinctive competencies or advantages it has or plans to develop.

Culture. Organizational values direct and sustain the behaviour that translate the mission and the strategy into action.

The vision is the picture of the future we want to create. It establishes an overarching goal and helps keep the learning organization on track when stresses and conflicts develop. The shared vision is different from the 'vision statements' that we will present below. When there is shared vision, the reason that people learn and excel is because they want to, not because they are told to. It is what provides focus and energy. Building a shared vision is what builds a commitment to the long term. Senge (1990: 206) describes shared vision as follows:

> A vision is truly shared when you and I have a similar picture and are committed to one another having it, not just to each of us, individually, having it. When people truly share a vision they are connected, bound together by a common aspiration. Personal visions derive their power from an individual's deep caring for the vision. Shared visions derive their power from a common caring.

All types of organizations are developing and publicizing organizational vision statements. These organizations cover the diverse range of industrial manufacturers, schools, voluntary organizations, police departments, military units, municipalities and government agencies, to name just a few. The content and complexity of the statements vary and, although it is impossible to know for certain from an external perspective, it is probably safe to assume that the way the statements were developed also varied from organization to organization. Some statements include mission statements, some organizations present mission statements separately. In Table 5.1 we present some examples of vision statements, selected fairly randomly from organization sites on the Internet. The organizations are grouped according to whether they are equipment or technology driven (R), product driven (G), rule driven (I) or discovery driven (M), as explained in Chapter 4. The last column presents the focus of the mission statement. 'Outward' refers to a statement directed towards the environment, clients and customers; 'Inward', to an internally focused statement explaining how the organization will function internally and develop its culture; and 'Mixed', to a statement presenting both foci. All of the examples are from US organizations.

From the table it is possible to see that all but one of the statements are at least partially outwardly directed. Only the vision statement of the 18th Communications Squadron is totally directed inward, towards its own internal mode of operations. Of course, it must be remembered that all of these statements were taken from the Internet – that is, they are public representations of the organization and are probably intended, at least in part, more for customers than organization members.

It can also be seen in the table that our a priori division of organizations on the basis of functional analysis matches the organizations' self-representation. That is, we categorized the organizations as technology, product, rule or discovery driven on the basis of their name and assumed objectives. These categorizations are supported by the vision statements for the main part. Although it may seem strange to find chemical companies, business associations, municipalities, health service providers, broadcasting systems and educational institutions all categorized under the same heading of product-driven organizations, that choice becomes clearer when the vision statements are examined. All of these organizations focus on the 'customer' and the products (or services) they are to deliver to that customer. In contrast, the rule-driven organizations talk about upholding rules – law enforcement, prosecution and the administration of justice. Neither of these things seems to be the focus of the discovery-driven organizations which talk about research and technology development. The one category which is slightly unaligned is the first one, equipment- and technology-driven organizations. Within our sample there is one statement which is totally inward directed and another statement which is non-descriptive and presents a defensive posture without specification. The third organization, however, does show its technological dependency.

Up until now we have basically been saying that it is possible to classify organizations according to functional analysis and that most of the time this classification is supported by the organization's vision statement. However, we also found an exception to this point. As mentioned above, law-enforcement agencies and law firms are considered to be rule driven. But, as shown here, we have found an example of a law firm which views itself as product driven:

. . . to be recognized as the premier mortgage banking law firm in the state of [X].
Associated with that vision statement, the partners have developed certain core values that express our commitment to attaining that vision. They are as follows:
We believe in providing exceptional service to both our internal and external customers.
We believe in the importance of providing our employees with the resources they require to best serve our clients.
We believe that innovation is the key for responding to our customer's needs as they encounter the business challenges of the twenty-first century.
We believe in the personal dignity of each one of our employees and acknowledge their value as a member of our team.
We believe in creating a proactive environment where profit is the result of both personal and business growth.
We believe that demonstrating servant leadership in the firm and in the community enables us all to be a hope and a help to one another.

Table 5.1 *Examples of organizational vision statements*

Organization	Vision statement	Focus
R – equipment or technology driven		
Gaines Metzler Kriner & Company, Buffalo (accounting and investment)	'To be recognized as the best with the best for the best.'	Outward
Port Hueneme Division Naval Surface Warfare Center, Ventura County, California	'We will be the Navy's premier in-service engineering organization as a result of our high quality and cost effective performance to sustain weapon and combat system readiness in the surface maritime forces of our nation and its allies. We will be a highly trained, cohesive team universally committed to integrity, innovation, and the relentless pursuit of improvement. We will be known for our responsiveness as an advocate for the Fleet and the eyes and ears of our sponsors.'	Mixed
18th Communications Squadron, Network Control Center, based in Kadena AB, Okinawa, Japan	'Innovative leadership fostering teamwork and an organization capable of transforming itself to meet the future . . .'	Inward
G – product driven		
Roham and Haas, Philadelphia	'Rohm and Haas is a highly innovative, growing global speciality polymer and chemical company building on an ever-broadening technical base. Our customers regard us as indispensable to their success. We are their best and most consistent supplier of products and services. The general public views the company as a valued corporate citizen and a good neighbour. Our employees behave as owners and feel accountable for their performance and the success of the company. Ethical behaviour, teamwork, fast action, and a passion for constant improvement are the hallmarks of our culture.'	Mixed
National Association of Women Business Owners, Chicago Area Chapter	'. . . propels women entrepreneurs into economic, social, and political spheres of power.'	Outward

Organization	Statement	Type
Small Business Administration (US federal government agency)	The U.S. Small Business Administration (SBA) was created in 1953 as an independent agency of the federal government to aid, counsel, assist and protect the interests of small business concerns to preserve free competitive enterprise and to maintain and strengthen the overall economy of our Nation. Small business is critical to our economic recovery, to building America's future, and to helping the United States compete in today's global marketplace. Our vision for the SBA revolves around two principles: customer-driven outreach and quality focused management. We are determined to reach out to small businesses in an unprecedented way to listen to their needs, to report those needs back to President Clinton, and to suggest appropriate initiatives to help small businesses. We also recognize the need to change our management culture, our organizational structure, and the way we do business to improve the quality of our work. Through these changes, we will create a more entrepreneurial, customer-driven, and efficient SBA.'	Mixed
Scott County, Minnesota	'We create our own future. The future we envision is to make Scott County a great place for people to live and work, a place where families grow and thrive. By creating an environment that supports people, where our citizens live free of fear, where citizens are well informed and where county government is the true expression of the people's will, our vision will begin to take shape. Our vision is to make Scott County government a model of the American Principle of government: of the people, by the people, and for the people'.	Outward
City of Des Moines, Washington	'A friendly and safe waterfront community.'	Outward
Blanchard Valley Health Association, Ohio	'As perceived by all, by 1998 the Blanchard Valley Health Association will be the preferred provider of the highest *quality, cost effective, integrated health services in Northwest Ohio. *Quality is striving to meet or exceed the needs and expectations of those we serve.'	Outward
KPBS, San Diego, California (broadcasting system)	'It is the purpose of KPBS to educate, inform, entertain and empower our audience by acquiring, producing and delivering high quality programming which is of value and worthy of support.' *KPBS Guiding Principles* 'KPBS values community building, lifelong learning, and providing a service that is accessible to all. KPBS believes in being a responsive and professional organization. KPBS staff are committed to creating engaging and appealing programs and services, and through their endeavors, reflect the values of civility, respect, integrity and individual responsibility.' *KPBS Mission* 'KPBS will continue to thrive in a time of radical change.'	Mixed

Table 5.1   *Continued*

Organization	Vision statement	Focus
Oxnard Public Libraries, California	'The Oxnard Public Libraries will be a friendly, vital presence in the community, and a center of information. It will offer quality customer service, print and non-print materials, and cultural opportunities.'	Outward
Lennox School District, California	'We, the Lennox School Community of parents, staff, and students, celebrate learning and the lifelong quest for knowledge. We celebrate and nurture the talents and uniqueness of each individual. We are committed to creating a challenging educational experience that empowers all members to strive for excellence and to achieve their personal bests as contributors to the future of the community, nation and humanity.'	Mixed
I – rule driven		
Department of Police and Security, University of Wisconsin, Madison	'Our vision is to become a nationally recognized leader in campus policing, security services and law enforcement methods. Through continuous improvement, training and innovation, we will become proficient in problem solving and conflict resolution, and in the use of advanced technology. We will heighten our profile as an integral part of the university community, widely respected and trusted by its people. We will work in partnership with the community and continue to expand our cooperative efforts with other organizations in order to provide high quality professional service. We will stress employee development. We will establish a cohesive, friendly and supportive work environment for our employees; one that encourages creativity and the free exchange of ideas.'	Mixed

Wisconsin District Attorneys' Association, Wisconsin	'Deliver fair and effective prosecution and associated services for the betterment of the community by: leading the effort to improve the administration of justice; demanding integrity and professionalism; fostering communication and cooperation within the justice system; managing state and county resources efficiently; making optimal use of technology.'	Mixed
M – discovery driven		
Northern Great Plains Research Lab (agricultural research service – part of US Department of Agriculture)	'Our vision is economically sustainable and environmentally sound agricultural systems based on science.'	Outward
Dryden Flight Research Center (NASA)	'The world leader in flight research for discovery, technology development and technology transfer for US Aeronautics and Space Preeminence.'	Outward
Gas Research Institute, Chicago	'To provide the leadership in gas research and technology development to move the industry into a new era of opportunity and challenge by improving service to existing gas customers and significantly expanding major new market opportunities. Toward these ends, GRI will foster a climate that emphasizes technology transfer and that nurtures and rewards teamwork, innovation, and personal growth in order to provide value to all stakeholders.'	Mixed

Why is this distinction between a product-driven and a rule-driven organization important? It is important because the vision of the organization is part of the organization's culture. It is shaped by the values and goals of the organization and helps shape them. When values come into conflict and priorities have to be set, it is the culture which tells us what to do. By their vision statements, we would assume that the culture of the Wisconsin District Attorneys' Association and that of the mortgage banking law firm, and therefore their definitions of 'success', would be very different. One appears to focus on upholding the law, the other on satisfying the customer.

It is probable that most of the 'vision statements' in Table 5.1 were the vision of one person or one group within the organization, not true shared vision. If that is so, then the most we can expect is compliance, not commitment. A statement written at the top and pushed down the organizational hierarchy has little hope of success. Developing a vision is a tricky process. If it is developed in a vacuum, it may ignore the needs of those who are expected to bring it to life. If it is not grounded in reality, ignoring the environment or the abilities and problems of the organization, it will be rejected. The evolution of a final vision statement (final at a single point in time) requires consensus building, dialogue, listening and questioning.

Shared visions can be extrinsic, or as Senge (1990: 207) calls them, 'defensive goals', such as 'Blanchard Valley Health Association will be the preferred provider.' The problem with defensive goals is that once the goal is reached, the vision achieved, there is no further force for creativity, for further striving. The goal becomes 'defensive', protecting what has already been achieved.

Intrinsic visions are those such as the Lennox School District vision which includes: 'We are committed to creating a challenging educational experience that empowers all members to strive for excellence and to achieve their personal bests as contributors to the future of the community, nation and humanity.' In a case like this (Senge, 1990: 207–8), 'work becomes part of pursuing a larger purpose embodied in the organization's products or services'.

A shared vision has a number of effects besides creating excitement. It changes the individual's relationship to the organization from 'their company' to 'my company', creating a common identity. It leads people to do whatever needs to be done in order to pursue that vision and encourages risk taking and experimentation, necessary ingredients not only for organizational learning but also for creativity. Lastly, it encourages a long-term view and long-term commitment. But the power of a vision should not be overestimated. If it is seen as a wonder pill for all organizational problems, it will only make the organization worse off. Building shared vision is an important, ongoing, leadership activity. Although Senge (1990) acknowledges that there are no formulas, there are principles and guidelines for building shared vision as follows:

Encouraging personal vision. Shared visions derive their energy from personal visions and foster commitment because of them. When the shared vision is rooted in an individual's own set of values, concerns, hopes and dreams, then that individual will personally care about the vision. Without personal vision, there is only compliance with someone else's vision, not commitment.

Moving from personal visions to shared visions. Leaders must remember that their visions are personal visions and not automatically the organization's vision. Leaders wanting to build shared vision must be willing to share their personal vision and ask for support by opening up the vision for examination and testing by others. They must also be willing to listen to what these others are telling them. But not all shared visions start at the top of the organization. When they begin in the middle, the process of sharing and listening is the same but the process may take longer. Truly shared visions do not emerge quickly but rather grow as a result of the interactions of individual visions. Without openness, patience and a refusal to bring premature closure there is no chance that there will be shared vision.

Spreading visions. The goal is commitment – a desire to see the vision fulfilled and a feeling of responsibility for making that happen. More often, what we get is compliance, which may look like commitment but isn't. With compliance, the individual will do what's expected but that's where it stops. Compliant people may accept the vision – committed people *want* it. You cannot get another person to be committed to a vision. Commitment requires free choice.

Anchoring visions in a set of governing ideas. These governing ideas include the 'what' (the vision), the 'why' (the mission) and the 'how' (the values). If the vision is not consistent with the day-to-day values of the organization, it will not inspire anything but cynicism or ridicule.

Consensus

If an individual or group is making a decision about a matter of fact, then, in Western societies, the scientific method is used. This was discussed earlier in this chapter. However, when commitment to a decision is required, for example to the mission statement or vision of an organization, then another decision rule is best. In our review of the literature we find that we are warned against having the vision statement simply asserted by management for the members of the organization to follow. Nor is majority vote mentioned. Over and over again the decision method is given as *consensus*. But the details of the method are not given. You will not be surprised if here we will provide a set of guidelines for group and organizational decisions in terms of functional analysis (Hare, 1992b: 36–43).

The process of gathering opinions in a group to reach consensus begins with a recognition of the basic concerns of each individual. The outcome of the consensus process can take two forms. The first choice is a decision that each member of the group can identify with and feels commitment for, and thus there is a unanimity of opinion. A second choice is a decision that seems to be the best possible at the time, all things considered, even though some members might wish for a different version of the solution if it were possible. With either form, members are able to unite and will be committed to carry out the decision. The steps in reaching a decision follow the five phases in group development, described earlier. Step 1 involves commitment to making the decision by consensus (M); Step 2 the gathering of facts (R); Step 3 considering the relations between the members of the group (I); Step 4 reaching a decision (G); and Step 5 commitment to the implications of the new decision (M again).

In somewhat more detail, the five steps are as follows:

1   Meaning (M)
    Do: Secure agreement to follow the decision rules for consensus to create a decision that incorporates all points of view or one that all members agree is best for the group at this time.
    Avoid: A zero-sum solution or using majority vote, averaging or trading as conflict reduction devices.
2   Resources (R)
    Do: Give your own opinion on the issue. Seek out differences of opinion to obtain more facts, especially from low-status members.
    Avoid: Arguing for your own opinions.
3   Integration (I)
    Do: Address remarks to the group as a whole. Show concern for each individual opinion.
    Avoid: Confrontation and criticism.
4   Goal-attainment (G)
    Do: The group may have a *coordinator* whose main function is to help to formulate a consensus on each issue and a *recorder* to record each decision as it is reached and read back to the group (rather than wait for the next meeting to discover that some members do not agree with the wording). However, all members should help formulate statements about solutions to which all can agree. Even if there appears to be initial agreement, explore the basis of agreement to make sure there is agreement at a fundamental level.
    Avoid: Changing your mind only to allow the group to reach agreement.
5   Meaning (M) again
    Do: If consensus is reached, make it clear that each group member is responsible to apply the principle in new situations.
    Avoid: Pressing for a solution because time for the meeting is over. If consensus is not reached, postpone the decision until another meeting and do more homework on the problem.

Early in the 1960s, Leavitt, in *Managerial Psychology* (1972), had urged managers in organizations to consider the advantages of consensus as a method of reaching group decisions. He noted that most businessmen at that time favoured the method of limited discussion and acceptance of majority vote in the parliamentary fashion. When the decision is forced quickly, the minority might psychologically reject the decision and may feel challenged to prove that the majority is wrong. When the time comes for action, they may act in ways to 'prove' that the decision cannot be made to work. Leavitt emphasized that 'if the group's problems require that every member carry out of the group a desire to act positively on the group's decision, then it is imperative that everyone accept, both consciously and unconsciously, the decisions reached by the group' (1972: 216). He also noted that if total agreement could not be reached, an acceptable form of consensus is that everyone agree that there is a need for some kind of decision: 'Then, at least, the minority has expressed its opinion, has announced that it is not ready to change that position, has had a chance to express its own feelings about its position, and has agreed that some decision short of unanimity is necessary' (1972: 217).

If a group chooses to make decisions by consensus, rather than by majority vote or by leaving some decisions to subgroups, the meaning of consensus should be considered carefully. Dyer (1987: 103–4) recognizes two forms of consensus when he suggests that group members should realize that consensus does not necessarily mean that all persons think alike, but that after a decision each person can at least agree that 'this is a sound decision – one I am willing to support and implement. It is not exactly what I personally want, but given the range of opinions, the time factor, and the kinds of personalities involved, it is a good, working decision.' If consensus is not reached, discussion should continue.

Patten (1981: 129, 133) suggests that for union–management disputes one might ask whether 'accommodations to conflict reached through collective bargaining are on the same plane as a consensus developed under conditions of trust, openness, risk-taking, authenticity, receptivity to feedback, and focus of change that are characteristic of OD (organizational development)'. He also recommends consensus as an alternative to majority rule or to sweeping messy issues under the carpet.

Whatley and Hoffman (1987: 89, 93) report that when quality circles were first introduced into a government installation, the union felt threatened since the workers might solve problems on their own. As a result the steering committee that was formed to introduce quality circles included union members. The union members agreed to use consensus rather than majority rule, assuring that any agreements would be supported by all members of the committee. Although the method of consensus was time consuming, it helped ensure smooth implementation of committee decisions. In this case, the process was further facilitated by the consultant, who acted as a neutral party.

It is important that 'consensus' be understood as a process leading up to a group decision and not just the final outcome. McGregor (1960: 232–5) listed 11 characteristics for effective decision making in effective teams. In brief, they are as follows:

1   The atmosphere is informal, comfortable and relaxed.
2   Everyone participates in the discussion.
3   The objective is well understood.
4   Every idea is given a hearing.
5   Disagreements are not suppressed or overridden, but examined.
6   Simple majority is not accepted as a proper basis for action.
7   Criticism is frequent and frank without personal attack.
8   Feelings are expressed on the problem and on the group's process.
9   When action is taken, clear assignments are made and accepted.
10 The issue is not who controls but how to get the job done.
11 The group is self-conscious about its own operations.

Unfortunately, many procedures recommended for decision making, such as the use of 'nominal groups' (Ulschak et al., 1981: 85–96), only provide for group agreement on the rank order of given items. There is no possibility to combine items into a new idea, much less look for an overarching solution that combines all points of view in a new perspective. Contributors who 'own' ideas that do not receive high rank are left out of the process.

The same problem occurs for tasks, often used in management training sessions, such as the NASA moonwalk problem. Group members are asked to agree on a rank order of items of equipment needed for survival. There is no provision for the introduction of new ideas, and therefore no possibility of reaching 'consensus' on a higher level of creativity.

Tasks that are suggested for workshops to demonstrate group decision making are often in the form of 'eureka' tasks, where once group members have shared information on their slips of paper, only one individual is needed to find a solution. Then all will agree with that solution (Steiner, 1972). Practice with more complicated and realistic training tasks would be required for a team with maximum role differentiation and a high degree of integration.

Socializing New Employees

The learning of new skills and new rules of the game is especially important for newcomers as employees of the organization, since organizations have encoded inferences from history into routines that guide behaviour (Levitt and March, 1988). The rate of turnover of employees affects the attention that must be given to skill learning. Carley (1992) used a computer simulation to examine the impact of personnel turnover on organizational learning and problem solving for individuals working either in teams or hierarchies. She found that teams learned faster and better, but hierarchies were less affected by high turnover rates.

Katz (1988) records that individuals undergoing a transition to a new organization are placed in a high anxiety-producing situation. The supervisors and colleagues of new employees have a very special and important role to fulfil in inducting and socializing them. If the ultimate objective is to learn how to provide newcomers with a better 'joining-up' process, one that is not only less stressful but also more meaningful and personally developmental, then it is necessary to understand more fully how individual needs and concerns should be met throughout this important introductory period of organizational careers. Socialization is a social process that takes place through interaction, with other key organizational employees and relevant clientele, and the experiences are highly influential and long lasting. The content of socialization includes establishing one's organizational role identity, learning to deal with one's boss and other employees, and deciphering reward systems and situational norms. Through the process of socialization individuals are strongly motivated to organize their work lives in a manner that reduces the amount of uncertainty they must face and that is therefore low in stress. New employees can only reduce uncertainty through interpersonal activities and interpersonal feedback processes.

Evaluation and Feedback

For the learning process to be effective, feedback is very important. While some process is going on, feedback indicates whether or not the organization is on course toward its goals and allows adjustments to be made. Lawson and Ventriss (1992) report on a programme designed to strengthen the future productivity of a public-sector organization (a 10,000-student university) by identifying new goals and outlining a plan to implement change. The results indicated that in addition to having systematic and structured programmes based on well-defined and specific organizational goals, performance measures and incentives, performance feedback mechanisms are important for increased organizational productivity. The timing of feedback is crucial during disasters such as earthquakes (Comfort, 1993).

At the end of a process, feedback is again necessary for evaluation. DiBella (1990) discusses both problems and strategies connected with attempts to maximize programme evaluation impact in a research organization. Three major orientations affect evaluation utilization: (1) evaluator focus on technical demands and requirements of his/her academic training; (2) evaluator focus on concerns and needs of evaluation users rather than technical demands of the research; (3) a matrixed role whereby the evaluator bridges the gap between technical concerns of staff researchers and the information/organizational demands of users. The research manager must take the responsibility of utilization and facilitate the process of organizational change and learning and change. The utilization of evaluation requires personal action, changed behaviour or policies, political activity and ongoing systems to engender evaluation use.

Forss et al. (1994) provide an example from experiences in Norwegian aid administration. They find that evaluation generates learning in two modes: via involvement and via communication. If an organization wants to maximize its learning, it should pursue strategies to let the two modes supplement each other. Learning must be related to what people know, their knowledge structures, and to what they need to know to do their job well. Evaluation systems may be only marginally effective when there is a need to change knowledge structures rapidly, particularly if the organization lacks dominating knowledge structures.

Examples of Organizational Learning

Probst and Buechel (1997) provide examples of different types of organizational learning. We have selected three cases: first, Jakob Schlaepfer, an organization that has characteristics that support organizational learning (1997: 26–9); second, Hewlett-Packard, an organization that developed a system for 'learning to learn' (1997: 49–52); and third, NASA, an often-cited example of an organization that did not learn in time to prevent a disaster as it launched the Challenger space shuttle (1997: 73–4).

Supporting Organizational Learning – Jakob Schlaepfer (Probst and Buechel, 1997)

Jakob Schlaepfer Ltd has a modern network structure and a culture which is creative and strongly oriented towards learning. With 140 employees the organization is one of the best-known Swiss exporters of embroidery. The firm has branches in St Gallen, Paris, Los Angeles and Osaka. Almost all of its products go to leading fashion houses. The firm has been a leading influence in textile technology for the manufacture of embroidery and similar fashion products. Their designers produce four collections each year, or more than 1,400 designs, using embroidery, sequins and designer fabrics. This level of creativity is supported by a network concept, with a management hierarchy that is a flat pyramid functioning primarily as a network group and which has no permanent director. Committed employees with many years of experience form a wider circle of advisors and leaders, thus extending the network principle. In the firm's own 'school', in the Creative Centre, employees have an opportunity to develop their creativity and to form a cohesive community.

With the aim of promoting organizational learning, workshops were held in the Creative Centre to analyse theories of leadership and ways of working together and making decisions. Anomalies were identified and discussed, for example in connection with unavoidable redundancies, new sales concepts and financial decisions on projects. These discussions led to an increase in shared knowledge and a changed frame of reference, thus laying the foundation for further action.

Learning to Learn – Hewlett Packard (Probst and Buechel, 1997)

In 1988 Hewlett-Packard had 87,000 employees and sold more than 10,000 products for measurement and data processing. The company's motto was 'Tomorrow's world will probably be no better and no worse than today's, but at least we know that it will be different'. Knowing that success in the past was no guarantee of success in the future, the largest overseas branch in Germany launched a project to examine its central information system and to prepare it to meet the future.

First they took stock of all the planning, control and information systems in use. They discovered duplications and internal contradictions between data sets. Most of the available information was technical and related to the past. A project team was set up to develop an 'early warning system' that would show up probable future conflicts and dependencies.

Records of orders were chosen as a basis for the system as well as the image of the organization held by customers and employees. In response to a number of early warning signals, Hewlett-Packard was able to enter the 1990s as a successful company.

Failing to Learn – NASA (Probst and Buechel, 1997)

The disaster which befell NASA's Challenger space shuttle in 1986 is an example of how defensive routines operating throughout an organization can prevent learning from taking place. NASA had known for years that the O-rings on the launching rocket were unreliable in cold weather. Prior to the launch and on the day of the launch, engineers drew attention to the fact that the temperatures on that day were below those that were guaranteed for safety. After the space shuttle blew up, the investigation showed that the early warnings of the engineers had not been taken seriously by their superiors because there had been no problems during previous flights. Moreover, postponement of the flight would have had grave financial consequences. At a final meeting before the flight, the engineers were asked if there were any problems. They kept quiet because they thought no one was going to listen to them. In this case both NASA and the engineers used organizational defensive mechanisms. Because of the financial implications, NASA did not want to take the engineers' doubts seriously and the engineers, for their part, stopped expressing their anxieties because they thought nobody would listen.

Probst and Buechel (1997: 74) conclude that the Challenger disaster illustrates that defensive routines were also used after the accident investigation. The engineers were fired because they provided evidence to the commission, and were thus punished for their justified anxieties. NASA then set up even more comprehensive and rigorous safety regulations to guard against human error. Higher-level learning processes did not take place because the underlying norms and values were not questioned. Rather than

undertake an analysis of the behaviour which would have made it possible
for new points of view to be considered, the authorities tried to improve
safety simply by improving the rules.

The Challenge of Organizational Change

Organizational change is a subject about which there is a lot of disagreement. There is no one widely accepted theory of change and no agreed
guidelines for how to go about doing it (Dunphy, 1996). Like many other
areas in the organizational field (and probably in most fields of human
behaviour), organizational change is value laden.

> Theories of organizational change have not developed by some dispassionate,
> uncommitted, and unemotional form of cerebral inquiry. Rather, major change
> theories have been developed by change agents and practitioners who have
> sought to develop frameworks for understanding and directing change based
> on their practical experiences in organizations. In the organizational change
> field, the process of theory building has primarily occurred through an active
> interchange between agents of change and the organizations that have been
> the objects of their change attempts. The developers of the dominant approaches
> have often been passionate advocates of particular approaches to organiza-
> tional reform (for example, Taylor, Trist, Emery, and Deming). . . . In the field
> of organizational change, theories are necessarily infused with ideology. Our
> theories are value driven, often self-serving, grounded in social movements
> and driven by social forces. While this may be seen as a limitation of theories
> of organizational change, the fact that they are infused with ideologies does
> not mean that they are any less relevant or scientifically impure. (Dunphy,
> 1996: 542)

The implication of this is that the values which lie behind our
commitment to change have to be made explicit. In fact, one of the
authors of this book teaches courses on organizational change and places
the values she believes in before the students during the first or second
class. This often leaves them rather bewildered – they cannot understand
why she is doing it because at that point the change process still seems
value free to them.

Enough of the moralizing – so what is this thing called organizational
change all about and how do we do it?

In their book *The Challenge of Organizational Change*, Kanter et al. (1992)
refer to their scheme as the 'Big Three' model: three kinds of motion,
three forms of change and three roles in the change process. They see
these three sets of three as interconnected aspects of organizations: the
forces, both external and internal, that set events in motion; the major
kinds of changes that correspond to each of the external and internal
change pressures; and the principal tasks involved in managing the
change process.

The three kinds of movement are:

1 The motion of the organization in relation to motion in the environment. The change is macro-evolutionary, historical and typically related to clusters or whole industries. (Meaning)
2 The motion of parts of the organization in relation to one another as the organization grows, ages and progresses through its life cycle. The change is micro-evolutionary, developmental, typically related to the organization's size and shape, resulting in coordination issues. (Integration)
3 The struggles for power and control among individuals and groups with a stake in the organization. The change is focused on political dimensions and involves revolutionary activity. (Goal-attainment)

Each of the three kinds of movement is related to a corresponding form of change:

1 *Identity* changes in the relationships between the organization as an entity and its environment: the assets it owns and the markets it approaches, the niches it occupies, the relationships it has with its customers and to the organizations that fund it, supply it and confer legitimacy on it. Organizations can change their identity by reformulating any of these relationships. The most extreme form of identity change is when an organization becomes something completely different (in its business, products, ownership, etc.) to allow some portion of its asset base, know-how, employment base or tax carry-over to endure. (Meaning)
2 *Coordination* changes, which involve the internal array of parts or activity sets that constitute the organization. The result is reshaping or revitalizing. (Integration)
3 Changes in *control* with regard to the dominant coalition, set of interests or ownership. These lead to makeover through takeover. The changes are often dramatically revolutionary in their impact on many aspects of the organization. (Goal-attainment)

The three kinds of movement also correspond to three action roles in the change process, the phases in the change sequence and to traditional organizational levels.
The three action roles in the change process are:

1 *Change strategists* who have a concern for the connection between the organization and its environment and for the organization's overall direction in the light of macro-evolutionary forces. The role is often played at the beginning of a change sequence by top leaders. (Meaning)
2 *Change implementors* who are responsible for the internal structure and coordination as the organization moves through its life cycle.

They are active in the middle of a change sequence or at middle levels of the organization. (Integration)

3   *Change recipients* are usually involved toward the end of a change sequence at the 'bottom' of the organization. They are strongly affected by the change and its implementation, but without much opportunity to influence the effects. Their position reflects the political and control dimensions of organizations, such as who benefits and which interests are served. Tension can arise between those directing the change and the powerless, passive recipients. For more effective change, the recipients should be included among the implementors and strategists. (Goal-attainment)

Kanter et al. (1992) spell out their model in their book, examining each element with illustrations drawn from a wide range of companies, industries and countries. They indicate why there are so many possibilities for failure in making change. The three kinds of motion may be leading in different directions. The three action roles not only involve different responsibilities but they also reflect different perspectives and interests that can interfere with any one group's ability to realize its intentions. They stress that many changes happen to organizations and their members without any planning. But, they conclude, it also helps to understand both the opportunities and the difficulties of planned or intentional change.

They caution that often change programmes are presented as if they were recipes that will produce the results desired. Nothing could be farther from the truth. Every change programme is full of opportunities for alternative courses of action. There is not 'one best way' but many paths for implementation of innovation, each of which might be useful in some given set of circumstances. They suggest that there are four types of critical choices facing the change manager. These are identified along with detailed lists of factors to be taken into account when making each choice.

1   *Everywhere versus pilot sites?* Should the change be introduced across the organization (rolled out) or step by step?
2   *Fast versus slow?* How useful is it to attempt to move very quickly, for example, by devoting greater resources?
3   Is it better to *work through existing structures and roles*, or to *create new roles*, or groupings, or structures?
4   Should the changes be *mandatory* or *voluntary*?

Heckscher et al. (1994) define four change processes which are defined by two dimensions, sharing of information and sharing of power:

Command. Commands are issued without seeking agreement and full reasons for the actions are not communicated to the organization. Even in cases in which some power is transferred through 'empowerment' to teams, the changes can be easily subsumed within the bureaucratic, hierarchical structure. The sizes and shapes of the boxes in the organizational chart may change but the logic remains.

Cascade. Information is opened up although power is not. There is an attempt to create shared commitment to the change through explanations of the rationale and strategy and training. Problems with this approach include a loss of meaning and 'steam' as the idea progresses downwards through the organization. It is also highly dependent on top management and, therefore, to changes in top management.

These first two types of change are linear – the endpoint is defined and then what remains is to figure out how to get there. Not all organizational change can be planned and implemented in a relatively straight line. Sometimes we need nonlinear forms of change in which the endpoint is not clearly defined in advance. For example, Heckscher et al. (1994: 134–5) describe the change to the post-bureaucratic organization (described in Chapter 4) as a developmental change with the constraint that 'one cannot envision it before experiencing it. It is a matter not of clarifying and then implementing a vision but rather of structuring a series of experiences that move toward a vague "sense" of the future.'

The next two types of change are nonlinear, a type of change whose cyclical spiralling can be explained in three steps (Heckscher et al., 1994):

1 *Fuzzy visioning.* Developing consensus on an imprecise picture of the future that sets a general direction but leaves wide scope for exploration.
2 *Experimentation.* Trying out various approaches toward the broad vision.
3 *Reflection.* Systematic review of the experience and preparation to enter the next cycle.

This imprecision and lack of simple and definable outcomes does nothing to calm the nerves of most managers since it relies on faith in the process – a belief that the inquiry and reflection cycles will lead to the emergence of a good solution.

Private politics and leadership. This approach works toward consensus but without open sharing of information. It is based on private politics and coalition building. The only person with an overall picture of the goal is the leader. This process is nonlinear because there are stages of reflection, revision, adaptation and refinement but it is only the leader who participates. Because there is no public picture of the future, the leader can shift directions more easily.

Collaborative process. This process opens up both information and power and is open and consensual. Dialogue is conducted across boundaries of formal power and status and the entire process demands a lot of time, energy and patience. The power of the collaborative process comes

LIVERPOOL JOHN MOORES UNIVERSITY

from its combining high degrees of openness, which produces unity, and consensus, which produces commitment. Heckscher et al. (1994) propose that only a process of open and public self-examination without a predefinition of the solution can establish the conditions for successful transition to a post-bureaucratic organization. The purpose of the self-examination is to develop a deeper understanding of the challenges the organization faces and the capabilities it has to deal with them. Collaborative processes also increase the level of organizational learning because of the dialogue process involved. In the terminology of the first part of this chapter, this type of transition demands double-loop learning.

Organizational Culture

As noted above, Cook and Yanow (1993) suggest that the results of organizational learning are to be found in the organizational culture. Thus it becomes important to look more closely at organizational culture and the way in which it influences the behaviour of individuals and groups in organizations.

Hawkins (1997), based on a review of books on organizational culture and his own experience as a consultant in the UK, provides several sets of categories that can be useful for the analysis of organizational culture. One set, based on the work of Schneider (1994), fits well with the 'four functions' approach that we have been using to bring together various findings in the literature on individuals and groups in organizations. Hawkins reviews seven studies that propose four types of emphasis in organizational cultures. For five of the studies the fit with the four functional categories is very direct, while for two of the studies the authors each left out one function but gave two versions of another. Hawkins concludes that no one culture type is intrinsically better than any other, but different cultures are more suitable to different enterprises and environments. In the following list we give the functional area, the label of the area that Hawkins uses, in parentheses a comparable label from another study, the description of the area and, last, the kind of organization for which this type of culture is best suited.

Resources: competence (rational). It pays most attention to potentially, imagined alternatives, creative notions and theoretical concepts. Its decision-making process is analytically detached, formula oriented, scientific and prescriptive. It thrives in research organizations, advertising agencies, partnerships and consultancies in organizations where there is a strong emphasis on achievement.

Goal-attainment: control (hierarchical). What it pays attention to most is concrete, tangible reality, actual experience and matters of practical utility. Its decision-making process is analytically detached, formula

oriented and prescriptive. These cultures are best suited to large production companies or financial institutions.

Integration: collaboration (consensus). Like the control culture it pays a
great deal of attention to concrete, tangible reality, actual experience and
matters of practical utility. However, its decision-making process is
people driven, organic and informal. It is more suited to some of the
helping professions, or companies that are highly people focused.

Meaning: cultivation (ideological). It pays attention chiefly to potential-
ity, ideals and beliefs, aspirations and inspirations, and creative options.
Its decision-making method is people driven, organic, open-minded and
subjective. It flourishes in religious and therapeutic organizations where
there is a strong emphasis on personal development.

Developing an Organizational Culture

Having outlined the four types of cultures, Hawkins cites Schneider's list
of five steps that might be taken to develop an organizational culture
based on the four-fold typology:

Step 1: Determine your core culture.
Step 2: Capture your culture's strengths.
Step 3: Determine your core culture's level of integration.
Step 4: Determine your core culture's degree of wholeness.
Step 5: Determine your core culture's degree of balance.

This approach, like that of Denison (1990) and Burt et al. (1994),
emphasizes the importance of a strong unitary culture that is integrated
throughout all parts and levels of the organization, with leadership being
the 'fundamental process' by which organizational cultures are formed
and changed (Schein, 1985). However, Hawkins warns that this approach
has a danger of becoming overdetermined and thus killing the 'butterfly'
that it seeks to nourish. He is basically concerned about the taxonomic
approach itself. Is culture something an organization *has*, or is it an
integral part of what an organization is. For some anthropologists culture
is seen as the ongoing process of 'organizing and negotiating meaning'.
Consultants who attempt to help organizations develop 'a strong unitary
culture', often fail to look at the richness of the culture as it already exists
with its multiple and complex meaning-making processes.

The consulting group of which Hawkins is a part has developed a
methodology of culture change which they feel honours the richness and
depth of the organization's culture and the complexity of the change
process. They identify five levels of culture:

Level 1: *Artefacts*. Policy statements, mission statements, dress codes,
  furnishings, buildings, PR, etc.
Level 2: *Behaviour*. What people do and say. What is rewarded. How
  conflict is resolved. How mistakes are treated, etc.

Level 3: *Mind-set*. Organizational 'world view', ways of thinking that constrain behaviour. Organizational values-in-use, basic assumptions, etc.
Level 4: *Emotional ground*. Mostly unconscious emotional states and needs that create a context within which events are perceived.
Level 5: *Motivational roots*. Underlying sense of purpose that links the organization and the individuals.

The most noticeable elements of a culture are the artefacts and the behaviour. The artefacts demonstrate the espoused values and the behaviours show the values in action. Hawkins reports that many organizations have run into difficulties when there has been a rift between their rhetoric (what they say) and the reality of what they do. Below the artefacts and behaviour are the 'mind-sets' that hold in place the belief systems of the culture. These in turn are enacted in the 'emotional ground' or climate of an organization. The 'motivational roots' provide the alignment of individual purpose and motivations with those of the organization.

Hawkins advises organizational leaders that they have a clear role in organizational change. They are encouraged to be sensitive to the needs of the various stakeholders and confront discrepancies between the current dominant culture of the organization and the demands of those at the environmental boundary, be they customers, clients, competitors or political agencies. Leaders should represent the need of the future while valuing the past. Culture change is thus a double dialogue process across the boundary of the organization between insiders and outsiders, and across the time boundary between past and future.

Alongside of the five-level model, culture is expressed through three levels of consciousness:

Espoused culture. The public presentation of the collective self; the organizational persona.
Enacted conscious culture. The lived culture that is noticed and can be verbalized.
Unconscious culture The unthought unknown that is collectively experienced but unnoticed by conscious reflection and not able to be verbalized.

Rumours can pose a special problem for organizations. Rumours flourish when there is a gap between the rhetoric (espoused culture) and the reality (enacted conscious culture) of an organization. The concept of rumour is used to illustrate how an organizational unknown thought can, step-by-step, emerge into the public domain. Hawkins lists eight steps, from the unthought unknown at the bottom, through gossip, to public behaviour, with 'enshrined in procedures, policies, and artifacts' at the top. He suggests that powerful felt experiences in the collective pre-reflective subconscious would first be thought about by individuals, but remain unspoken. Next, they would be spoken about in the form of gossip, as rumours, before being discussed in public but in encoded form. A meeting might discuss the problem of 'democratic decision making' as a way of bringing the gossip about a dictatorial manager to the edge of the public domain. Hawkins feels that his step-by-step model could help consultants realize the dangers of taking information directly from the reality of the pre-reflective unconscious into direct attention and the importance of developing facilitative methods that respect the natural flow of the emergence of data from the pre-reflective unconscious, through the enacted conscious culture, into the area of the publicly espoused culture.

Hawkins concludes that, just as individuals are most creative, productive and energized when their root motivation and sense of purpose, their feelings and emotions, and their mental frame are all in relationship with each other, so it is with cultural levels. Thus the relationship between cultural levels is at the heart of synergistic teamwork and organizational performance.

National Culture

Descriptions of organizations focus on aspects that are overt and clearly recognizable, while the larger national 'culture' may have a less conscious influence on behaviour. Nussbaum (1994) conducted an ethnographic study of Mitsubishi Heavy Industry (MHI) in Japan to discover the extent to which organizational control was subconscious. Based on interviews and field observations, he concluded that MHI was typical of Japanese companies that have strong organizational cultures, characterized by a high degree of coherence between management and employee goals. Employees subconsciously conduct themselves in line with organizational goals and do not need authoritarian control. Employees have low absenteeism, high overtime and an unwillingness to take vacation or leave time. The commitment to the company exhibited by MHI employees is seen to be a direct reflection of the values of Japanese culture: the subordination of the individual to the group and the importance of harmony, duty and loyalty. These values are evident in the individual Japanese and in the firm's organization. The fear of normative social punishment (isolation or seclusion from the work group) underscores the commitment and is symbolically manipulated by the organization.

Culture and Creativity

Since, according to Hawkins's five levels of culture, all patterns of activity in an organization which serve to guide behaviour can be considered as part of culture, we will not be surprised to discover, in the next chapter on creativity in organizations, that the factors in an organization that enhance or limit creativity are essentially part of the organizational culture. To save a bit of duplication, the factors influencing productivity and creativity that are discussed by some authors in relation to culture will be covered in the next chapter as they relate to characteristics of the organization. Some example of these variables as they are attributed to culture are on the importance of shared meanings (Blunt, 1991; Feldman, 1993), shared goals (Haas et al., 1992; Hermans, 1990), subcultures (Kinnunen, 1990) and the fit with external conditions (Arogyaswamy and Byles, 1987).

Learning – Some Final Words

In the previous chapter, 'Groups', we touched on the topic of learning briefly as it applied to groups within an organization under the headings 'building productive groups' and 'self-managing work groups' as group members learned to become more productive and to share the leadership functions. In this chapter we have summarized literature on learning in organizations since that has been the focus of much research. Since what is learned by individuals will not be carried over from one generation to the next unless it becomes embodied in the organization's culture, we then discussed organizational culture. If what is learned is the result of new ideas from within the organization, we are then dealing with organizational creativity, the subject of the next chapter. Essentially the same points are being made three times since the factors that enhance learning also make change possible and provide a framework for creativity.

In this chapter two levels of learning have been identified and in the next chapter the levels of learning (creativity) will be run up to five. The two levels are represented as a 'double loop', where the first loop consists of learning that takes place within an organization's system of values and the second, higher loop, involves changes in values that provide frames for action. In functional terms, the first loop includes learning related to the sub-functions of resources, integration and goal-attainment in each of the major four functional areas. The second loop is associated with changes in meaning in each functional area. Learning in all four functional areas will be involved since the most effective learning requires that activity in each area needs to be understood and evaluated.

A given organization may place the emphasis in its culture on one of the functional areas, on competence, control, collaboration or ideals. The richness and depth of an organization's culture can be seen at five levels, in artefacts, behaviour, mind-set, emotional ground and motivational roots, and is expressed through three levels of consciousness: espoused culture, enacted conscious culture and unconscious culture.

6

CREATIVITY

Bartunek (1988) defines creativity as 'transformation through reframing'. The concept 'reframing' applies to having a new idea, providing a new definition of the situation, a new meaning. However the new idea must be put into practice to be useful. Many ideas are presented 'before their time' if no process is in place by which they may be implemented.

Groups and organizations that find themselves in situations of increasing paradoxical demands with scarce resources, a radically changing workforce, rapid communications and global competition are under pressure to find more creative solutions to be effective in this complex and turbulent environment (Smith and Gemmill, 1991).

The theories used to explain creativity (innovation) in organizations are guided by three basic assumptions: (1) innovation is universally desirable in organizations; (2) once an organization increases in size beyond a critical mass it becomes more inert, less capable of meaningful organizational change and only haltingly proficient at innovation; and (3) certain structures and practices can overcome inertia and increase the generation rate of innovation (Drazin and Schoonhoven, 1996). The speed at which innovations are adopted is especially important during periods of incremental technological change in industries similar to the microcomputer industry where the speed of innovation adoption enhances a firm's performance (Drazin and Schoonhoven, 1996).

A Theoretical Perspective on Creativity

After reviewing theories of creativity, Arbet (1991) concluded that the analysis of levels of creativity is essential, even though it has been overlooked by most writers on the subject. We base our own analysis on five levels of creativity, as they would appear in art and science, that were identified by Taylor (1975). Each problem faced by an organization has an implied level of creativity necessary for its solution. There are ways to warm up for each level (Hare, 1982). Taylor's categories have been applied to creativity in group discussion and negotiation, with examples of each of the levels (Hare, 1992a).

In brief, the five levels, as they would appear in art and science, with Taylor's examples, are as follows:

High   5   *New meaning (paradigm)*. A contribution that involves the most abstract ideational principles that underlie a body of knowledge. Examples: Einstein, Freud, Picasso.

4   *Extension of theory*. Basic principles are understood so that older theories can be extended to cover new areas and modification through alternative approaches is possible. Examples: Jung and Adler elaborate on Freud.

3   *Combination of known elements*. Ingenuity with materials, providing combinations to solve old problems in new ways. Examples: Edison's light, Bell's telephone.

2   *Demonstration of skill*. Contribution or solution that involves skill and a new level of proficiency. Example: Stradavari's violin.

Low   1   *Spontaneity*. An action that is different where the originality and quality of the product are unimportant. Examples: children's drawings.

Creativity is a form of problem solving. The steps required for the development of a new idea are essentially the same as the steps in the scientific method. The steps in the scientific method are, in turn, the same as those used for the development of any idea from a functional perspective:

Scientific method	*Function*
1 State problem	M
2 Gather facts	R
3 Test relationships	I
4 Draw conclusions	G
5 Solution leads to new problems	M new meanings

The M, R, I, G functional categories are based on the work of Parsons (1961) as defined by Effrat (1968). Examples of positive and negative behaviour in each of these categories are:

Meaning	+ Seeks or provides basic categories or ultimate values.
	− Seeks to deny, take away or inhibit the development and recognition of values.
Integration	+ Seeks or provides solidarity or norms.
	− Seeks to deny, inhibit or prevent the formation of norms and movement toward group solidarity.
Goal-attainment	+ Seeks or provides relatively specific direction, goal-definition or problem solutions relevant to the group's goals.

	− Seeks to prevent or inhibit movement toward the group's goals.

Resources + Seeks or provides facilities for goal-attainment.
             − Seeks to deny, inhibit or prevent the provision of facilities and relevant information.

Although the categories are listed above in their cybernetic hierarchical order, from high to low, as phases in group development or problem solving, the categories usually appear in the order M, R, I, G with a final phase of M as indicated above. (See Chapter 4 for a discussion of phases in group and organizational development.)

For problem solving, the first phase involves the statement of the problem to be solved, the definition of the situation. The second phase involves gathering resources, usually in the form of information about the subject. The third phase involves formulating and testing hypotheses about the relationships between the various factors of the problem that have been identified. The fourth phase consists of formulating a new perspective or implementing a solution. In a final phase, the solution of the initial problem and its evaluation suggests a new set of problems.

It is assumed that the amount of creativity required to solve a problem depends on the type of problem and the phase in problem solving. This leads to two hypotheses: (1) different problems have different starting levels and require different levels of creativity for their solution; and (2) ideally the creativity level of the solution should be as high as, or higher than, that of the problem.

Three examples:

1 A problem involving the development of a 'new, improved' product in order to retain customers who are showing signs of 'defecting' to another manufacturer. No new concepts or new interpersonal relationships are required. The problem is to find the right *combination* of rules (creativity level 3).
2 A problem involving adapting an idea to local conditions, such as transplanting Disneyland to Europe or Japan. Although much of the work may be to select the right location and personnel (creativity level 3), changes in roles or relationships may be required (creativity level 4).
3 A problem involving interdepartmental conflict, such as mediating between the sales and manufacturing departments. The initial situation is defined as one of conflict. The problem is to change the definition of the situation (creativity level 5).

In each case the level of creativity required in phase R, gathering facts, is lowest. A higher level of creativity is required for the I phase, testing relationships. For the G phase, drawing conclusions, ideally the creativity level of the solution should be as high as, or higher than, that of the problem. A solution involving a trade-off (level 3) does not last as long as one involving new units or new relationships (level 4). The acceptance of a new definition of the situation lasts longest.

At any level of creativity there is typically an 'aha' experience as a new insight occurs. This 'creative shift' in perception takes the form of a new perspective or a new formulation of an idea, and can occur to an individual acting alone or as a member of a group (Hare, 1982). In either case there is a prior state of conformity to the common perception of things or to common forms of behaviour, then a period of 'spontaneity' when proactive and reactive behaviour becomes more frequent and immediate with considerable variety, then the 'creative shift', then the consolidation of the idea, and finally its transmission and acceptance by others. Stein (1974) has noted the importance of supporters, patrons, or the presence of a 'psychegroup' to help with the creation and diffusion of an innovation.

For a creative shift to take place, the boundaries of old categories of perception must be blurred. If the 'old categories' of perception apply to the self and others they may be locked in by strong emotional feelings. Then some form of emotional catharsis will be necessary before new insights can occur. However, no emotional catharsis may be required when dealing with impersonal objects for the creation of a new work or art or a new scientific theory.

Creative Persons

In the search for potentially creative children and adults, social scientists who have developed psychological tests have looked for the presence of four variables: fluency, flexibility, originality and elaboration. In one of the tests used by organizational consultants, creative persons are found to be highly intuitive (Agor, 1991).

In a summary of research on the characteristics of productive scientists, Barron (1969) finds 10 traits that are associated with creativity:

1   High ego strength and emotional stability.
2   A strong need for independence and autonomy; self-sufficiency; self-direction.
3   A high degree of control of impulse.
4   A superior general intelligence.
5   A liking for abstract thinking and a drive towards comprehensiveness and elegance in explanation.
6   High personal dominance and forcefulness of opinion, but a dislike of personally toned controversy.
7   Rejection of conformity pressures in thinking (although not necessarily in social behaviour).

8   A somewhat distant or detached attitude in interpersonal relations, though not without sensitivity or insight; a preference for dealing with things and abstractions rather than with people.

9   A special interest in a kind of 'wagering' that involves pitting oneself against the unknown, so long as one's own efforts can be a deciding factor.

10 A liking for order, method and exactness, together with excited interest in the challenge presented by contradictions, exceptions and apparent disorder.

Steiner (1965) and Stein (1991) list similar sets of characteristics of the creative person.

Drawing on their practical experience, rather than psychological research, managers of the Sony Corporation, a Japanese company making electronic devices, look for people who are *neyaka*, which translates roughly as optimistic, open-minded and wide ranging in their interests (Schlender, 1992).

Frohman (1997) studied successful examples of incremental change in over 24 companies, including service companies and consumer and industrial manufacturers. He looked at changes that showed effective recognition and adaptation to problems, opportunities or changed circumstances, rather than major changes in strategy or structure. To be included in the research, changes had to have a positive impact on the 'bottom line' and had to become part of the part the organization operated, not just a one-shot activity. Who were the people who initiated these changes? They can be characterized in the following ways:

They were easily identified by their peers and superiors. They had independent but loyal attitudes, were respectful yet questioning of the status quo, and were determined to make a constructive impact.

They were usually not seen as having potential for high promotion. They had ambition but it was problem focused, not promotion focused.

They were directed by organization needs to go beyond their jobs. They did not simply do their jobs, but took initiative that went beyond job requirements and persisted even when there was resistance or disapproval.

Their learning focused on meeting the organization need. They had to learn something new within the context of the change they were effecting. Their growth and learning were driven by a need to make a difference.

They were driven internally to make a difference. The need to make a difference was internally, not externally, motivated.

They were action oriented. They acted with a sense of urgency and attacked problems without waiting for orders or approval. They felt a sense of responsibility for and to the organization but not blind acceptance of the way things were done.

They expected success in their efforts. They were patient and set realistic expectations about the rate of change.

They focused on results more than teamwork. They were not blind to the impact of their action on others but had little interest in politics and impression management.

In sum, the creative person is essentially a nonconformist with the capacity to pursue nonconforming and creative ideas in the face of societal pressures to see things as others have seen them and leave things as others have found them. However, different levels of creativity call for different sets of traits. Persons can be creative at the skill level without being creative at the combinatorial level or without being able to extend current theories or envision paradigm shifts. For example, product development managers at the Sony Corporation believe that the answer to creativity is to match the right kind of engineer to the right kind of product. 'There's an appropriate role for everyone,' says Kozo Ohsone, 58, senior managing director of the audio group, who was a key executive on both the original Walkman and the Discman portable CD. But he also shepherds the development of hundreds of less revolutionary products. Says Ohsone: 'If you want to lower the cost of an existing product or find a better way to manufacture it, you assign it to experienced engineers who like what they are doing. If you are designing something new that is higher priced, with lots of features, you give it to the rookies.'

Encouraging Creativity

Yong (1994) identifies three steps that are necessary to encourage creativity in organizations. The first step is to understand the creative process which has four characteristics: (1) problem sensitivity (recognizing the problem that exists); (2) idea fluency (generating a large number of ideas assisted by notetaking and the use of special times or places); (3) originality (finding new ways to adapt existing ideas to new conditions); and (4) flexibility (considering a wide range of options). Abraham and Boone (1994) focus on idea generation using brainstorming and evaluation. However, they accept any idea without a criterion for selecting higher levels of creativity.

Proctor (1995), in a book entitled *The Essence of Management Creativity*, describes many additional techniques that can be used to stimulate the reorganization of thoughts leading to creativity. Although Proctor does not indicate the level of creativity that might be achieved using these methods, any checklist that forces a person or group to be more systematic in the search for a solution to a problem is bound to provide some improvement.

The second step of appreciating the creative person involves developing trust by giving freedom within a set of parameters, harnessing creative employees' intensity and energy, and encouraging warmth and tact in communicating with others. Finally, a creative work environment should be encouraged, especially developing good supervisor–subordinate relationships. As an example of one form of encouragement, a public utility company gives awards for ideas that can be implemented and bring about significant improvements in operations (Smith et al., 1990).

Although you may not always get what you want, for creativity in organizations, apparently you may get what you reinforce. West (1990) proposed that four psychological constructs (vision, participative safety, climate for excellence and norms of – and support for – innovation) can be used to enable prediction of innovation at work. However, two of the concepts, which are group process variables (norms for innovation and participative safety) are more likely to encourage the quantity of attempts to introduce new ideas. Vision and climate for excellence are more product oriented and are more likely to affect the quality of the innovation.

Burningham and West (1995) examined the influence of these four climate factors on rated group innovativeness in a study of 59 members of 13 teams in an oil company. Support for innovation was the most consistent predictor, with negotiated vision and an aim for excellence also serving as predictors.

After reviewing the literature on 'organizing for innovation', Dougherty (1996) concluded that there were four sets of activities that formed the basis for the development of commercially successful new products by an organization. For each of these activities she identifies an underlying tension, a problem of normal functioning that disrupts the tension and particular practices which perpetuate disruption.

1   The innovators must work with potential new customers to identify needs and link these needs with technological possibilities. This activity deals with the 'outside vs inside' tension, to keep operations efficient, and avoids an inward emphasis on departmental thought worlds and units and a fixed sense of business.
2   They must organize the flow of work to collaborate across boundaries over problems, and solve them within the context of the whole system of attributes that comprise the product. This activity deals with the 'new vs old' tension, by managing complexity, and avoids segmentalist thinking and compartmentalization of work, with power based on current work.
3   They must monitor and evaluate their progress. This activity deals with the 'determined vs emergent' tension, by controlling multiple activities, and avoids abstracting work into generic standards, with no strategy making.
4   They must develop a sense of commitment which enables partici-pants to take more responsibility without feeling overwhelmed. This activity deals with the 'freedom vs responsibility' tension, by

accounting for work and results, and avoids the designation of innovation and inclusion as illegitimate.

Whatever the organization can do formally to enhance creativity, the informal group can do or undo. The major finding of the Western Electric Studies in the 1930s (Roethlisberger and Dickson, 1939) was that informal groups could either encourage or discourage individual productivity. The same is true for creativity. Ford (1996) reminds us that it is not only informal groups that may support or discourage creativity, but that multiple social domains may be involved. His advice to managers is that the challenge of providing for creativity and innovation requires them to (a) consistently empower the individual processes that facilitate creative action, while holding the temptations that draw people toward habitual responses at bay; and (b) identify and utilize the ways within the multiple social domains (of subunits, groups, organizations, institutional environments and markets) by which innovations are selected to be implemented.

In Norway, workers from a project-based engineering company were interviewed about aspects of the organization that inhibited or facilitated creativity (Wesenberg, 1994). The workers reported little satisfaction of their essential needs through their work. Instead they sought satisfaction through close relationships in their tightly defined and isolated work groups. Thus, senior managers who advocated a structural orientation toward stimulating creativity were overlooking the potential influence of the informal group. Mueller (1991) agrees as he reports that a 'growing body of evidence' indicates that traditional hierarchies are not the most conducive structure for enhancing creativity and innovation at work. Many innovations happen because of the information and support offered by informal channels of communication within an organization. This can be done through 'networking' using electronic means of communication. With the advent of the 'virtual group' and the 'virtual organization', the members of an informal group need no longer be sitting side by side or in the front or back of the room, as they were in the Western Electric study days.

Managing Creativity

For a national industry, such as shipping, the industry's ability to innovate in social and organizational terms determines that industry's ability to survive in world competition. Walton (1987) compared innovative change in the shipping industry in eight countries: the USA, Denmark, Japan, the Netherlands, Sweden, Norway, West Germany and the UK. He describes four adaptive changes (flexibility in work assignments, employee participation in management, social integration of employees and continuity of employment in shipboard organization) that each of the eight countries made or failed to make between 1966 and 1983. The capacity for innovative change is found to have five components: guiding models, social context, economic necessity, institutional forms and individual competence in the innovation process.

Benveniste (1987) adds his name to the list of those who caution organizations about creating inappropriate rules, regulations and routines to control the use of the expertise and experience of their professional staff. Using examples from organizations as diverse as the US National Aeronautics and Space Administration and a small community medical clinic, he describes specific management approaches that allow professional staff to be more effective in solving problems and dealing with emergencies, to approach projects with greater flexibility and to develop an increased commitment to the organization. These approaches involve choosing management structures and incentives to ensure professional commitment and encouraging risk taking and professional responsibility.

Similar results are found in surveys of American workers and managers who are asked to describe the ideal conditions employees need to do their best work and the conditions actually provided by management (Hall, 1994; Mullin and Sherman, 1993).

Adopting Innovations

In the research noted above, some examples are given of the types of management approaches that are used to encouraged innovation in organizations. Other studies emphasize the capacity of an organization to adopt an innovation once it has been suggested.

Glynn (1996) sees the process of creating innovations and adopting them as two phases of one process. She stresses the part played by individual and organizational intelligence, both of which involve adaptive, purposeful information processing, in both phases of the process.

Using data from 694 US manufacturing establishments, Osterman (1994) examined the incidence of innovative work practices, such as using teams, job rotation, quality circles and total quality management. About 35 per cent of private sector establishments with 50 or more employees made substantial use of flexible work organization. The two factors associated with an establishment's adoption of these practices were being in an internationally competitive market and following a 'high road' strategy that emphasizes variety and quality rather than low cost.

Mechanisms for the successful adoption of process innovation by manufacturing organizations was investigated by Ettlie and Reza (1992). Successful organizations appear to use two types of mechanisms to capture the value from process innovations: (1) making process innovation a unique occasion for significant restructuring; and (2) creating effective new patterns from the many alternative ways of accomplishing these changes.

The introduction of dry photocopying provides an example of organizational tendencies to resist accepting an innovation (Brown and
Duguid, 1991). In this case the acceptance of the innovation involved a
new form of organizational practice. Most of the innovative corporations
at the time were approached. All turned down the idea of a dry copier.
They agreed that the machine worked but rejected the concept of an
office copier since the new device seemed to have no role in current
office practice. They did not need an expensive machine to make a record
copy of original documents since carbon paper already did that. What
they failed to see was that a copier allowed one to make many copies and
copies of copies. The quantitative leap in copies then produced a qualitative leap in the way they were used. They no longer served merely as
records of an original. Instead, they participated in the productive interactions of an organization's members in an unprecedented way.

Dougherty and Hardy (1996) examined the problems with sustained
product innovation in 13 firms with headquarters in the USA, one in
Canada and one in the UK, that averaged 96 years of age, 54,000
employees and $9.4 billion in annual revenues. The firms included
chemical, food and equipment companies as well as data processing,
banking and consulting organizations. They defined sustained product
innovation as the generation of multiple new products, as strategically
necessary over time, with a reasonable rate of commercial success. New
products were those intended for customers who were unfamiliar with
the organization or who required unfamiliar product or process
technologies.

They interviewed 134 innovators in depth, and the majority in follow-
up interviews two years later, to explore whether and how resources
flowed to innovation projects, whether and how structures connected the
innovations to ongoing work in other functions, divisions and managerial levels, and whether and how innovative projects became embodied
in the organization's strategies. They found that the inability to connect
new products with organizational resources, processes and strategy
thwarted innovation in these large, mature organizations and that innovators lacked the power to make these connections. Their suggested
answer to these problems is for the organizations to reconfigure their
systems of power to become capable of sustained innovation.

In an example of a shut-down of a new product unit, a marking
manager reported that, as a result of a merger, the new firm was 'much
more conservative and less willing to try new things'. Regarding resources, a corporate planner in a chemical company described how he
provided a young researcher with access to senior managers, who in turn
provided support to develop a new plastic material: 'I told the executive
vice president that I had a gut feel that we had a success here.' The
planner than set up meetings so that the young engineer could explain
the product. To keep the vice president informed, the planner would
drop hints whenever they met in the men's room: 'Gee, we're looking at

new breakthroughs.' Unfortunately, two years later, the project lost support due to routine corporate belt-tightening.

In some cases the innovators were successful in creating 'bubbles' as self-contained, micro-configurations in which resources, processes and meanings were aligned with innovation. A manufacturing manager in a food corporation described his team: 'The team sits as a group to make decisions, which gives us more responsibility. . . . No one is really in our way, because we make our own decisions.' A senior scientist in a chemical company said: 'Our top management should get a lot of credit for this because they set us up and then left us totally alone.' Unfortunately, even these 'bubbles' are vulnerable, especially as a result of downsizing, when fewer resources are available and reporting relationships and networks are disrupted.

Klein and Sorra (1996) see innovation implementation as a challenge. They observe that implementation is a process of gaining targeted organizational members' appropriate and committed use of an innovation. They propose a model where the variables are:

1   Implementation effectiveness which includes the difficulties of introducing innovations. It refers to the consistency and quality of targeted organizational members use of a specific innovation.
2   Innovation effectiveness which focuses on the benefits that may accrue to an organization as a result of innovation of a given implementation (e.g. improvements in profitability, productivity, customer service and employee morale). Implementation effectiveness is a necessary but not sufficient condition for innovation effectiveness.
3   Organizational climate for innovation which refers to the targeted employees' shared perceptions of the extent to which their use of a specific innovation is rewarded, supported and expected.
4   The fit of the innovation to target users' values. The organizational values are implicit or explicit shared views about both the external adaptation of the organization (i.e. how the organization should relate to external customers, constituencies and competitors) and the internal integration of the organization (i.e. how members of the organization should relate to and work with one another).

They suggest that implementation effectiveness is a function of the strength of an organization's climate for the implementation of that innovation and the fit of the innovation to targeted users' values. They note that there is a range of possible outcomes from resistance and avoidance through compliance and commitment.

Klein and Sorra provide a number of examples of different variations of the relationship of the variables in their model. As an example of a company where the climate for implementation is weak they describe a large engineering and construction company that experienced difficulty in implementing three-dimensional computer-aided design and drafting (3D CADD). Although the managers complained of employee resistance to change, the employees thought the innovation 'was the greatest thing since sliced bread' but felt that they were given few opportunities to use the new software and were not rewarded for doing so.

Having introduced one innovation, how soon can the next innovation be introduced? Kessler and Chakrabarti (1996) report that many organizations, especially in industries with shortened product life cycles, have recognized the importance of speeding up operations to build a competitive advantage. They suggest that innovative speed is most appropriate in environments characterized by competitive intensity, technological and market dynamism, and low regulatory restrictiveness. The innovation speed can be positively or negatively affected by strategic orientation factors and organizational capability factors and has an influence on development costs, product quality and ultimately product success.

If the speed of innovation is related to competition within a 'hot spot' of fast-growing geographical clusters of competing firms (for example, the laser and electro-optics industry in Orlando, Florida, or the biotechnology and communications industries in San Diego, California), then Pouder and St John (1996) warn that over time the same forces that motivated innovation may create a homogeneous macroculture that suppresses innovation, making hot spot competitors more susceptible than non-hot spot competitors to environmental jolts.

Diffusion of Innovation

If one organization introduces an innovation, is it wise for another organization to adopt it? Based on their analysis of cross-national survey data from 1,719 businesses, Cohen and Levinthal (1990) argue that the ability of a firm to recognize the value of new external information, assimilate it and apply it to commercial ends is critical for the firm's innovative capacities.

In contrast, Abrahamson and Rosenkopf (1993) produced a mathematical model, as yet to be tested, to explore innovation diffusion according to the characteristics of a set of organizations that form a 'collective'. They reach a somewhat depressing conclusion that 'bandwagons' can prompt most organizations in a collective to adopt an innovation, even when most of them expect this adoption to yield negative returns.

A survey of organizational personnel practices indicated that factors outside the organization can influence the adaptation of innovation in this area. Johns (1993) reports that innovation is not strongly influenced by technical merit. Rather environmental threat, governmental regulation, and political influence often dominated the highly uncertain adoption process.

Creative Organization

Ambrose (1995) compared creatively intelligent post-industrial organizations and intellectually impaired bureaucracies. His conclusions reinforce the hypothesis that the most creative organizations provide a clear meaning for the work, a well-developed integration of roles and appropriate leadership. In his terms, using a brain metaphor, the most effective organizations function much like the most effective individual minds. The creatively intelligent organization has a robust and balanced neocortex, which is powerfully integrated (I) with inspiring emotion (M) and visionary leadership (G). By contrast, the intellectually impaired bureaucracy suffers from fragmentation and its subsystems are poorly integrated, particularly at the microscopic level.

A meta-analysis of the relationship between organizational innovation and its potential determinants by Damanpour (1991) emphasizes the meaning, integration and goal-attainment functions listed by Ambrose and adds technical knowledge and other resources (R) to complete the list of the four necessary functions.

In addition to the way an organization is effective in meeting the requirements of the basic functions of an organization, the culture of the society of which the organization is a part can enhance or detract from the possibility of innovation. For example, in Japan the interpersonal communication system in corporations is shaped by cultural values in line with the traditional patterns of communication in Japanese society. This congruence intensifies the smooth flow of communication with two important consequences: on the motivational level, sharing common values results in more consensus on and commitment to the values; on the cognitive level, sharing of knowledge, ideas and information enhances the level of productivity and innovation (Erez, 1992).

Various aspects of working have been discussed in earlier chapters in this volume and organizational learning in the previous chapter. Brown and Duguid (1991) conclude that for an organization working, learning and innovation are interrelated and compatible. They suggest that there may be a difference between an organization's formal descriptions of work and the actual work practices. Reliance on espoused practice can blind an organization to the actual, and usually valuable, practices of its members. A composite concept of 'learning-in-working' is suggested as best representing the evolution of learning through practice. From this practice-based standpoint, learning is viewed as the bridge between working and innovating. They conclude that to understand working and learning, it is necessary to focus on the sites of innovating, the communities in which work takes place.

Most reports on organizations whose members are able to produce many creative ideas do not examine activity in all four functional areas at the four system levels and thus only provide evidence for part of the ideal organization. In their research to test a dynamic model of the causes of organizational innovation, Monge et al. (1992) correlated five variables with the number of innovative ideas contributed by members of five firms. Two variables were related to the content and form of communication – level of information (*resources* at group level) and group communication (*integration* at group level); and three variables were related to motivation – perceptions of equity (*resources* at individual level), expectations of benefits (*resources* at individual level) and perceived social pressure (*integration* at group level). Their results indicate that the 'communication' variables were causes of organizational innovation, but the 'motivational' variables were not. Although the authors did not sort their variables according to the cybernetic hierarchy, we note that the two communication variables at the group level did have an effect, while two of the three motivational levels, at the individual level, did not.

Each system level has some effect, although this may be countered by conditions at a higher system level. Generally there is a positive relationship between the extent to which systems of employment and compensation favour creativity and a firm's propensity to innovate. Quinn and Rivoli (1991) argue that the propensity of a firm to innovate is related to the attitudes of its employees toward risk and that these attitudes will vary systematically according to the employment and compensation systems that are in place. Thus commercial innovation will occur more often under the Japanese system than the American system, especially in volatile markets. However, under stable market conditions, firms and employees prefer the American system over the Japanese system, despite its reduced incentive for innovation. Yamada (1991) reaches a different conclusion, calling attention to the Japanese education system that can discourage creativity by focusing on entrance examinations and the human resources management in Japanese companies that places too much emphasis on harmony and conformity, which discourages the implementation of innovation.

In innovation, experimentation is crucial. Kanter (1983) showed that, in innovation, experiments have a double purpose. First, they are the keys to breakthroughs and, second, successful experiments give organizational decision-makers choices or options. Innovative organizations operate in turbulent environments which are unanalysable *because* of their turbulence (Daft and Weick, 1994). Therefore, organizations have to enact their environments. They try new behaviours and see what happens.

Kanter (1983) found that during the early period of an industry's growth, innovation takes place in the products and services themselves and in how to tailor them to meet customer desires. As the industry matures, innovation tends to concentrate more around saving costs and improving performance. In an attempt to reduce uncertainty in a turbulent environment, historically most industries have sacrificed innovation in an attempt to close off their core technologies from environmental disturbances. These are what Kanter (1983) calls segmentalist organizations, and she shows that innovation and change cannot occur in them since they are more interested in controlling what they already know rather than focusing on what they do not know.

After reviewing a number of studies on innovation and organizations, Drazin and Schoonhoven (1996) propose an 'integrated' model that places the strategic focus of an organization in a critical causal role in the innovation process. They list five strategic initiatives that may be taken at the corporation level: acquisitions, mergers, divestitures, downsizing and cost reduction. They note that these strategies are a result of institutional forces that have shaped organizations from the mid-1980s to the early 1990s. Their adoption has had a direct effect on the behaviour of senior executives. When faced with implementing any of these strategies, executives are likely to: (1) increase financial controls; (2) decrease strategic controls; and (3) reduce the time and attention they devote to innovation-related activities. The behaviour of the senior managers, in turn, affects the culture of innovation and resource availability at the organizational level, since the adoption of one or more of the five strategies implies that an organization is purposefully restricting or redirecting its resources away from internal innovation.

An organization will find it especially difficult to be innovative if the society (nation) does not supply basic resources, such as electricity, or has a strong central control of government and the economy. In one 'less developed country' sociopolitical factors were seen by managers in private and public organizations as the primary barriers to innovation producing high levels of cost, risk and uncertainty (Munene, 1995).

The society does not need to be less developed to be influenced by social and political factors. Suarez (1990) analysed the contrasting performances of individual and corporate invention from a long-term perspective by exploring, first, the process of resource allocation for invention. The process of invention was then related to the macrosocial innovative capacity by analysing inventive performance over the period 1880 to 1986 with US invention patent data. National income trends were found to be important statistical predictors of new annual corporate inventive output, exposing the latter's potential vulnerability to major economic crises.

Research by Oldham and Cummings (1996) provides evidence that when variables that affect organizational creativity are ranked according to their position in the cybernetic hierarchy, those variables that are nearest the top of the hierarchy have the most influence. Oldham and Cummings set out to examine the independent and joint contributions to creative performance of employees' creativity-relevant personality characteristics (personality level) and three characteristics of the organizational context: job complexity (role level), controlling supervision (group level, G) and supportive supervision (group level, I). They used three

measures of creative performance: patents, contributions to the organization's suggestion programme, and supervisory ratings of creativity.
The participants in the study were 171 employees from two manufacturing facilities. They found that the employees produced the most
creative work when they had appropriate creativity-relevant characteristics, worked on complex, challenging jobs and were supervised in a
non-controlling, supportive fashion. Their main interest was in the fact
that most of these variables had significant positive correlations. However their research also reveals that once a person was placed in a
complex, challenging job, with non-controlling and supportive supervision, the person was likely to be creative, regardless of whether the
Creative Personality Scale indicated that the person was high or low on
being self-confident and reflective, with wide interests. Thus aspects of
role and group support were more important than personality.

In addition, although again not noticed by Oldham and Cummings,
the results of a series of hierarchical regression analyses showed that for
five variables related to creativity (rated creativity, patents, suggestions,
rated performance and intentions to quit), the rank order of the variables
used to explain creativity was the same in every case (although differences between ranks were small). Creativity-relevant personality characteristics had the least influence, then job complexity, then non-controlling
supervision, and then supportive supervision with the largest amount of
influence.

Fiol (1996) offers the metaphor of the sponge to visualize the relationship between an organization inputs and outputs with regard to creativity.
The 'absorptive capacity' of an organization is its ability to recognize the
value of new and external information and its ability to assimilate and
exploit it. Much of the literature on organizations focuses on the ways
you can squeeze the sponge through specialization, functional differentiation, professionalism, participatory work environments, administrative intensity and slack resources. However, Fiol (1996) notes that how
much one can squeeze out of a sponge depends secondarily on the
various means of squeezing it. It depends more fundamentally on what,
how much and how continuously the sponge has absorbed to begin
with. A sponge that has been left to dry out to the point where it can no
longer absorb anything new will not generate outputs no matter how
effectively one squeezes it.

Additional studies reporting positive correlations at different system
levels include: Scott and Bruce (1994), on leadership, individual problem-
solving style and group relations; Feldman (1989), on the need to balance
control and autonomy; Woodman et al. (1993), on contextual influences,
including those that come from the environment; and Feldman (1993), on
organizational culture.

For those readers who wish to move up a level and inject some
creativity into their theory of organizational behaviour, Das (1984) suggests that you use 'inter-idea ideas' by joining two or more differing

words so that much more than the characteristics of the words are expressed. His examples of this type of 'loose coupling' include: horizontal delegation, deferred-action decision making and flexible-horizon planning. Good luck.

3M – Encouraging Organizational Innovation (3M, 1997a, 1997b, 1997c)

One company which is often mentioned when the subject of organizational creativity and innovation comes up is 3M. According to their *Innovation Network* web site:

Creating innovative products and services that respond to customer needs has always been a way of life at 3M.
    For nearly a century, 3M's culture has fostered creativity and given employees the freedom to take risks and try new ideas. This culture has led to a steady stream of products. With no boundaries to imagination and no barriers to cooperation, one good idea leads swiftly to another. So far there have been more than 50,000 innovative products that help make our world better. (3M, 1997a)

Some of the mechanisms they use to encourage innovation are (3M, 1997b):

The 30 per cent challenge – a corporate goal to obtain 30 per cent of annual sales from products introduced within the last four years.
Pacing plus programme – setting worldwide priorities and providing laboratories and financial funding for products that show high potential.
Genesis grants – grants of up to $85,000 for innovative research projects not readily funded through normal channels.
15 per cent rule – allowing researchers to spend up to 15 per cent of their time on projects of their own choice.
Bootlegging – development of ideas in the employee's own time which may include using 3M equipment and facilities during off hours and on weekends
Dual ladder system – allowing researchers, sales staff and other professionals to climb a career ladder identical to the management ladder in terms of prestige, position and compensation.
Leading edge academic programme – funding for members of 3M's technical community to collaborate on advanced technical assignments at government laboratories or academic institutions.
Consulting with customers – asking customers for ideas in order to better understand their needs.
International teamwork – taking advantage of the diverse talent and worldwide resources available to the organization.
Technical forum – worldwide network of 3M's technical community which uses education programmes, chapter meetings and symposia to facilitate the free flow of information to its more than 10,000 members.
Sharing technology – encouraging researchers to help each other by sharing their knowledge.

The 3M management approach is a legacy of William McKnight, who joined the company in 1907, became its president in 1929 and served as chairman of the board from 1949 to 1966. His basic rule of management was laid out in 1948:

As our business grows, it becomes increasingly necessary to delegate responsibility and to encourage men and women to exercise their initiative. This requires considerable tolerance. Those men and women to whom we delegate authority and responsibility, if they are good people, are going to want to do their jobs in their own way.

Mistakes will be made. But if a person is essentially right, the mistakes he or she makes are not as serious in the long run as the mistakes management will make if it undertakes to tell those in authority exactly how they must do their jobs.

Management that is destructively critical when mistakes are made kills initiative. And it's essential that we have many people with initiative if we are to continue to grow. (3M, 1997c)

As we can see, 3M has taken this message to heart. It understands that in order to get creativity and innovation, it must allow people to take initiative and to learn, and provides resources and opportunities that enable them to do so.

Creativity – Some Final Words

In the literature on creativity in general, and creativity in organizations in particular, usually only two levels of creativity at most are differentiated. However, five levels in group or organizational creativity can be identified that form a cybernetic hierarchy: from new meanings at the top, through extensions of theory, combinations of known elements and demonstrations of skill, to individual work unrelated to the group at the bottom. Creativity is a form of problem solving. The steps in the scientific method for solving problems follow the same order that is apparent in the development of a group or organization in terms of functional categories. Various mechanisms can be used to stimulate a 'creative shift' resulting in a new perspective or a new idea.

Creative persons tend to be open minded with a wide range of interests. However, creativity at the skill level does not make as many demands on the individual as creativity at the level of the paradigm shift. To encourage creativity, organizations need to provide the same four types of functional support as do organizations facilitating learning or culture change. However, relatively few ideas are generated within an organization – most of the change comes about by adopting innovations from other organizations. In addition to whatever an organization can do to support creativity, the culture of the society in which the organization is a part also has an influence.

SOME FINAL, FINAL WORDS

It is time for evaluation. We have written a book and you have read it. Have any of us learned anything? Is there a possibility for 'second loop' learning? For any form of evaluation, one always compares what is expected with what is observed. Statistical tests do this in a formal way. We will be less formal. Expectations about behaviour or the results of a project, in this case a book, can come from the stated purpose of the project (as stated in our introduction), or by comparison with some other similar project (another text on organizational behaviour), or from some theory about the way a project should develop to be effective (a functional or learning theory perhaps). We do not know what you had in mind when you began reading the book, although we can assume that your evaluation up to this point cannot have been all bad, or you would never have read this far (or maybe some of you started here). So we can only use as a criterion for evaluating the book the expectations set out in the introduction.

But what about that second loop? In writing this book the authors formed a 'virtual team', drawing on the resources of the 'virtual library' at our university using our computers and the even larger 'virtual library' represented by the Internet Web where additional unpublished information is available. True, we occasionally spoke with each other face-to-face (which we highly recommend), but our offices are 45 kilometres apart on different campuses of the university, so much of the communication was by email or by leaving drafts of chapters in mail boxes. We worked as a 'virtual team' to produce this book – we have no other formal relationship. So where is the organizational culture that will become the repository of any 'second-loop' learning that we acquire? This is not just our problem. It is and will be a problem for all the 'virtual teams' and 'virtual organizations' that networking, using new methods of communication, makes possible.

To be sure our miniature organization, in keeping with the current trend, had a 'flat and lean' organizational hierarchy, with each of us being 'empowered' since all information about the project was available to both of us. We did not have to take turns in communicating. We could send messages at the same time or, not at all, depending upon our own pace of work. We had 24 hours a day of 'flexitime' since we were not required to be seen at work in any particular place. We could supply peer support without waiting for recognition by our supervisor, since we had none. All in all an ideal team reflecting the spirit of the times. But where is the organizational culture? If we learn anything about the system problems of our little group, how will they be passed on to the next generation? Enough questions. What is the answer? Time out while we think about it and you think about it.

As a diversion, since we know that often the creative insight occurs when you stop focusing intently on the task at hand (something may not be working with your computer application but you only realize what it is after you have turned off the computer and walked out of the door of your office), we return to the problem of evaluation at the level of the first loop. In our introduction, which was written before we began writing the book, not after, we chose six topics having to do with individuals and groups in organizations that seemed relevant for persons who wished to maintain organizations, to make them more effective, or to implement change. To provide a contemporary perspective we limited our search of the literature, for the most part, to the previous six years. In line with our concern for practitioners in organizations, most of the references were drawn from field research rather than from laboratory studies. You might wish to add more topics to the list, and so did we. At first we included 'ethics and responsibility' as a topic, but left it out when we did not find enough current literature that specifically applied to organizations to warrant a separate chapter. The topics of organizational culture and organizational change were also considered as candidates for separate chapters, but when finally combined with the topic of organizational learning, we discovered that the three topics were closely related.

We proposed to use a functional perspective for organizing the results of our search of the literature with the additional notion that each of us, alone and together with others, creates our own reality. Our perception of this reality and the meaning we attach to it is important to understand our own behaviour and that of others. We warned that we would not be able to use either of these perspectives to bring a single order into all of the theoretical and applied literature on organizations. One reason for this is that only in rare cases did an observer of organizational behaviour use categories that were similar to the four functional categories. Some observers leave out one or more categories, or combine the results of observations into different categories that cut across the four functions. Another reason is that we still have some distance to go to compile a theoretical social–psychological perspective that is comprehensive enough to include all aspects of individual, group and organizational behaviour. Do not wait up for the final result. We believe that we are further along than when we started, as we shall note below, but there is still much to do. We urge you to join in. It is a game that any number may play.

The First Loop

Chapter 1, about people in organizations, focuses on identity and whether one's identity, and therefore meaning, is completely tied to an organization, or whether one can have several selves with separate identities, allowing for more self-expression in different areas. Since most of the research on people in organizations deals with a single type of organization, usually business or manufacturing, there is relatively little literature comparing issues related to identity in different organizations. The type of information we need is the model proposed by Karasek and Theorell (1990), who categorize types of work according to the extent to which they are high or low on psychological demand and decision latitude. They are concerned with the resulting stress on the job.

We could also look at the figure in Chapter 1 in terms of identity. Occupations with high decision latitude (architect, lawyer, doctor) probably rank higher in their influence on the overall identity of a person that those with low decision control (watchman, waiter). Many of these occupations are primarily associated with one of the four functional areas in a society. Meaning, at the top of the cybernetic hierarchy, is the main province of religious organizations. Integration is provided by organizations dealing with law (which defines the rights and duties of roles), health and welfare (which are concerned with the individual's ability to take part in informal relationships) and education (which serves both meaning and resources since it is concerned with both the transmission of culture and skills). Goal-attainment is the main function of political organizations that provide, at least in principle, the coordination in a society between resources and roles to accomplish the overall meaning of the society. Resources, at the bottom of the cybernetic hierarchy, are provided by economic organizations, including business and manufacturing.

We would expect that people actively involved in religious organizations would find that much of the meaning of their daily life (their identity) is prescribed by their religion, which may provide norms for food, dress and all aspects of the daily round. People whose main involvement is with an economic organization would find that pre-scripted behaviour covers only their working hours. At home and at play they can enact other identities. We might say that at the bottom of the cybernetic hierarchy, in the economic area, people earn a living. That is, what they earn allows them to live fully their other identities outside of work. At the top of the hierarchy, in promoting a system of values, the living earns the people. That is, ideas about the 'meaning of all this' need people to enact them, to serve as models for the next generation, otherwise they decline and fall. Organizations involved with integration and goal-attainment would take their place in the middle of the cybernetic hierarchy with regard to the extent to which individual identity was primarily associated with membership in the organization.

In Chapter 2, on gender, we find that the functional categories and the cybernetic hierarchy are useful in sorting out the differences between the parts played by women and men in organizations. Usually there is an expectation that they will have differences in skills, methods of asserting power and influence, roles, and in the balance of meaning between home and work. Some of the stresses for individuals in organizations can be attributed to three system levels – biological, organizational and societal – with the stresses attributed to society having the most effect and being the most difficult to change. The general conclusion from this review of the literature is that women are under-utilized with regard to their contribution to all four functional areas in organizations.

In our consideration of flexibility in organizations, we again find it useful to note the functional area associated with the type of flexibility under consideration. Much of the literature deals with physical, temporal and technological flexibility (resources) and career, role and relationship flexibility (integration), and the advantages of an organization in having people with many skills who can play many parts. We note that the key motives associated with the four patterns of career experience described by Brousseau et al. (1996) are related to the four-fold cybernetic hierarchy, with 'expertise and security' related to resources, 'power and achievement' related to goal-attainment, 'variety and independence' related to integration, and 'personal growth and creativity' related to meaning. Careers are also 'anchored' in different functional areas. Here, again, we would expect that the higher the anchor in the cybernetic hierarchy and the more it is related to the individual rather than the organization, the easier it will be for the person to shift from traditional careers to 'boundaryless' careers which appear to be required by the current pace of change in organizations and their environment.

Chapter 4, on groups, provides many examples of the necessity of groups to provide adequate solutions to the four functional problems if they are to be effective. When work groups are sorted according to the extent to which they are driven by activity in one of the functional areas, we find that crews of boats, planes and other forms of transportation are at the bottom of the hierarchy since their activity is closely associated with the resources (technology) that they manage. At the top of the hierarchy, with the most degrees of freedom, are the research and development teams, driven by meaning, whose function it is to discover new concepts and new relationships between old concepts.

Whereas the summary of the literature in Chapter 4 relied primarily on ideas we had about groups before beginning this book, the 'big idea' in Chapter 5, on organizational learning, only occurred in the process of combining information about organizational learning, organizational culture and organizational change. We had collected the summaries of books and journal articles under the three different headings because they are usually discussed in different chapters in texts on organizations and the research in each area is usually carried out by different people. Although you, the reader, may already have been aware of this, we found that the same theme appeared in each of the three sets of studies, and again in the last chapter on creativity. Namely, if you have an organization with appropriate resources, distribution of roles, leadership and a definition of the goal to which the members are committed, together with a willingness to change the means of achieving the goal or even the goal itself, should this be required, then you have an organization where learning is possible, where the learning will find its place in the organizational culture and the culture will be open to change, and if new ideas are generated, you have enhanced creativity at one or more levels.

The Second Loop

In our case, learning can occur (or not occur) for different parties. There are us the authors (individually and as a group), you the readers and third parties who may be affected by the learning done by the first two parties. We cannot tell you what you learned and are not sure we can even tell you what we have learned now when the work is still so new. But perhaps we can throw out some hints which may make learning more probable for those as yet unknown third parties.

Looking back over the final product one word jumps out as the unifying thought – flexibility. The idea comes up over and over again but not always through using that exact word. Sometimes it appears as something material, sometimes as something intangible. In the first chapter we saw the necessity of flexibility in personal expression and employment arrangements. The second chapter emphasized the need for flexibility in how we perceive individuals and groups. The third chapter was totally and openly devoted to flexibility in a number of forms. The theme was continued in the fourth chapter through seeing that groups must be flexible and move to fulfil all of the different functions. Flexible organizational arrangements come into play with self-managed teams. Learning, our fifth topic, is also basically about flexibility and being able to allow new information to enter our cognitive structures. But the greatest cognitive flexibility is probably found in the sixth chapter, on creativity.

All in all, it appears that without personal and organizational flexibility organizations and individuals will remain stuck and eventually stagnate. The realization of the necessity for flexibility in all its forms, learning how to achieve it and not allowing it to degenerate into anarchy and chaos are possibly the elements of the second-loop learning which has to be done. It is the challenge of the next few years which cannot be ignored. For many organizations it will demand precisely what is meant by second-loop learning – a re-examination of the governing variables, the values and norms, that inform action, a reformulation of the organizational and individual theories of action. We are not going to presume to tell you how to do that for at least two reasons: this is not a 'how-to' recipe book; and sticking to the theme of flexibility means that there is no recipe which will work in all cases. The most we can advise you and ourselves to do is to embrace that flexibility (particularly perceptive and cognitive flexibility), to keep ourselves open to all types of input and not to try to bend it to fit our predetermined categories and answers. And now, before we become overly preachy, we will just say goodbye.

INTERNET APPENDIX

There are many sites on the Internet which deal with subjects covered in this book. Some contain references to academic research or information, some are companies which are promoting goods and services, some are propaganda, some are basically uninformed ramblings and some are just interesting. A partial list of some of these sites (trying to leave out the more obviously commercial or baseless) can be found below. A word of warning: Internet addresses change faster than can be imagined. Addresses were correct at the time of this writing but it is possible that some have changed or disappeared in the interim. Most of the sites present a wide variety of offerings and many include links to related sites. Since the selections are extensive and most are in a relatively constant cycle of change, only a few examples will be mentioned for each subject. Astutely used search engines can turn up additional pointers.

General Sites for Organizational Subjects

Name and address	Special features
Academy of Management Online http://www.aom.pace.edu	Links to web sites of Academy divisions and interest groups Placement service
Society for Industrial-Organizational Psychology (Division 14 of the American Psychology Association) http://www.siop.org	TIP – the official newsletter of the society Other links of interest to I/O students, academics and practitioners
Internet Survival Guide of Industrial/Organizational Psychology http://allserv.rug.ac.be/~flievens/guide.htm	Links to Internet resources in areas of organizational psychology, human resource management, statistics and methodology
International Association of Applied Psychology http://allserv.rug.ac.be/~pcoets/div/home.htm	Recent table of contents for a variety of journals in the field of organizational psychology and management
Business Week http://www.businessweek.com	Current issue – article viewing for subscribers Searchable archives – pay per view Variety of free services

Fortune
  http://www.fortune.com   Current issue and searchable archives
                                                      back to September 1995 – Free
Fast Company
  http://www.fastcompany.com   Current issue and archives – Free

@BRINT (A Business Researcher's Interests)   Access to full-text articles and papers,
  http://www.brint.com/   magazines and journals, case stud-
                                                      ies and tools in a wide variety of
                                                      areas, including a virtual library on
                                                      knowledge management, sections
                                                      on emergent organizational forms
                                                      and virtual organizations
Harvard Business School – Department of Research   Abstracts of Working Papers 1996–7
  http://www.hbs.edu/dor/papers9697.html

Foundation for Enterprise Development   Emphasis on company profiles and
  http://www.fed.org   case studies
                                                      Articles in areas of compensation,
                                                      leadership, employee motivation
                                                      and empowerment
                                                      US employee ownership research
                                                      and policy
                                                      Leading Companies e-zine

Stress

Name and address	Special features
Job Stress Network (Center for Social Epidemiology) http://www.workhealth.org	Reference list Models of job stress and job strain Information on risk factors for heart disease and other stress outcomes
NIOSH (National Institute for Occupational Health and Safety http://www.cdc.gov/niosh	General information on health and safety aspects of work Search engine connected to the Center for Disease Control Extensive links

Work/life Policies

Name and address	Special features
US Department of Labor Corporate Citizenship Resource Center http://www.ttrc.doleta.gov/citizen	Principles of corporate citizenship (one principle is a family-friendly workplace) White House press releases and other speeches and articles on the subject Profiles of companies (self-submitted) with a commitment to one or more of the principles List of not-for-profit organizations that offer related assistance and resources

Netmarquee Family Business Center
http://NMQ.com

Working Mother Magazine
http://www.womweb.com/sitwmm.htm

Work and Family: A Research Bibliography by John H. Bosma
http://ccwf.cc.utexas.edu/~worklife/wfbib.htm

Children Youth and Family Consortium Electronic Clearinghouse
http://www.cyfc.umn.edu/Work/trend.html

Bibliography and abstracts of research, books and other reference material
Current events and trends
Links to related web sites
References to several papers dealing with work–family issues within family businesses.
Searchable database of the results of their survey of Best (US) Companies for Working Mothers
Articles from the magazine
Extensive current bibliography (copyright 1997)

Reports on work–family trends

Gender

Name and address	Special features
Women's Web http://www.womweb.com	Articles from *Working Mother Magazine*, *Working Woman* and *MS* Areas dealing with technology issues
Information Technology and Women's Lives Bibliography gopher://silo.adp.wisc.edu:70/11/.uwlibs/.womenstudies/.infotech	Sections on computer science and education, employment and health and other resources
University of Maryland – Women's Studies Resources http://www.inform.umd.edu/EdRes/Topic/WomensStudies/	US Department of Labor Glass Ceiling Commission report Other documents on women in the workplace

Computers and Work

Name and address	Special features
Journal of Computer-Mediated Communication http://shum.huji.ac.il/jcmc/citesite.html	Links to on-line bibliographies about computer-mediated communication

Telecommuting

Name and address	Special features
European Telework Online (ETO) http://www.eto.org.uk	Sections on telework, teletrade and telecooperation Definitions and FAQs Links to related sites throughout the world.
MIRTI (Models of Industrial Relations in Telework Innovation) http://www.iess-ae.it/mirti	Pages in English, German and Italian Bibliographies, case studies and research information Links to other sites

Teams

Name and address	Special features
Center for the Study of Work Teams http://www.workteams.unt.edu/	Annotated team bibliography Academic papers Links
Self-directed Work Teams Page http://users.ids.net/~brim/	Extensive resource links Case examples of SDWT

Discussion Group

TeamNet – an email list dedicated to discussions about teamwork and team-related topics.	To subscribe, send an email message to :majordomo@mail.cas.unt.edu with message: subscribe teamnet-L or: subscribe teamnet-L-digest (digest version is sent out once per day)

Organizational Learning

Name and address	Special features
Stanford Learning Organization Web http://www-leland.stanford.edu/group/SLOW/	Resource lists of books, articles and videos related to organizational learning Links to other related sites and information about mailing lists and discussion groups
The Society for Organizational Learning http://learning.mit.edu	Online working papers and articles A guided tour of organizational learning concepts Idea exchange
The Fifth Discipline Fieldbook http://www.fieldbook.com	Study groups – worldwide list of study groups on the learning organization Wide variety of related links 'Lost chapters' that didn't make it into the fieldbook
The Leadership Alliance http://www.tlainc.com/tlaolr.htm	Many learning and knowledge management links

Discussion Group

Learning Organization	To subscribe, send an email to: majordomo@world.std.com for individual messages send message with two lines: subscribe learning-org end for daily digest of messages send message with two lines: subscribe learning-org-digest end

Organizational Culture

Name and address	Special features
SCOS – Standing Conference on Organizational Symbolism http://www.it.com.pl/scos/	Full text of presented papers from 1997 conference in Poland Link to papers presented at 1996 conference in Los Angeles

Creativity

Name and address	Special features
Creativity Web Home Page http://www.ozemail.com.au/~caveman/Creative/	Extensive link site – techniques, books, software, people and other Internet resources
Lucia Chamber's links page http://www.waterw.com/~lucia/awlinks.html	Very extensive list of links relating to creativity
Routing – The Creative Nordic Light http://www.routing.se/avica/secres.htm	Swedish creative resources (in Swedish)
Mind Games http://www.q-net.net.au/~gihan/mindgames/index.html	Set of interactive exercises to help expand and unleash your creative thinking skills

Discussion Group

CREA-CPS: Discussion list for Creativity and Creative Problem Solving practitioners	To subscribe, send an email message to: **Listserv@Surfnet.nl** with message: **Subscribe Crea-CPS your-name**

BIBLIOGRAPHY

Abraham, T. and Boone, L.W. (1994) 'Computer based systems and organizational decision making: an architecture to support organizational innovation', *Creativity Research Journal*, 7: 111–23.

Abrahamson, E. and Rosenkopf, L. (1993) 'Institutional and competitive bandwagons: using mathematical modeling as a tool to explore innovation diffusion', *Academy of Management Review*, 18: 487–517.

Abrams, D. and Hogg, M.A. (eds) (1990) *Social Identity Theory: Constructive and Critical Advances*. Hemel Hempstead: Harvester Wheatsheaf.

Adelmann, P.K. and Zajonc, R.B. (1989) 'Facial expression and the experience of emotion', *Annual Review of Psychology*, 40: 249–80.

Adler, N.J. and Izraeli, D.N. (eds) (1988) *Women in Management Worldwide*. New York: M.E. Sharpe.

Agor, W.H. (1991) 'How intuition can be used to enhance creativity in organizations', *Journal of Creative Behavior*, 25: 11–19.

Albin, P. and Applebaum, E. (1988) 'The computer rationalization of work: implications for women workers', in J. Jenson, E. Hagen and C. Reddy (eds), *Feminization of the Labour Force: Paradoxes and Promises*. Cambridge: Polity Press. pp. 137–52.

Alfredsson, L and Theorell, T. (1983) 'Job characteristics of occupations and myocardial infarction risk: effect of possible confounding factors', *Social Science and Medicine*, 17: 1497–503.

Allen, T.J. (1977) *Managing the Flow of Technology: Technology Transfer and the Dissemination of Technology Information within the Research and Development Organization*. Cambridge, MA: MIT Press.

Allred, B.B., Snow, C.C. and Miles, R.E. (1996) 'Characteristics of managerial careers in the 21st century', *Academy of Management Executive*, 10 (4): 17–27.

Ambrose, D. (1995) 'Creatively intelligent post-industrial organizations and intellectually impaired bureaucracies', *Journal of Creative Behavior*, 29: 1–15.

Ancona, D.G. and Caldwell, D.F. (1992) 'Demography and design: predictors of new product team performance', *Organization Science*, 3: 321–41.

Antonovsky, A. (1987) *Unraveling the Mystery of Health: How People Manage Stress and Stay Well*. San Francisco, CA: Jossey-Bass.

Arbet, L. (1991) 'Reflections on creativity', *Studia Psychologica*, 33 (3–4): 175–80.

Argyris, C. (1996). *On Organizational Learning*. Cambridge, MA: Blackwell.

Argyris, C. and Schön, D.A. (eds) (1996) *Organizational Learning II: Theory, Method, and Practice*. Reading, MA: Addison-Wesley.

Arogyaswamy, B. and Byles, C.M. (1987) 'Organizational culture: internal and external fits', *Journal of Management*, 13: 647–58.

Ashforth, B.E. and Humphrey, R.H. (1993) 'Emotional labor in service roles: the influence of identity', *Academy of Management Review*, 18: 88–115

Ashforth, B.E. and Humphrey, R.H. (1995) 'Emotion in the workplace: a reappraisal', *Human Relations*, 48: 97–125.

Ashkanasy, N.M. (1994) 'Automatic categorization and causal attribution: the effect of gender bias in supervisor responses to subordinate performance', *Australian Journal of Psychology*, 46: 177–82.

Attewell, P. (1992) 'Technology diffusion and organizational learning: the case of business computing', *Organization Science*, 3: 1–19.

Auerbach, J.D. (1990) 'Employer-supported child care as a women-responsive policy', *Journal of Family Issues*, 11: 384–400.

Bacharach, S.B., Bamberger, P. and Conley, S. (1991) 'Work–home conflict among nurses and engineers: mediating the impact of role stress on burnout and satisfaction at work', *Journal of Organizational Behavior*, 12: 39–53.

Bales, R.F. (1955) 'How people interact in conferences', *Scientific American*, 192 (3): 31–5.

Bales, R.F. and Strodtbeck, F.L. (1951) 'Phases in group problem solving', *Journal of Abnormal and Social Psychology*, 46: 485–95.

Balshem, M. (1988) 'The clerical worker's boss: an agent of job stress', *Human Organization*, 47: 361–7.

Barker, D.B. (1991) 'The behavioral analysis of interpersonal intimacy in group development', *Small Group Research*, 22: 76–91.

Barnett, R.C. and Baruch, G.K. (1987) 'Social roles, gender, and psychological distress', in R.C. Barnett, L. Biener and G.K. Baruch (eds), *Gender and Stress*. New York: Free Press. pp. 122–43.

Barron, F. (1969) *Creative Person and Creative Process*. New York: Holt, Rinehart & Winston.

Bartunek, J.M. (1988) 'The dynamics of personal and organizational reframing', in R.E. Quinn and K.S. Cameron (eds), *Paradox and Transformation*. Cambridge, MA: Ballinger. pp. 137–162

Becker, T.E. and Billings, R.S. (1993) 'Profiles of commitment: an empirical test', *Journal of Organizational Behavior*, 14: 177–90.

Beehr, T.A., Johnson, L.B. and Nieva, R. (1995) 'Occupational stress: coping of police and their spouses', *Journal of Organizational Behavior*, 16: 3–25.

Beena, C. and Poduval, P.R. (1992) 'Gender differences in work stress of executives', *Psychological Studies*, 37 (2–3): 109–13.

Bem, S. (1981) 'Gender schema theory: a cognitive account of sex typing', *Psychological Review*, 88: 354–64.

Bennett, P., Evans, R. and Tattersall, A. (1993) 'Stress and coping in social workers: a preliminary investigation', *British Journal of Social Work*, 23: 31–44.

Bennis, W.G. and Shepard, H.A. (1956) 'A theory of group development', *Human Relations*, 9: 415–37.

Benokraitis, N.V. and Feagin, J.R. (1986) *Modern Sexism: Blatant, Subtle, and Covert Discrimination*. New York: Harper & Row.

Benveniste, G. (1987) *Professionalizing the Organization: Reducing Bureaucracy to Enhance Effectiveness*. San Francisco, CA: Jossey-Bass.

Bessant, J. (1991) *Managing Advanced Manufacturing Technology: The Challenge of the Fifth Wave*. Manchester: NCC/Blackwell.

Bessant, J. (1993) 'Towards factory 2000: designing organizations for computer-integrated technologies', in J. Clark (ed.), *Human Resource Management and Technical Change*. London: Sage. pp. 192–211.

Blum, T.C., Fields, D.L. and Goodman, J.S. (1994) 'Organization-level determinants of women in management', *Academy of Management Journal*, 37: 241–68.

Blunt, P. (1991) 'Organizational culture and development', *International Journal of Human Resource Management*, 2: 55–71.

Bohlen, C. (1996) 'Where every day is mother's day', *New York Times*, 12 May.

Bramwell, R.S. and Davidson, M.J. (1992) 'A review of current evidence concerning possible reproductive hazard from VDUs', *Journal of Reproductive and Infant Psychology*, 10: 3–17.

Branegan, J. (1996) 'Why a good job is hard to find', *Time*, 26 February: 21–6.

Bridges, W. (1994) *JobShift: How to Prosper in a Workplace without Jobs*. Reading, MA: Addison-Wesley.

Brooks, A.K. (1994) 'Power and the production of knowledge: collective team learning in work organizations', *Human Resource Development Quarterly*, 5: 213–35.

Brousseau, K.R., Driver, M.J., Eneroth, K. and Larsson, R.L. (1996) 'Career pandemonium: realigning organizations and individuals', *Academy of Management Executive*, 10 (4): 52–66.

Brown, J.S. and Duguid, P. (1991) 'Organizational learning and communities of practice: toward a unified view of working, learning, and innovation', *Organizational Science*, 2: 40–57.

Burke, R.J. (1986) 'Occupational and life stress and the family: conceptual frameworks and research findings', *International Review of Applied Psychology*, 35: 347–69.

Burke, R.J. (1996) 'Work experiences, stress and health among managerial and professional women', in M.J. Schabracq, J.A.M. Winnubst and C.L. Cooper (eds), *Handbook of Work and Health Psychology*. New York: Wiley. pp. 205–30.

Burke, R.J. and Greenglass, E.R. (1987) 'Work and family', in C.L. Cooper and I. Robertson (eds), *International Review of Industrial and Organizational Psychology*. New York: Wiley. pp. 273–320.

Burke, R.J. and McKeen, C.A. (1990) 'Mentoring in organizations: implications for women', *Journal of Business Ethics*, 9: 317–22.

Burlingame, G., Fuhriman, A. and Drescher, S. (1984) 'Scientific inquiry into small group process', *Small Group Behavior*, 15: 441–70.

Burningham, C. and West, M.A. (1995) 'Individual, climate, and group interaction processes as predictors of work team innovation', *Small Group Research*, 26: 106–17.

Burt, R.S., Gabbay, S.M., Holt, G. and Moran, P. (1994) 'Contingent organization of a network theory: the culture-performance contingency function', *Acta Sociologica*, 37: 345–70.

Byrne, J., Brandt, R. and Port, O. (1993) 'The virtual corporation: the company of the future will be the ultimate in adaptability', *Business Week*, 8 February: 98–102.

Callaghan, P. and Hartmann, H. (1992) *Contingent Work: A Chart Book on Part-time and Temporary Employment*. Washington, DC: Institute for Women's Policy Research/Economic Policy Institute.

Capel, S.S. (1987) 'The incidence of and influences on stress and burnout in secondary school teachers', *British Journal of Educational Psychology*, 57: 279–88.

Cappelli, P. and Sherer, P.D. (1989) 'Spanning the union/nonunion boundary', *Industrial Relations*, 28: 206–26.

Carley, K. (1992). 'Organizational learning and personnel turnover', *Organization Science*, 3: 20–46.

Carson, K.D. and Carson, P.P. (1997) 'Career entrenchment: a quiet march toward occupational death?', *Academy of Management Executive*, 11 (1): 62–75.

Cartwright, D. and Zander, A. (eds) (1968) *Group Dynamics: Research and Theory.* New York: Harper & Row.

Cartwright, S. and Cooper, C.L. (1996) 'Coping in occupational settings', in M. Zeidner and N.S. Endler (eds), *Handbook of Coping.* New York: Wiley. pp. 202–20.

Carver, C.S. and Scheier, M.F. (1981) *Attention and Self-Regulation: A Control Theory Approach to Human Behavior.* New York: Springer-Verlag.

Child, J. (1972) 'Organizational structure, environment, and performance: the role of strategic choice', *Sociology*, 6: 1–22.

Christensen, K.E. and Staines, G.L. (1990) 'Flextime: a viable solution to work/ family conflict?', *Journal of Family Issues*, 11: 455–76.

Church, G. (1996) 'Disconnected', *Time*, 15 January: 38–9.

Chusmir, L.H., Moore, D.P. and Adams, J.S. (1990) 'Research on working women: a report card of 22 journals', *Sex Roles: A Journal of Research*, 22: 167–75.

Cissna, K.N. (1984) 'Phases in group development', *Small Group Behavior*, 15: 3–32.

Clark, J. (1993) 'Full flexibility and self-supervision in an automated factory', in J. Clark (ed.), *Human Resource Management and Technical Change.* London: Sage. pp. 116–36.

Clark, K. (1996) 'Women, men and money', *Fortune*, 5 August: 60–1.

Clark, T., Varadarajan, P.R. and Pride, W.M. (1994) 'Environmental management: the construct and research propositions', *Journal of Business Research*, 29 (1): 23–38.

Clegg, S. (1990) *Modern Organizations: Organization Studies in the Postmodern World.* London: Sage.

Cobb, S. (1976) 'Social support as a moderator of life stress', *Psychosomatic Medicine*, 38: 300–14.

Cobb, S. and Kasl, S.V. (1977) *Termination: The Consequence of Job Loss.* Washington, DC: US Department of Health, Education and Welfare, US Government Printing Office.

Cohen, B.P. and Zhou, X. (1991) 'Status processes in enduring work groups', *American Sociological Review*, 56 (2): 179–88.

Cohen, S. and Wills, T. (1985) 'Stress, social support, and the buffering hypothesis', *Psychological Bulletin*, 98: 310–57.

Cohen, S.G. and Ledford, G.E. (1994) 'The effectiveness of self-managing teams: a quasi-experiment', *Human Relations*, 47: 13–43.

Cohen, W.M. and Levinthal, D.A. (1990) 'Absorptive capacity: a new perspective on learning and innovation', *Administrative Science Quarterly*, 35: 128–52.

Collins, L. (1997). 'Army refuses to let male soldier serve as nurse', *Jerusalem Post*, 1 January.

Comfort, L.K. (1993) 'Integrating information technology into international crisis management and policy', *Journal of Contingencies and Crisis Management*, 1 (1): 15–26.

Cook, S.D.N. and Yanow, D. (1993) 'Culture and organizational learning', *Journal of Management Inquiry*, 2: 373–90.

Cooper, C.L. and Melhuish, A. (1984) 'Executive stress and health: differences between women and men', *Journal of Occupational Medicine*, 26: 99–104.

Cordes, C.L. and Dougherty, T.W. (1993) 'A review and integration of research on job burnout', *Academy of Management Review*, 18: 621–56.

Corse, S.J. (1990) 'Pregnant managers and their subordinates: the effects of gender expectations on hierarchical relationships', *Journal of Applied Behavioral Science*, 26: 25–47.

Craig, J.M. and Jacobs, R.R. (1985) 'The effect of working with women on male attitudes toward female firefighters', *Basic and Applied Psychology*, 6: 61–74.

Curtis, R.L., Jr (1989) 'Cutbacks, management, and human relations: meanings for organizational theory and research', *Human Relations*, 42: 671–89.

Daft, R.L. and Huber, G.P. (1987) 'How organizations learn: a communication framework', *Research in the Sociology of Organizations*, 5: 1–36.

Daft, R.L. and Weick, K.E. (1994) 'Strategic change and the environment', in C. Hard (ed.), *Managing Strategic Action: Mobilizing Change*. London: Sage. pp. 80–93.

Dalton, D.R. and Mesch, D.J. (1990) 'The impact of flexible scheduling on employee attendance and turnover', *Administrative Science Quarterly*, 35: 370–87.

Damanpour, F. (1991) 'Organizational innovation: a meta-analysis of effects of determinants and moderators', *Academy of Management Journal*, 34: 555–90.

Daniel, W.W. and Millward, N. (1993) 'Findings from the Workplace Industrial Relations Surveys', in J. Clark (ed.), *Human Resource Management and Technical Change*. London: Sage. pp. 43–77.

Das, T.K. (1984) 'Discussion note: portmanteau ideas for organizational theorizing', *Organization Studies*, 5: 261–67.

Davidson, M.J. and Cooper, C.L. (1986) 'Executive women under pressure', *International Review of Applied Psychology*, 35: 301–26.

Davidson, M.J. and Cooper, C.L. (1992) *Shattering the Glass Ceiling: The Woman Manager*. London: Paul Chapman.

Davis-Blake, A. and Pfeffer, J. (1989) 'Just a mirage: the search for dispositional effects in organizational research', *Academy of Management Review*, 14: 385–400.

Dean, J., Yoon, S. and Susman, G. (1992) 'Advanced manufacturing technology and organization structure: empowerment or subordination?', *Organization Science*, 3: 203–29.

Deaux, K. (1984) 'From individual differences to social categories', *American Psychologist*, 39: 105–16.

Denison, D.R. (1990) *Corporate Culture and Organizational Effectiveness*. New York: Wiley.

Dewe, P., Cox, T. and Ferguson, E. (1993) 'Individual strategies for coping with stress at work: a review', *Work and Stress*, 4: 17–27.

DiBella, A.J. (1990) 'The research manager's role in encouraging evaluation use', *Evaluation Practice*, 2 (June): 115–19.

Dipboye, R.L. (1987) 'Problems and progress of women in management', in K.S.

Kaziora, M.H. Moskow, and L.D. Tanner (eds), *Working Women: Past, Present, Future*. Washington, DC: Bureau of National Affairs. pp. 118–53.

DiTomaso, N. (1989) 'Sexuality in the workplace: discrimination and harassment', in J. Hearn, D. Sheppard, P. Tancred-Sheriff and G. Burrell (eds), *The Sexuality of Organization*. London: Sage. pp. 71–90.

Donnellon, A. and Scully, M. (1994) 'Teams, performance, and rewards: will the post-bureaucratic organization be a post-meritocratic organization?', in C. Heckscher and A. Donnellon (eds), *Post-Bureaucratic Organization: New Perspectives on Organizational Change*. Thousand Oaks, CA: Sage. pp. 63–90.

Dougherty, D. (1996) 'Organizing for innovation', in S.R. Clegg, C. Hardy and W.R. Nord (eds), *Handbook of Organization Studies*. London: Sage. pp. 424–39.

Dougherty, D. and Hardy, C. (1996) 'Sustained product innovation in large mature organizations: overcoming innovation-to-organization problems', *Academy of Management Journal*, 39: 1120–53.

Drazin, R. and Sandelands, L. (1992) 'Autogenesis: a perspective on the process of organizing', *Organization Science*, 3: 230–49.

Drazin, R. and Schoonhoven, C.B. (1996) 'Community, population, and organization effects on innovation: a multilevel perspective', *Academy of Management Journal*, 39: 1065–83.

Dunahoo, C.L., Geller, P.A. and Hobfell, S.E. (1996) 'Women's coping: communal versus individualistic orientation', in J.A.M. Schabracq and C.L. Cooper (eds), *Handbook of Work and Health Psychology*. New York: Wiley. pp. 183–204.

Dunkel-Schetter, C. and Skokan, L. (1990) 'Determinants of social support provision in personal relationships', *Journal of Social and Personal Relationships*, 7: 437–50.

Dunphy, D. (1996) 'Organizational change in corporate settings', *Human Relations*, 49: 541–52.

Dyer, W.G. (1987) *Team Building: Issues and Alternatives* (2nd edn). Reading, MA: Addison-Wesley.

Eagley, A.H. and Johnson, B.T. (1990) 'Gender and leadership style: a meta-analysis', *Psychological Bulletin*, 111: 3–32.

Edwards, J.R. (1988) 'The determinants and consequences of coping with stress', in C.L. Cooper and R. Payne (eds), *Causes, Coping and Consequences of Stress at Work*. Chichester: Wiley. pp. 233–63.

Effrat, A. (1968) 'Editor's introduction', *Sociological Inquiry* (special issue: applications of Parsonian theory), 38: 97–103

Eisenberger, R., Fasolo, P. and Davis-LaMastro, V. (1990) 'Perceived organizational support and employee diligence, commitment, and innovation', *Journal of Applied Psychology*, 75: 51–9.

Ekman, P. (1973) 'Cross-culture studies of facial expression', in P. Ekman (ed.), *Darwin and Facial Expression: A Century of Research in Review*. New York: Academic Press. pp. 169–222.

Ekman, P. (1992) 'Facial expressions of emotion: new findings, new questions', *Psychological Science*, 3: 34–8.

Ely, R.J. (1995) 'The power in demography: women's social constructions of gender identity at work', *Academy of Management Journal*, 38: 589–634.

Enarson, E. (1993) 'Emotion workers on the production line: the feminizing of casino card dealing', *NWSA Journal*, 5: 218–32.

Erera, I.P. (1991) 'Supervisors can burn-out too', *Clinical Supervisor*, 9: 131–48.

Erez, M. (1992) 'Interpersonal communication systems in organizations, and their relationships to cultural values, productivity and innovation: the case of Japanese corporations', *Applied Psychology: An International Review*, 41: 43–64.

Ettlie, J.E. (1986) 'Innovation in manufacturing', in D. Gray, T. Solomon and W. Hetzner (eds), *Technological Innovation: Strategies for a New Partnership*. Amsterdam: North-Holland. pp. 135–44.

Ettlie, J.E. and Reza, E.M. (1992) 'Organizational integration and process innovation', *Academy of Management Journal*, 35: 795–827.

Feldman, D.C. and Doerpinghaus, H.I. (1992) 'Missing persons no longer: managing part-time workers in the '90s', *Organizational Dynamics*, 21 (1): 59–72.

Feldman, D.C., Doerpinghaus, H.I. and Turnley, W.H. (1994) 'Managing temporary workers: a permanent HRM challenge', *Organizational Dynamics*, 23 (2): 49–63.

Feldman, M.S. and March, J.G. (1981) 'Information in organizations as sign and symbol', *Administrative Science Quarterly*, 26: 171–86.

Feldman, S.P. (1989) 'The broken wheel: the inseparability of autonomy and control in innovation within organizations', *Journal of Management Studies*, 26 (2): 83–102.

Feldman, S.P. (1993) 'How organizational culture can affect innovation', in L. Hirschhorn and C.K. Barnett (eds), *The Psychodynamics of Organizations: Labor and Social Change*. Philadelphia, PA: Temple University Press. pp. 85–97.

Fidell, L.S. (1975) 'Empirical verification of sex discrimination in hiring practices in psychology', in R.K. Unger and F.L. Denmark (eds), *Women: Dependent or Independent Variable?* New York: Psychological Dimensions.

Fierman, J. (1994) 'The contingency work force', *Fortune*, 24 January: 20–5.

Fine, M.G., Johnson, F.L. and Ryan, M.S. (1990) 'Cultural diversity in the workplace', *Public Personnel Management*, 19: 305–19.

Fineman, S. (1993) 'Organizations as emotional arenas', in S. Fineman (ed.), *Emotion in Organizations*. London: Sage. pp. 9–35.

Fiol, C.M. (1996) 'Squeezing harder doesn't always work: continuing the search for consistency in innovation research', *Academy of Management Review*, 21: 1012–21.

Fiol, C.M. and Lyles, M.A. (1985) 'Organizational learning', *Academy of Management Review* 10: 803–13.

Fisher, S. (1984) *Stress and the Perception of Control*. Hillside, NJ: Erlbaum.

Fishman, C. (1996) 'Whole foods is all teams', Fast Company Online [http://www.fastcompany.com/02/team1.htm] (first appeared in *Fast Company*, April/May, 1996).

Flam, H. (1990) 'Emotional man: II – corporate actors as emotion-motivated emotion managers', *International Sociology*, 5: 225–34.

Fletcher, J.K. (1996) 'A relational approach to the protean worker', in D.T. Hall and Associates, *The Career is Dead – Long Live the Career: A Relational Approach*. San Francisco, CA: Jossey-Bass.

Fletcher, J.K. and Rapoport, R. (1996) 'Work–family issues as a catalyst for organizational change', in S. Lewis and J. Lewis (eds), *The Work–Family Challenge: Rethinking Employment*. London: Sage. pp. 142–58.

Flynn, G. (1996) 'Hallmark cares', *Personnel Journal*, 75 (3): 50–9.

Ford, C.M. (1996) 'A theory of individual creative action in multiple social domains', *Academy of Management Review*, 21: 1112–42.

Forss, K., Cracknell, B. and Samset, K. (1994) 'Can evaluation help an organization learn?', *Evaluation Review*, 18: 574–91.

Fortune (1995) 'A thought for the shower', 15 May: 51.

Foushee, H.C. (1984) 'Dyads and triads at 35,000 feet: factors affecting group
process and air crew performance', *American Psychologist*, 39: 885–93.

Francis, D. and Young, D. (1979) *Improving Work Groups: A Practical Manual for
Team Building*. San Diego, CA: University Associates.

Freedman, D.H. (1992) 'Is management still a science?', *Harvard Business Review*,
November–December: 26–38.

Freedman, S.J.M. (1990) *Managing Lives: Corporate Women and Social Change*.
Amherst, MA: University of Massachusetts Press.

Frijda, N.H. (1986) *The Emotions*. Cambridge: Cambridge University Press.

Frohman, A.L. (1997) 'Igniting organizational change from below: the power of
personal initiative', *Organizational Dynamics*, 25 (3): 39–53.

Ganster, D.C. and Schaubroeck, J. (1991) 'Work, stress and employee health',
Journal of Management, 17: 235–71.

Gash, D.C. (1991) 'Information technology and the redefinition of organizational
roles', *Research in the Sociology of Organization*, 9: 21–48.

George, J.M., Brief, A.P. and Webster, J. (1991) 'Organizationally intended and
unintended coping: the case of an incentive compensation plan', *Journal of
Occupational Psychology*, 64: 193–205.

Gergen, K.J. (1965) 'Interaction goals and personalistic feedback as factors
affecting the presentation of self', *Journal of Personality and Social Psychology*, 1:
413–24.

Gersick, C.J. (1988) 'Time and transition in work teams: toward a new model of
group development', *Academy of Management Journal*, 1: 9–41.

Gilbert, L. (1993) *Two Careers/One Family*. Beverly Hills, CA: Sage.

Ginnett, R.C. (1993) 'Crews as groups: their formation and their leadership', in
E.L. Wiener, B.G. Kanki and R.L. Helmreich (eds), *Cockpit Resource Management*.
San Diego, CA: Academic Press. pp. 71–98.

Giordano, L. (1988) 'Beyond Taylorism: computerization and QWL programmes
in the production process', in D. Knights and H. Willmott (eds), *New Technology
and the Labour Process*. London: Macmillan. pp. 163–96.

Glaser, R. (1992) 'Helping your organization gear up for self-managed teams', in
R. Glaser (ed.), *Classic Readings in Self-managing Teamwork*. King of Prussia, PA:
Organization Design and Development. pp. 374–99.

Glynn, M.A. (1996) 'Innovative genius: a framework for relating individual and
organizational intelligences to innovation', *Academy of Management Review*, 21:
1081–111.

Goffman, E. (1959) *The Presentation of Self in Everyday Life*. Garden City, NY:
Doubleday.

Golembiewski, R.T. and Kim, B.S. (1990) 'Burnout in police work: stressors,
strain, and the phase model', *Police Studies*, 13 (2): 74–80.

Gonyea, J.G. and Googins, B. (1996) 'The restructuring of work and family in the
United States: a new challenge for American corporations', in S. Lewis and J.
Lewis (eds), *The Work–Family Challenge: Rethinking Employment*. London: Sage.
pp. 63–78.

Goodstein, J.D. (1994) 'Institutional pressures and strategic responsiveness:
employer involvement in work–family issues', *Academy of Management Journal*,
37: 350–82.

Gordon, F.M. (1994) 'Bureaucracy: can we do better? We can do worse', in C. Heckscher and A. Donnellon (eds), *Post-Bureaucratic Organization: New Perspectives on Organizational Change*. Thousand Oaks, CA: Sage. pp. 195–210.

Gottfried, H. (1991) 'Mechanisms of control in the temporary help service industry', *Sociological Forum*, 6: 699–713.

Grant, J. (1988) 'Women as managers: what they can offer to organizations', *Organizational Dynamics*, 16 (3): 56–63.

Greenberg, J. and Baron, R.A. (1997) *Behavior in Organizations: Understanding and Managing the Human Side of Work* (6th edn). Upper Saddle River, NJ: Prentice-Hall.

Greenglass, E.R. (1985) 'Psychological implications of sex bias in the workplace', *Academic Psychology Bulletin*, 7: 227–40.

Greenhalgh, L. and Rosenblatt, Z. (1984) 'Job insecurity: toward conceptual clarity', *Academy of Management Review*, 9: 438–48.

Greenhaus, J.H. and Parasuraman, S. (1994) 'Work–family conflict, social support and well-being', in M. Davidson and R. Burke (eds), *Women in Management: Current Research Issues*. London: Paul Chapman. pp. 213–29.

Greller, M., Parsons, C. and Mitchell, D. (1992) 'Additive effects and beyond: occupational stressors and social buffers in a police organization', in J. Quick., L. Murphy and J. Hurrell (eds), *Stress and Well-Being at Work: Assessment and Interventions for Occupational Mental Health*. Washington, DC: American Psychological Association. pp. 33–47.

Grover, S.L. and Crooker, K.J. (1995) 'Who appreciates family-responsive human resource policies: the impact of family-friendly policies on the organizational attachment of parents and non-parents', *Personnel Psychology*, 48: 271–88.

Gutek, B.A. (1985) *Sex and the Workplace: The Impact of Sexual Behavior and Harassment on Women, Men and Organizations*. San Francisco, CA: Jossey-Bass.

Gutek, B.A. (1989) 'Sexuality in the workplace: key issues in social research and organizational practice', in J. Hearn, D. Sheppard, P. Tancred-Sheriff and G. Burrell (eds), *The Sexuality of Organization*. London: Sage. pp. 56–70.

Gutek, B.A. and Stevens, D. (1979) 'Differential responses of males and females to work situations which evoke sex role stereotypes', *Journal of Vocational Behavior*, 14: 23–32.

Gutek, B.A., Repetti, R.L. and Silver, D.L. (1988) 'Nonwork roles and stress at work', in C.L. Cooper and R. Payne (eds), *Causes, Coping and Consequences of Stress at Work*. Chichester: Wiley. pp. 141–74.

Guzzo, R.A. and Dickson, M.W. (1996) 'Teams in organizations: recent research on performance and effectiveness', *Annual Review of Psychology*, 47: 307–38.

Gwartney-Gibbs, P.A. and Lach, D.H. (1991) 'Workplace dispute resolution and gender inequality', *Negotiation Journal*, 7: 187–200.

Gwartney-Gibbs, P.A. and Lach, D.H. (1994) 'Gender differences in clerical workers' disputes over tasks, interpersonal treatment, and emotion', *Human Relations*, 47: 611–39.

Gyan-Baffour, G. (1994) 'Advanced manufacturing technology, employee participation and economic performance: an empirical analysis', *Journal of Managerial Issues*, 6: 491–505.

Haas, J.W., Sypher, B.D. and Sypher, H.E. (1992) 'Do shared goals really make a difference?', *Management Communication Quarterly*, 6: 166–79.

Hackett, E.J., Mirvis, P.H. and Sales, A.L. (1991) 'Women's and men's expectations about the effects of new technology at work', *Group and Organization Studies*, 16: 60–85.

Hackman, J. (ed.) (1990) *Groups that Work (and Those that Don't Work)*. San Francisco, CA: Jossey-Bass.

Hall, D.T. (1996) 'Protean careers of the 21st century', *Academy of Management Executive*, 10 (4): 8–16.

Hall, J. (1994) 'Americans know how to be productive if managers will let them', *Organizational Dynamics*, 33 (4): 33–46.

Hare, A.P. (1967) 'Small group development in the relay assembly test room', *Sociological Inquiry*, 37: 169–82.

Hare, A.P. (1973) 'Theory of group development and categories for interaction analysis', *Small Group Behavior*, 4: 259–304.

Hare, A.P. (1976) *Handbook of Small Group Research* (2nd edn). New York: Free Press.

Hare, A.P. (1982) *Creativity in Small Groups*. Beverly Hills, CA: Sage.

Hare, A.P. (1992a) 'Group development and functional theory', in R.T. Golembiewski (ed.), *Handbook of Organizational Consultation*. New York: Marcel Dekker. pp. 407–13.

Hare, A.P. (1992b) *Groups, Teams, and Social Interaction*. New York: Praeger.

Hare, A.P. (1993) 'Small groups in organizations', in R.T. Golembiewski (ed.), *Handbook of Organizational Behavior*. New Brunswick, NJ: Transaction. pp. 61–77.

Hare, A.P. and Davies, M.F. (1994) 'Social interaction', in A.P. Hare, H.H. Blumberg, and M.F. Davies and M.V. Kent (eds), *Small Group Research: A Handbook*. Norwood, NJ: Ablex. pp. 169–93.

Harker, L. (1996) 'The family-friendly employer in Europe', in S. Lewis and J. Lewis (eds), *The Work–Family Challenge: Rethinking Employment*. London: Sage. pp. 48–62.

Hart, P.M., Wearing, A.J. and Headey, B. (1995) 'Police stress and well-being: integrating personality, coping and daily work experiences', *Journal of Occupational and Organizational Psychology*, 68: 133–56.

Haslett, B., Geis, F. and Carter, M. (1993) *The Organizational Woman: Power and Paradox*. Norwood, NJ: Ablex.

Hawkins, P. (1997) 'Organizational culture: sailing between evangelism and complexity', *Human Relations*, 50: 417–40.

Hearn, J. (1993) 'Emotive subjects: organizational men, organizational masculinities and the (de)construction of emotions', in Stephen Fineman (ed.), *Emotion in Organizations*. London: Sage. pp. 142–66.

Heckscher, C. (1994) 'Defining the post-bureaucratic type', in C. Heckscher and A. Donnellon (eds), *Post-Bureaucratic Organization: New Perspectives on Organizational Change*. Thousand Oaks, CA: Sage. pp. 14–62.

Heckscher, C., Eisenstat, R.A. and Rice, T.J. (1994) 'Transformational processes', in C. Heckscher and A. Donnellon (eds), *Post-Bureaucratic Organization: New Perspectives on Organizational Change*. Thousand Oaks, CA: Sage. pp. 129–77.

Helmers, S. and Buhr, R. (1994) 'Corporate story-telling: the buxomly secretary, a pyrrhic victory of the male mind', *Scandinavian Journal of Management*, 10: 175–91.

Hennig, M. and Jardim, A. (1977) *The Managerial Woman*. New York: Simon & Schuster.

Hermans, H.J.M. (1990) 'Who shares whose values: identity and motivation in organizations', in U. Kleinbeck, H.H. Quast, H. Thierry and H. Hacker (eds), *Work Motivation*. Hillsdale, NJ: Lawrence Erlbaum. pp. 247–55

Herriot, P. and Pemberton, C. (1996) 'Contracting careers', *Human Relations*, 49: 757–90.

Hildebrandt, E. (1988) 'Work, participation and co-determination in computer-based manufacturing', in D. Knights and H. Willmott (eds), *New Technology and the Labour Process*. London: Macmillan. pp. 50–65.

Hirschhorn, L. (1984) *Beyond Mechanization: Work and Technology in a Postindustrial Age*. Cambridge, MA: MIT Press.

Hirsh, M. (1995) 'Slice! Cut! Slash!', *Newsweek*, 6 February: 36–42.

Hochschild, A.R. (1983) *The Managed Heart: Commercialization of Human Feelings*. Berkeley, CA: University of California Press.

Hogg, C. and Harker, L. (1992) *The Family Friendly Employer: Examples from Europe*. London: Daycare Trust.

Holmes, T.H. and Rahe, R.H. (1967) 'The social readjustment rating scale', *Psychosomatic Medicine*, 11: 213–18.

Holt, H. and Thaulow, I. (1996) 'Formal and informal flexibility in the workplace', in S. Lewis and J. Lewis (eds), *The Work–Family Challenge: Rethinking Employment*. London: Sage. pp. 79–92.

Homans, G.C. (1950) *The Human Group*. New York: Harcourt, Brace.

Hood, J. and Chusmir, H. (1986) 'Factors determining type A behavior among employed men and women', paper presented at the Annual Meeting of the Academy of Management, Chicago, August.

Hood, J.N. and Koberg, C.S. (1994) 'Patterns of differential assimilation and acculturation for women in business organizations', *Human Relations*, 47: 159–81.

Huber, G.P. (1991) 'Organizational learning: the contributing processes and the literatures', *Organization Science*, 2: 88–115.

Hutchins, E. (1990) 'The technology of team navigation', in J. Galegher, R.E. Kraut and C. Egido (eds), *Intellectual Teamwork: Social and Technological Foundations of Cooperative Work*. Hillsdale, NJ: Lawrence Erlbaum. pp. 191–220.

Instone, D., Major, B. and Bunker, B.B. (1983) 'Gender, self confidence, and social influence strategies: an organizational simulation', *Journal of Personality and Social Psychology*, 44: 322–33.

Isaacs, W.N. (1993) 'Taking flight: dialogue, collective thinking, and organizational learning', *Organizational Dynamics*, 22 (2): 24–39.

Ivancevich, J.M. and Matteson, M.T. (1988) 'Promoting the individual's health and well being', in C.L. Cooper and R. Payne (eds), *Causes, Coping and Consequences of Stress at Work*. Chichester: Wiley. pp. 267–99.

Izraeli, D. and Adler, N. (1994) 'Competitive frontiers: women managers in a global economy', in N. Adler and D. Izraeli (eds), *Competitive Frontiers: Women Managers in a Global Economy*. Cambridge, MA: Basil Blackwell. pp. 3–21.

Jaroff, L. (1995) 'Age of the road warrior', *Time*, Spring: 35–6.

Jerusalem Post (1987) 'Computer-induced heart attack recognised as work accident', *Jerusalem Post*, 7 September.

Johns, G. (1993) 'Constraints on the adoption of psychology-based personnel practices: lessons from organizational innovation', *Personnel Psychology*, 46: 569–92.

Johns, G. (1996) *Organizational Behavior: Understanding and Managing Life at Work* (4th edn). New York: HarperCollins College.

Jones, C. and DeFillippi, R.J. (1996) 'Back to the future in film: combining industry and self-knowledge to meet the career challenges of the 21st century', *Academy of Management Executive*, 10 (4): 89–103.

Jones, E.E. and Davis, K.E. (1965) 'A theory of correspondent inferences: from acts to dispositions', in L. Berkowitz (ed.), *Advances in Experimental Social Psychology* (vol. 2). New York: Academic Press. pp. 219–66.

Jones, E.E. and Pittman, T.S. (1982) 'Toward a general theory of strategic self-presentation', in J. Suls (ed.), *Psychological Perspectives on the Self* (vol. 1). Hillside, NJ: Erlbaum. pp. 231–62.

Jones, E.E., Rhodewalt, F., Berglas, S. and Skelton, J.A. (1981) 'Effects of strategic self-presentation on subsequent self-esteem', *Journal of Personality and Social Psychology*, 41: 407–21.

Kahn, R.L. and Byosiere, P. (1992) 'Stress in organizations', in M.D. Dunnette and L.M. Hough (eds), *Handbook of Industrial and Organizational Psychology* (2nd edn) (vol. 3). Palo Alto, CA: Consulting Psychology Press. pp. 571–650.

Kahn, W.A. (1993) 'Caring for the caregivers: patterns of organizational caregiving', *Administrative Science Quarterly*, 38: 539–63.

Kahneman, D. and Tversky, A. (1979) 'Prospect theory: an analysis of decision under risk', *Econometrica*, 47: 263–91.

Kanter, R.M. (1977) *Men and Women of the Corporation*. New York: Basic Books.

Kanter, R.M. (1983) *The Change Masters: Innovation and Entrepreneurship in the American Corporation*. New York: Touchstone.

Kanter, R.M., Stein, B.A. and Jick, T.D. (1992) *The Challenge of Organizational Change*. New York: Free Press.

Karasek, R.A., Jr and Theorell, T. (1990) *Healthy Work: Stress, Productivity, and the Reconstruction of Working Life*. New York: Basic Books.

Katz, R. (1988) 'Organizational socialization', in R. Katz (ed.), *Managing Professionals in Innovative Organizations*. Cambridge, MA: Ballinger. pp. 355–69.

Katzenbach, J.R. and Smith, D.K. (1993) *The Wisdom of Teams*. Boston, MA: Harvard Business School Press.

Kelly, K.E. and Houston, B.K. (1985) 'Type A behavior in employed women: relation to work, marital, and leisure variables, social support, stress, tension and health', *Journal of Personality and Social Psychology*, 48: 1067–79.

Kessler, E.R. and Chakrabarti, A.K. (1996) 'Innovation speed: a conceptual model of context, antecedents, and outcomes', *Academy of Management Review*, 21: 1143–91.

Kew, F. (1987) 'Contested rules: an explanation of how games change', *International Review for the Sociology of Sport*, 22: 125–35.

Kinnunen, J. (1990) 'The importance of organizational culture on development activities in a primary health care organization', *International Journal of Health Planning and Management*, 5: 65–71.

Kirchmeyer, C. (1995) 'Managing the work-nonwork boundary: an assessment of organizational responses', *Human Relations*, 48: 515–36.

Kirkman, B.L. and Shapiro, D.L. (1997) 'The impact of cultural values on employee resistance to teams: toward a model of globalized self-managing work team effectiveness', *Academy of Management Review*, 22: 730–57.

Klein, K.J. and Sorra, J.S. (1996) 'The challenge of innovation implementation', *Academy of Management Review*, 21: 1055–80.

Kofman, F. and Senge, P.M. (1993) 'Communities of commitment: the heart of learning organizations', *Organizational Dynamics*, 22 (2): 5–23.

Krackhardt, D. (1994) 'Constraints on the interactive organization as an ideal type', in C. Heckscher and A. Donnellon (eds), *Post-Bureaucratic Organization: New Perspectives on Organizational Change*. Thousand Oaks, CA: Sage. pp. 211–22.

Kraut, A. (1990) 'Some lessons on organizational research concerning work and family issues', *Human Resource Planning*, 13: 109–18.

Kuhnert, K. and Vance, R. (1992) 'Job insecurity and moderators of the relation between job insecurity and employee adjustment', in J. Quick., L. Murphy and J. Hurrell (eds), *Stress and Well-Being at Work: Assessment and Interventions for Occupational Mental Health*. Washington, DC: American Psychological Association. pp. 48–63.

Kuypers, B.C., Davies, D. and Glaser, K.H. (1986) 'Developmental arrestations in self-analytic groups', *Small Group Behavior*, 17: 269–302.

Lambert, S.J. (1993) 'Workplace policies as social policy', *Social Service Review*, June, 237–60.

Lawson, R.B. and Ventriss, C.L. (1992) 'Organizational change: the role of organizational culture and organizational learning', *Psychological Record*, 42 (2): 205–19.

Lazarus, R.S. (1981) 'The stress and coping paradigm', in C. Eisdorfer, D. Cohen, A. Kleinman and P. Maxim (eds), *Models for Clinical Psychopathology*. New York: Spectrum. pp. 177–214.

Lazarus, R.S. and Folkman, S. (1984) *Stress, Appraisal, and Coping*. New York: Springer.

Leavitt, H.J. (1972) *Managerial Psychology: An Introduction to Individuals, Pairs, and Groups in organizations* (3rd edn). Chicago, IL: University of Chicago Press.

Leiter, M.P., Clark, D. and Durup, J. (1994) 'Distinct models of burnout and commitment among men and women in the military', *Journal of Applied Behavioral Science*, 30: 63–82.

Levering, R. and Moskowitz, M. (1993) *The 100 Best Companies to Work for in America*. New York: Currency Doubleday.

Levitt, B. and March, J.G. (1988) 'Organizational learning', *Annual Review of Sociology*, 14: 319–40.

Lewis, S. (1994) 'Role tensions and dual career families', in M. Davidson and R. Burke (eds), *Women in Management: Current Research Issues*. London: Paul Chapman.

Lewis, S. (1996) 'Rethinking employment: an organizational culture change framework', in S. Lewis and J. Lewis (eds), *The Work–Family Challenge: Rethinking Employment*. London: Sage. pp. 1–19.

Liebig, P.S. (1993) 'Factors affecting the development of employer-sponsored eldercare programs: implications for employed caregivers', *Journal of Women and Aging*, 5: 59–78.

Liff, S. (1993) 'Information technology and occupational restructuring in the office', in E. Green, J. Owen and D. Pain (eds), *Gendered by Design? Information Technology and Office Systems*. London: Taylor & Francis. pp. 95–110.

Linville, P.W. (1985) 'Self-complexity and affective extremity: don't put all of your eggs in one cognitive basket', *Social Cognition*, 3: 94–120.

Linville, P.W. (1987) 'Self-complexity as a cognitive buffer against stress-related illness and depression', *Journal of Personality and Social Psychology*, 52: 663–76.

Lipman-Blumen, J. (1992) 'Connective leadership: female leadership styles in the 21st-century workplace', *Sociological Perspectives*, 35: 183–203.

Lipman-Blumen, J. (1996) *The Connective Edge: Leading in an Interdependent World*. San Francisco, CA: Jossey-Bass.

Lipshitz, O. (1995) 'Affirmative action needed', *Ha'daf Ha'yarok*, 3 March: 6–7 (Hebrew).

Lipton, M. (1996) 'Demystifying the development of an organizational vision', *Sloan Management Review*, 37 (4): 83–92.

Litt, M.D. (1988) 'Cognitive mediators of stressful experience: self-efficacy and perceived control', *Cognitive Therapy and Research*, 12: 241–60.

Little, L.F., Gaffney, I.C., Rosen, K.H. and Bender, M.M. (1990) 'Corporate instability is related to airline pilots' stress symptoms', *Aviation, Space, and Environmental Medicine*, 61: 977–82.

Loden, M. (1985) *Feminine Leadership, or How to Succeed in Business Without Being One of the Boys*. New York: Times Books.

Lorenz, E.H. (1992) 'Trust and flexible firm: international comparisons', *Industrial Relations*, 31: 455–72.

Lovell, R.D. and Turner, B.M. (1988) 'Organizational learning, bureaucratic control, preservation of form', *Knowledge*, 9: 404–25.

Lundberg, C.C. and Brownell, J. (1993) 'The implications of organizational learning for organizational communication: a review and reformulation', *International Journal of Organizational Analysis*, 1: 29–53.

MacCorquodale, P. and Jensen, G. (1993) 'Women in the law: partners or tokens?', *Gender and Society*, 7: 582–93.

MacDuffie, J.P. (1995) 'Human resource bundles and manufacturing performance: organizational logic and flexible production systems in the world auto industry', *Industrial and Labor Relations Review*, 48 (2): 197–221.

MacKinnon, C. (1979) *Sexual Harassment of Working Women*. New Haven, CT: Yale University Press.

Mael, F.A. and Aldkerks, C.E. (1993) 'Leadership team cohesion and subordinate work unit morale and performance', *Military Psychology*, 5 (3): 141–58.

Magnum, G., Mayall, D. and Nelson, K. (1985) 'The temporary help industry: a response to the dual internal labor market', *Industrial and Labor Relations Review*, 38: 599–611.

Markus, H. and Wurf, E. (1987) 'The dynamic self-concept: a social psychological perspective', *Annual Review of Psychology*, 38: 299–337.

Maslach, C. (1982) *Burnout: The Cost of Caring*. Englewood Cliffs, NJ: Prentice-Hall.

Maslach, C. and Jackson, S.E. (1981) 'The measurement of experienced burnout', *Journal of Occupational Behavior*, 2: 99–113.

Mason, E.S. (1994) 'Work values: a gender comparison and implications for practice', *Psychological Reports*, 74: 415–18.

Matteson, M.T. and Ivancevich, J.M. (1987) *Controlling Work Stress*. San Francisco, CA: Jossey-Bass.

Maurer, T.J. and Taylor, M.A. (1994) 'Is sex by itself enough? An explanation of gender bias issues in performance appraisal', *Organizational Behavior and Human Decision Processes*, 60: 231–51.

May, D.R. and Schwoerer, C.E. (1994a) 'Developing effective work teams: guidelines for fostering work team efficacy', *Organization Development Journal*, 12 (3): 29–39.

May, D.R. and Schwoerer, C.E. (1994b) 'Employee health by design: using employee involvement teams in ergonomic job design', *Personnel Psychology,* 47: 861–76.

McDaniel, S.A. (1993) 'Challenges to mental health promotion among working women in Canada', *Canadian Journal of Community Mental Health,* 12: 201–10.

McGrath, J.E. (1991) 'Time, interaction, and performance (TIP): a theory of groups', *Small Group Research,* 22: 147–74.

McGregor, D. (1960) *The Human Side of Enterprise.* New York: McGraw-Hill.

Meeker, B. and Weitzel-O'Neill, P. (1977) 'Sex roles and interpersonal behavior in task-oriented groups', *Sociological Review,* 42: 91–105.

Menaghan, E.G. (1991) 'Work experiences and family interaction processes: the long reach of the job?', *Annual Review of Sociology,* 17: 419–44.

Miller, J. (1992) 'Gender and supervision: the legitimation of authority in relationship to task', *Sociological Perspectives,* 35: 137–62.

Miller, M. and Robinson, C. (1994) 'Managing the disappointment of job termination: outplacement as a cooling-out device', *Journal of Applied Behavioral Science,* 30: 5–21.

Milliken, F.J., Dutton, J.E. and Beyer, J.M. (1990) 'Understanding organizational adaptation to change: the case of work-family issues', *Human Resource Planning,* 13: 91–107.

Mills, A. (1989) 'Gender, sexuality, and organization theory', in J. Hearn, D. Sheppard, P. Tancred-Sheriff and G. Burrell (eds), *The Sexuality of Organization.* London: Sage. pp. 29–44.

Miner, A.S. and S.J. Mezias. (1996) 'Ugly duckling no more: pasts and futures of organizational learning research', *Organization Science,* 7: 88–99.

Monge, P.R., Cozzens, M.D. and Contractor, N.S. (1992) 'Communication and motivational predictors of the dynamics of organizational innovation', *Organizational Science,* 3: 250–74.

Mordock, J.B. (1989) 'Organizational adaptation to policy and funding shifts: the road to survival', *Child Welfare,* 68: 589–603.

Morgan, G. (1986) *Images of Organization.* Beverly Hills, CA: Sage.

Morgan, H. and Milliken, F. (1993) 'Keys to action: understanding differences in organizations' responsiveness to work-and-family issues', *Human Resource Management Journal,* 31: 227–48.

Morris, J.A. and Feldman, D.C. (1996) 'The dimensions, antecedents, and consequences of emotional labor', *Academy of Management Review,* 21: 986–1010.

Morrison, A.M., White, R.P. and Van Velsor, E. (1987) *Breaking the Glass Ceiling: Can Women Reach the Top of America's Largest Corporations?* Reading, MA: Addison-Wesley.

Moss, P. (1996) 'Reconciling employment and family responsibilities: a European perspective', in S. Lewis and J. Lewis (eds), *The Work–Family Challenge: Rethinking Employment.* London: Sage. pp. 20–33.

Mueller, R.K. (1991) 'Corporate networking: how to tap unconventional wisdom', in J. Henry (ed.), *Creative Management.* London: Sage. pp. 153–62.

Mullin, R.F. and Sherman, R. (1993) 'Creativity and performance appraisal: shall never the twain meet?', *Creativity Research Journal,* 6: 425–34.

Munene, J.C. (1995) 'The institutional environment and managerial innovations: a qualitative study of selected Nigerian firms', *Journal of Occupational and Organizational Psychology,* 68: 291–300.

Murphy, L.R. (1988) 'Workplace interventions for stress reduction and prevention', in C.L. Cooper and R. Payne (eds), *Causes, Coping and Consequences of Stress at Work*. Chichester: Wiley. pp. 301–39.

Nandram, S.S. and Klandermans, B. (1993) 'Stress experienced by active members of trade unions', *Journal of Organizational Behavior*, 14: 415–31.

Nevis, E.C., DiBella, A.J. and Gould, J.M. (1995) 'Understanding organizations as learning systems', *Sloan Management Review*, 36 (2): 73–85.

Nicholson, N. (1996) 'Career systems in crisis: change and opportunity in the information age', *Academy of Management Executive*, 10 (4): 40–51.

Nieva, V.F. and Gutek, B.A. (1981) *Women and Work: A Psychological Perspective*. New York: Praeger.

Nohria, N. and Berkley, J.D. (1994) 'The virtual organization: bureaucracy, technology, and the implosion of control', in C. Heckscher and A. Donnellon (eds), *Post-Bureaucratic Organization: New Perspectives on Organizational Change*. Thousand Oaks, CA: Sage. pp. 108–28.

Northcott, J. and Rogers, P. (1984) *Microelectronics in British Industry: Patterns of Change*. London: Policy Studies Institute.

Nussbaum, G.M. (1994) 'The subconscious in organizational control: the case of Mitsubishi Heavy Industry', *International Journal of Comparative Sociology*, 35: 105–30.

O'Leary, V.E. and Ickovics, J.R. (1992) 'Cracking the glass ceiling: overcoming isolation and alienation', in U. Sekaran and F. Leong (eds), *Womanpower: Managing in Times of Demographic Turbulence*. Beverly Hills, CA: Sage. pp. 7–30.

Offermann, L.R. and Armitage, M.A. (1993) 'Stress and the woman manager: sources, health outcomes and interventions', in E.A. Fagenson (ed.), *Women in Management: Trends, Issues and Challenges in Managerial Diversity*. Beverly Hills, CA: Sage. pp. 131–61.

Ohlott, P.J., Ruderman, M.N. and McCauley, C.D. (1994) 'Gender differences in managers' developmental job experiences', *Academy of Management Journal*, 37: 46–67.

Oldham, G. R. and Cummings, A. (1996) 'Employee creativity: personal and contextual factors at work', *Academy of Management Journal*, 39: 607–34.

Olmsted, M.S. (1959) *The Small Group*. New York: Random House.

Olmsted, M.S. and Hare, A.P. (1978) *The Small Group* (2nd edn). New York: Random House.

Osborn, R. and Vicars, W. (1976) 'Sex stereotypes: an artifact in leader behavior and subordinate satisfaction analysis?', *Academy of Management Journal*, 19: 439–49.

Osterman, P. (1994) 'How common is workplace transformation and who adopts it?', *Industrial and Labor Relations Review*, 47: 173–88.

Parasuraman, S. and Hansen, D. (1987) 'Coping with work stressors in nursing', *Work and Occupations*, 14: 88–105.

Parsons, T. (1961) 'An outline of the social system', in T. Parsons, E.A. Shils, K.D. Naegele and J.R. Pitts (eds), *Theories of Society*. New York: Free Press. pp. 30–79.

Parthasarthy, R. and Sethi, S.P. (1992) 'The impact of flexible automation on business strategy and organizational structure', *Academy of Management Review*, 17: 86–111.

Pasmore, W. (1988) *Designing Effective Organization: The Sociotechnical Perspective*. New York: Wiley.

Patten, T. H., Jr. (1981) *Organizational Development through Teambuilding*. New York: Wiley.

Patten, T.H., Jr (1988) 'Team building, Part I: Designing the intervention', in W.B. Reddy with K. Jamison (eds), *Team Building*. San Diego, CA: University Associates. pp. 15–24

Pearlin, L.I. and Schooler, C. (1978) 'The structure of coping', *Journal of Health and Social Behavior*, 19: 2–21.

Perlow, L.A. (1995) 'Putting the work back into work/family', *Group and Organization Management*, 20: 227–39.

Piliavin, J.A. and Martin, R. (1978) 'The effects of the sex composition of groups on style of social interaction', *Sex Roles*, 4: 281–96.

Pines, A.M. and Aronson, E. (1981) *Burnout: From Tedium to Personal Growth*. New York: Free Press.

Pines, A.M. and Maslach, C. (1980) 'Combating staff burn-out in a day care center: a case study', *Child Care Quarterly*, 9: 5–16.

Piore, M.J. and Sabel, C. (1982) *The Second Industrial Divide: Possibilities for Prosperity*. New York: Basic Books.

Pliner, J. (1990) 'Staying with or leaving the organization', *Prevention in Human Services*, 8: 159–77.

Pliskin, N., Romm, C.T. and Markey, R. (1997) 'E-mail as a weapon in an industrial dispute', *New Technology, Work and Employment*, 12: 3–12.

Pouder, R. and St John, C.H. (1996) 'Hot spots and blind spots: geographical clusters of firms and innovation', *Academy of Management Review*, 21: 1192–225.

Poulin, J.E. and Walter, C.A. (1993) 'Burnout in gerontological social work', *Social Work*, 38: 305–10.

Powell, G.N. (1988) *Women and Men in Management*. Newbury Park, CA: Sage.

Powell, G.N. (1995) 'Vive la différence? Gender and management in the new workplace', in D.A. Kolb, J. Osland and I.M. Rubin (eds), *The Organizational Behavior Reader* (6th edn). Englewood Cliffs, NJ: Prentice-Hall. pp. 366–75.

Prasad, P. (1992) 'The symbolism of work computerization: an empirical investigation of the meanings and imagery around technological change', paper presented at the 52nd Annual Meeting of the Academy of Management, Las Vegas, 9–12 August.

Price, R. (1985) 'Work and Community', *American Journal of Community Psychology*, 13: 1–12.

Probst, G. and Buechel, B. (1997) *Organizational Learning: The Competitive Advantage of the Future*. London: Prentice Hall.

Proctor, T. (1995) *The Essence of Management Creativity*. London: Prentice Hall.

Putnam, L.L. and Mumby, D.K. (1993) 'Organizations, emotion and the myth of rationality', in S. Fineman (ed.), *Emotion in Organizations*. London: Sage. pp. 36–57.

Quinn, D.P. and Rivoli, P. (1991). 'The effects of American- and Japanese-style employment and compensation practices on innovation', *Organization Science*, 2: 323–41.

Quinn, R. (1988) *Beyond Rational Management*. San Francisco, CA: Jossey-Bass.

Raabe, P.H. (1996) 'Constructing pluralistic work and career arrangements', in S. Lewis and J. Lewis (eds), *The Work–Family Challenge: Rethinking Employment*. London: Sage. pp. 128–41.

Raber, M.J. (1994) 'Women in the workplace: implications for child care', *Employee Assistance Quarterly*, 9 (3–4): 21–36.

Rafaeli, A. and Sutton, R.I. (1987) 'Expression of emotion as part of the work role', *Academy of Management Review*, 12: 23–37.

Rafaeli, A. and Sutton, R.I. (1989) 'The expression of emotion in organizational life', in L.L. Cummings and B.M. Staw (eds), *Research in Organizational Behavior* (vol. 11). Greenwich, CT: JAI Press. pp. 1–42.

Ragins, B.R. (1989) 'Barriers to mentoring: the female manager's dilemma', *Human Relations*, 42: 1–22.

Ragins, B.R. and Sundstrom, E. (1990) 'Gender and perceived power in manager-subordinate dyads', *Journal of Occupational Psychology*, 63: 273–87.

Reuter (1996) 'Women work more but are paid less', *Jerusalem Post*, 30 July.

Rhodes, S.R. and Steers, R.M. (1990) *Managing Employee Absenteeism*. Reading, MA: Addison-Wesley.

Riley, P. (1983) 'A structurationist account of political culture', *Administrative Science Quarterly*, 28: 414–37.

Roche, G. (1979) 'Much ado about mentors', *Harvard Business Review*, 79: 14–28.

Roethlisberger, F.J. and Dickson, W.J. (1939) *Management and the Worker*. Cambridge, MA: Harvard University Press.

Rogers, T.B. (1981) 'A model of the self as an aspect of the human information processing system', in N. Cantor and J.F. Kihlstrom (eds), *Personality, Cognition, and Social Interaction*. Hillsdale, NJ: Erlbaum. pp. 193–214.

Roseman, I.J., Spindel, M.S. and Jose, P.E. (1990) 'Appraisals of emotion-eliciting events: testing a theory of discrete emotions', *Journal of Personality and Social Psychology*, 59: 899–915.

Rosen, R. (1991) *The Healthy Company*. Los Angeles, CA: Jeremy P. Tarcher.

Rosenberg, M. (1990) 'Reflexivity and emotions', *Social Psychology Quarterly*, 53: 3–12.

Rosner, J. (1990) 'Ways women lead', *Harvard Business Review*, 68 (6): 119–20.

Ross, R.R. and Altmaier, E.M. (1994) *Intervention in Occupational Stress: A Handbook of Counselling for Stress at Work*. London: Sage.

Rothman, R. (1979) 'Occupational roles: power and negotiation in the division of labor', *Sociological Quarterly*, Autumn: 495–515.

Rudolf, B. (1993) 'Monsieur Mickey', *Time*, 25 March: 48–9.

Rutter, D.R. and Fielding, P.J. (1988) 'Sources of occupational stress: an examination of British prison officers', *Work and Stress*, 2: 291–9.

Savery, L.K (1990) 'Men and women in the workplace: evidence of occupational differences', *Leadership and Organization Development Journal*, 11 (2): 13–16.

SC Johnson Wax on-line (1996a) 'A leader right from the start'. [http://www.scjohnsonwax.com:80/whoerovw.html]

SC Johnson Wax on-line (1996b) 'Johnson Wax child care center'. [http://www.scjohnsonwax.com:80/whochild.html]

Schaubroeck, J. and Merritt, D.E. (1997) 'Divergent effects of job control on coping with work stressors: the key role of self-efficacy', *Academy of Management Journal*, 40: 738–54.

Schein, E.H. (1985) *Organizational Culture and Leadership: A Dynamic View*. San Francisco, CA: Jossey-Bass.

Schein, E.H. (1993) 'On dialogue, culture, and organizational learning', *Organizational Dynamics*, 22 (2): 40–51.

Schein, E.H. (1996) 'Career anchors revisited: implications for career development in the 21st century', *Academy of Management Executive*, 10 (4): 80–8.

Scherer, K.R. (1988) 'Cognitive antecedents of emotion', in V. Hamilton, G.H. Bowers and N.H. Frijda (eds), *Cognitive Perspectives on Emotion and Motivation*. Dordrecht: Kluwer. pp. 89–126.

Schlender, B.R. (1992) 'How Sony keeps the magic going', *Fortune*, 24 February: 22–7.

Schlenker, B.R. (1985) 'Identity and self-identification', in B.R. Schlenker (ed.), *The Self and Social Life*. New York: McGraw-Hill. pp. 65–100.

Schneider, W.E. (1994) *The Reengineering Alternative: A Plan for Making Your Current Culture Work*. New York: Irwin.

Schulz, M. (1992) 'A depletion of assets model of organizational learning', *Journal of Mathematical Sociology*, 17 (2–3): 145–73.

Schutz, W.C. (1958) *FIRO: A Three-dimensional Theory of Interpersonal Behavior*. New York: Holt, Rinehart.

Schwartz, J.E. and Stone, A.A. (1993) 'Coping with daily work problems: contributions of problem content, appraisals and person factors', *Work and Stress*, 7: 47–62.

Schweiger, D.M. and DeNisi, A.S. (1991) 'Communication with employees following a merger: a longitudinal field experiment', *Academy of Management Journal*, 34: 110–35.

Scott, S. and Bruce, R.A. (1994) 'Determinants of innovative behavior: a path model of individual innovation in the workplace', *Academy of Management Journal*, 37: 580–607.

Scott, W.G. and Hart, D.K. (1989) *Organizational Values in America*. New Brunswick, NJ: Transaction.

Seers, A., Petty, M.M. and Cashman, J.F. (1995) 'Team-member exchange under team and traditional management: a naturally occurring quasi-experiment', *Group and Organization Management*, 20: 18–38.

Seifert, C.M. and Hutchins, E.L. (1992) 'Error as opportunity: learning in a cooperative task', *Human Computer Interaction*, 7: 409–35.

Selye, H. (1956) *The Stress of Life*. New York: McGraw-Hill.

Senge, P.M. (1990) *The Fifth Discipline: The Art and Practice of the Learning Organization*. Garden City, NY: Doubleday.

Shambaugh, P.W. (1978) 'The development of the small group', *Human Relations*, 31: 283–95.

Shapiro, L. (1997) 'The myth of quality time', *Newsweek*, 19 May: 42–8.

Shaw, M.E. (1981) *Group Dynamics* (3rd edn). New York: McGraw-Hill.

Sheppard, D.L. (1989) 'Organizations, power and sexuality: the image and self-image of women managers', in J. Hearn, D.L. Sheppard, P. Tancred-Sheriff and G. Burrell (eds), *The Sexuality of Organization*. London: Sage. pp. 139–57.

Shipper, F. and Manz, C.C. (1992) 'Employee self-management without formally designated teams: an alternative road to empowerment', *Organizational Dynamics*, 20 (3): 48–61.

Shulman, A.D., Penman, R. and Sless, D. (1990) 'Putting information technology in its place: organizational communication and the human infrastructure', in J.S. Carroll (ed.), *Applied Social Psychology and Organizational Settings*. Hillsdale, NJ: Lawrence Erlbaum. pp. 155–91.

Simpson, J.C. and Weiner, E.S.C. (comps) (1989) *The Oxford English Dictionary* (2nd edn). Oxford: Clarendon Press.

Sitkin, S.B. (1996) 'Learning through failure: the strategy of small losses', in M.D. Cohen and L.S. Sproull (eds), *Organizational Learning*. Thousand Oaks, CA: Sage. pp. 541–77.

Smith, C. and Gemmill, G. (1991) 'Change in the small group: a dissipative structure perspective', *Human Relations*, 44: 697–716.

Smith, J.C., Kaminski, B.J. and Wylie, R.G. (1990) 'May I make a suggestion? Corporate support for innovation', *Journal of Organizational Behavior Management*, 11: 125–46.

Smith, P.B., Peterson, M.F. and Misumi, J. (1994) 'Event management and work team effectiveness in Japan, Britain, and USA', *Journal of Occupational and Organizational Psychology*, 67: 33–43.

Smith, S. (1988) 'How much change at the store? The impact of new technology and labour processes on managers and staff in retail', in R. Hyman and W. Streeck (eds), *New Technology and Industrial Relations*. Oxford: Blackwell. pp. 143–63.

Smith, V. (1993) 'Flexibility in work and employment: the impact on women', *Research in the Sociology of Organization*, 11: 195–216.

Snizek, W.E. and Neil, C.C. (1992) 'Job characteristics, gender stereotypes and perceived gender discrimination in the workplace', *Organization Studies*, 13: 403–27.

Snyder, M. and Gangestad, S. (1982) 'Choosing social situations: two investigations of self-monitoring processes', *Journal of Personality and Social Psychology*, 43: 123–35.

Sokol, M.B. and Aiello, J.R. (1993) 'Implications for team focused stress management training', *Consulting Psychology Journal Practice and Research*, 45 (4): 1–10.

Sommer, A. (1996) 'The shortest commute', *Jerusalem Post Magazine*, 22 March: 13–15.

Spade, J.Z. and Reese, C.A. (1991) 'We've come a long way, maybe: college students' plans for work and family', *Sex Roles*, 24: 309–21.

Srivastva, S., Bilimoria, D., Cooperrider, D.L. and Fry, R.E. (1993) 'Management and organizational learning for positive global change', *Management Learning*, 26: 37–54.

Staw, B.M. and Ross, J. (1987) 'Behavior in escalation situations: antecedents, prototypes, and solutions', in B.M. Staw and L.L. Cummings (eds.), *Research in Organizational Behavior* (vol. 9). Greenwich, CT: JAI Press. pp. 39–78.

Steckler, N. and Fondas, N. (1995) 'Building team effectiveness: a diagnostic tool', *Organizational Dynamics*, 23 (3): 20–35.

Stein, M.I. (1974) *Stimulating Creativity: Individual Procedures* (vol. 1). New York: Academic Press.

Stein, M.I. (1991) 'Creativity is people', *Leadership and Organizational Development Journal*, 12 (6): 4–10.

Steiner, G. (ed.) (1965) *The Creative Organization*. Chicago, IL: University of Chicago Press.

Steiner, I.D. (1972) *Group Process and Productivity*. New York: Academic Press.

Steinhoff, P.G. and Tanaka, K. (1994) 'Women managers in Japan', in N.J. Adler and D.N. Izraeli (eds), *Competitive Frontiers: Women Managers in a Global Economy*. Cambridge, MA: Basil Blackwell. pp. 79–100.

Stenross, B. and Kleinman, S. (1989) 'The highs and lows of emotional labor: detectives' encounters with criminals and victims', *Journal of Contemporary Ethnography*, 17: 435–52.

Suarez, V.L. (1990) 'Invention, inventive learning, and innovative capacity', *Behavioral Science*, 35: 290–312.

Sullivan, S. (1995) 'Not so fast, ladies', *Newsweek*, 30 October: 30.

Sundstrom, E. and Altman, I. (1989) 'Physical environments and work-group effectiveness', *Research in Organizational Behavior*, 11: 175–209.

Sundstrom, E., de Meuse, K.P. and Futrell, D. (1990) 'Work teams: applications and effectiveness', *American Psychologist*, 45 (2): 120–33.

Sutton, C.D. and Moore, K.K. (1985) 'Executive women – 20 years later', *Harvard Business Review*, 63 (5): 42–66.

Sutton, R.I. (1991) 'Maintaining norms about expressed emotions: the case of bill collectors', *Administrative Science Quarterly*, 36: 245–68.

Sutton, R.I. and Kahn, R.L. (1987) 'Prediction, understanding and control as antidotes to organizational stress', in J.W. Lorsch (ed.), *Handbook of Organizational Behavior*. Englewood Cliffs, NJ: Prentice-Hall. pp. 272–85.

Swerdlow, M. (1989) 'Men's accommodations to women entering a nontraditional occupation: a case of rapid transit operatives', *Gender and Society*, 3: 373–87.

Tajfel, H. and Turner, J.C. (1985) 'The social identity theory of intergroup behavior', in S. Worchel and W.G. Austin (eds), *Psychology of Intergroup Relations* (2nd edn). Chicago, IL: Nelson-Hall. pp. 7–24.

Taylor, I.A. (1975) 'An emerging view of creative actions', in I.A. Taylor and J.W. Getzels (eds), *Perspectives in Creativity*. Chicago, IL: Aldine. pp. 297–325.

Tetrick, L. (1992) 'Mediating effect of perceived role stress: a confirmatory analysis', in J. Quick., L. Murphy and J. Hurrell (eds), *Stress and Well-Being at Work: Assessment and Interventions for Occupational Mental Health*. Washington, DC: American Psychological Association. pp. 134–52.

Thomas, L.T. and Ganster, D.C. (1995) 'Impact of family-supportive work variables on work–family conflict and strain: a control perspective', *Journal of Applied Psychology*, 80: 6–15.

3M (1997a) 'Innovation network: news & profile – innovation center'. [http://www.mmm.com/profile/innov/index.htm]

3M (1997b) 'Innovation quiz'. [http://www.mmm.com/quiz/]

3M (1997c) 'McKnight principles'. [http://www.mmm.com/profile/looking/mcknight.htm]

Torres, R.T. (1994) 'Evaluation and learning organizations: where do we go from here?', *Evaluation and Program Planning*, 17: 339–40.

Trope, Y. (1986) 'Identification and inferential processes in dispositional attribution', *Psychological Review*, 93: 239–57.

Tsang, E.W.K. (1997) 'Organizational learning and the learning organization: a dichotomy between descriptive and prescriptive research', *Human Relations*, 50: 73–89.

Tuckman, B.W. (1965) 'Developmental sequence in small groups', *Psychological Bulletin*, 63: 384–99.

Turner, J.C. (1982) 'Towards a cognitive redefinition of the social group', in H. Tajfel (ed.), *Social Identity and Intergroup Relations*. Cambridge: Cambridge University Press. pp. 15–40.

Turner, J.C. (1984) 'Social identification and psychological group formation', in H. Tajfel (ed.), *The Social Dimension: European Developments in Social Psychology* (vol. 2). Cambridge: Cambridge University Press. pp. 518–38.

Turner, J.C., Hogg, M.A., Oakes, P.J., Reicher, S.D. and Wetherell, M.S. (1987)

Rediscovering the Social Group: A Self Categorization Theory. Cambridge, MA: Basil Blackwell.

Ulschak, F.L., Nathanson, L. and Gillan, P.G. (1981) *Small Group Problem Solving*. Reading, MA: Addison-Wesley.

Van Maanen, J. and Kunda, G. (1989) ' "Real feelings": emotional expression and organizational culture', in L.L Cummings and B.M. Staw (eds), *Research in Organizational Behavior* (vol. 11). Greenwich, CT: JAI Press. pp. 43–104.

Vandenheuvel, A. (1993) 'Missing work to care for sick children', *Family Matters*, 34: 52–5.

Veugelers, W. and Zijlstra, H. (1996) 'Networks for modernizing secondary schools', *Educational Leadership*, 54 (3): 76–80.

Voydanoff, P. (1987) *Work and Family Life*. Beverly Hills, CA: Sage.

Voydanoff, P. (1988) 'Work roles, family structures, and work/family conflict', *Journal of Marriage and the Family*, 50: 749–61.

Wajcman, J. (1991a) 'Patriarchy, technology, and conceptions of skill', *Work and Occupations*, 18: 29–45.

Wajcman, J. (1991b) *Feminism Confronts Technology*. University Park, PA: Pennsylvania State University Press.

Waldron, V.R. and Krone, K. (1991) 'The experience and expression of emotion in the workplace: a study of a corrections organization', *Management Communication Quarterly*, 4: 287–309.

Waldrop, W.M. (1992) *Complexity*. New York: Simon & Schuster.

Walton, R.E. (1987) *Innovating to Compete: Lessons for Diffusing and Managing Change in the Workplace*. San Francisco, CA: Jossey-Bass.

Walton, R.E. (1989) *Up and Running: Integrating Information Technology and the Organization*. Boston, MA: Harvard Business School Press.

Walton, R.E. and Susman, G. (1987) 'People policies for the new machines', *Harvard Business Review*, 65 (2): 98–106.

Weber, M. (1947) *The Theory of Social and Economic Organization*. New York: Free Press.

Webster, J. (1990) *Office Automation: The Labour Process and Women's Work in Britain*. Hemel Hempstead: Wheatsheaf.

Weick, K.E. (1979) *The Social Psychology of Organizing*. Reading, MA: Addison-Wesley.

Weick, K.E. and Westley, F. (1996) 'Organizational learning: affirming and oxymoron', in S.R. Clegg, C. Hardy and W.R. Nord (eds), *Handbook of Organization Studies*. London: Sage. pp. 440–58.

Wesenberg, P. (1994) 'Bridging the individual–social divide: a new perspective for understanding and stimulating creativity in organizations', *Journal of Creative Behavior*, 28 (3): 177–92.

West, M.A. (1990) 'The social psychology of innovation in groups', in M.A. West and J.L. Farr (eds), *Innovation and Creativity at Work: Psychological and Organizational Strategies*. Chichester: Wiley. pp. 309–33.

Wharton, A.S. (1993) 'The affective consequences of service work', *Work and Occupations*, 20: 205–32.

Wharton, A.S. and Erickson, R.J. (1993) 'Managing emotions on the job and at home: understanding the consequences of multiple emotional roles', *Academy of Management Review*, 18: 457–86.

Whatley, A.A. and Hoffman, W. (1987) 'Quality circles earn union respect', *Personnel Journal*, 66 (11), 89–93.

Wheatley, M.J. (1994) *Leadership and the New Science: Learning about Organization from an Orderly Universe.* San Francisco, CA: Berrett-Koehler.

White, B., Cox, C. and Cooper, C.L. (1992) *Women's Career Development.* Oxford: Blackwell.

Whole Foods Market (1997) 'Declaration of Interdependence'. [http://www.wholefoods.com/wfm/whoweare/mission.htm]

Wolpert, L. and Richards, A. (1988) *A Passion for Science.* Oxford: Oxford University Press.

Wood, R. and Bandura, A. (1989) 'Impact of conceptions of ability on self-regulatory mechanisms and complex decision making', *Journal of Personality and Social Psychology,* 56: 407–15.

Wood, W. and Karten, S. (1986) 'Sex differences in interaction style as a product of perceived sex differences in competence', *Journal of Personality and Social Psychology,* 50: 341–7.

Woodman, R.W., Sawyer, J.E. and Griffin, R.W. (1993) 'Toward a theory of organizational creativity', *Academy of Management Review,* 18: 293–321.

Wortman, C., Biernat, M. and Lang, E. (1991) 'Coping with role overload', in M. Frankenhaeuser, U. Lundberg and M.A. Chesney (eds), *Women, Work and Health: Stress and Opportunities.* New York: Plenum. pp. 85–110.

Wouters, C. (1989) 'The sociology of emotions and flight attendants: Hochschild's Managed Heart', *Theory, Culture & Society,* 6: 95–123.

Yamada, K. (1991) 'Creativity in Japan', *Leadership and Organization Development Journal,* 12 (6): 11–14.

Yong, L.M.S. (1994) 'Managing creative people', *Journal of Creative Behavior,* 28 (1): 16–20.

Zammuto, R.F and Krakower, J. (1991) 'Quantitative and qualitative studies of organizational culture', *Research in Organizational Change and Development,* 5: 83–114.

Zammuto, R.F and O'Connor, E.J. (1992) 'Gaining advanced manufacturing technologies' benefits: the roles of organization design and culture', *Academy of Management Review,* 17: 701–28.

Zedeck, S., Maslach, C., Mosier, K. and Skitka, L. (1988) 'Affective response to work and quality of family life: employee and spouse perspectives', *Journal of Social Behavior and Personality,* 3 (4): 135–57.

Zeytinoglu, I.U. (1992) 'Reasons for hiring part-time workers', *Industrial Relations,* 21: 489–99.

Zhou, X. (1993). 'The dynamics of organizational rules', *American Journal of Sociology,* 98 (5): 1134–66.

INDEX